Windows NT Backup & Restore

Jody Leber

O'REILLY™

Cambridge · *Köln* · *Paris* · *Sebastopol* · *Tokyo*

Windows NT Backup & Restore
by Jody Leber

Copyright © 1998 O'Reilly & Associates, Inc. All rights reserved.
Printed in the United States of America.

Published by O'Reilly & Associates, Inc., 101 Morris Street, Sebastopol, CA 95472.

Editor: Robert Denn

Production Editor: Nancy Wolfe Kotary

Printing History:

      May 1998:   First Edition.

This book is printed on acid-free paper with 85% recycled content, 15% post-consumer waste. O'Reilly & Associates is committed to using paper with the highest recycled content available consistent with high quality.

ISBN: 1-56592-272-7

*This book is dedicated in loving memory
of my mom, Vivian Leber.*

*She was taken from this earth on January 24, 1998,
but she prevails everlastingly
in the hearts and souls she touched.*

Table of Contents

Preface

I had always thought it would be great to write a book. However, I never thought the topic of the book would be backup and restore. No one really likes to perform this task. I, on the other hand, find the topic very interesting, and believe it or not, I get excited about the topic. It requires a broad base of knowledge about a subject that is constantly changing. To properly design the backup and restore environment, you have to consider different aspects of computer systems, including the operating system, database software, backup software, networking, tape devices, tape media, and tape libraries, to mention a few. The design also requires interfacing with many different people in an organization to determine where the company's vital data is stored and how it should be backed up. Then, to get the backup and restore environment up and running efficiently, you have to apply good testing, troubleshooting, and integration methodology. Once you have an efficient solution, there are maintenance issues to contend with and training of others. I think the process exercises my technological and interpersonal skills and organizational diplomacy.

You may ask "How did this interest start?" Well, in late 1994 I took a job working for a former boss I had worked for twice before. He described a few cool projects he needed someone to work on, but I actually took the job without knowing exactly which project would be mine. Since I had known him for about eight years, at that time, I figured that we would work out the details when I came on board. Surprisingly, he assigned me to the centralized backup project. This was not a small site with rudimentary procedures. When I came into this picture, there were four backup servers backing up approximately 1,800 client systems. The project was in a bit of a pinch: because of the over-taxed backup infrastructure, the backups of all the client systems could not complete in the designated nightly processing window. Vital data was not being backed up, and in some cases, critical system start-up in the morning was being delayed pending the completion of backups. I analyzed the situation, and after a massive hardware and software upgrade the backup window was reduced and brought into appropriate operational parameters.

It was a painful process of no sleep at night and no fun on the weekends. The backup infrastructure overhaul took months, but I learned more about backups and restores than I thought possible. Toward the end of the project, I said to my boss, "If I knew what you were going to have me do before I started, I would never have taken the job in the first place." (When you have known your boss for eight years you can get away with that kind of forward and frank discussion!)

Two and a half years later, I was asked to be part of a team to completely redesign that first backup system and integrate about 600 more backup clients. The redesign was to use faster backup servers, more backup clients, faster tape technology, larger tape libraries, and an isolated backup network.

Shortly before publishing this book, a friend of mine, Curt Vincent, asked me to be his partner in a systems engineering consulting firm, Genorff Engineering Inc. I could not pass up the opportunity and jumped in with both feet. I am looking forward to going from client to client to implement backup and restore environments, and I am excited about my base of knowledge growing even more. The combination of implementing successful backup and restore environments and learning a ton in the process is what excites me the most about the work; not to mention that backups are only a small piece of the overall distributed storage management realm. Like any area in technology, there is always more to learn, no matter how much you know. Seeing myself going into this work full-time, as a consultant, I must have forgotten just how painful the first implementation was (like having a baby, I guess). As the saying goes: "no pain, no gain"—it may be corny, but it is so true.

Organization

This book starts out with a basic discussion of backups and restores. It then covers some concepts that are related to backups, to help you think about other things that affect backups. The next topic covered is things specific to Windows NT that affect backups. Finally, the book dives into the different phases associated with implementing a successful backup and restore environment. There are a total of seven phases covered in nine chapters.

Audience

As with so many of the O'Reilly books, this book is for the system administrator. However, there is information that may be valuable to information technology management. There are many aspects to backups and restores that cross organizational boundaries, and that is where management can get involved to assist technologists. Also, this book may help managers understand what a large task it is to implement the backups.

We'd Like to Hear from You

We have tested and verified all of the information in this book to the best of our ability, but you may find that features have changed (or even that we have made mistakes!). Please let O'Reilly know about any errors or suggestions for future editions by writing:

> O'Reilly & Associates, Inc.
> 101 Morris Street
> Sebastopol, CA 95472
> 800-998-9938 (in U.S. or Canada)
> 707-829-0515 (international/local)
> 707-829-0104 (fax)

You can also send us messages electronically. To be put on the mailing list or request a catalog, send email to:

> *nuts@oreilly.com*

To ask technical questions or comment on the book, send email to:

> *bookquestions@oreilly.com* or
> *jody@genorff.com*

Conventions

The following typographic conventions are used in this book:

Italic
> is used for filenames, pathnames, directory names, URLs, email addresses, command and program names, and variables within regular text.

`Constant width`
> is used for typed commands and Registry keys.

`Constant width italic`
> is used for placeholders within code or syntax formats.

Acknowledgments

I would like to dedicate this book to my mom, Vivian Leber. She was diagnosed with brain cancer and passed away while I was writing this book. She was always extremely supportive of the progression in my career and education. Over the past 15 years, she listened to what I was working on and asked lots of questions, even though she had a very limited knowledge of computers. During her illness, she still managed to continue to ask me about work and the progress of this book, even as she got sicker. I guess a mother always continues in her motherly ways, and that's what makes them so special. A friend of mine summarized her death in the most loving and caring way: "I think that in the long run, real immortality is measured by the effect someone has on the people around them. Your mother lives on inside you and your family, and in this way, she will never have truly died." I love her dearly and she will be with me, as a part of me, forever.

I would like to give my very first thanks to my editor, Robert Denn. He never pushed or pressured me through my mom's sickness and allowed me to take the book at my own pace. He is a real saint, and if he wasn't who he is I would have bailed out and never finished the book.

I would like to also say a special and heart-felt thanks to a crew of great friends and exceptional people who helped me through the outlining and editing process associated with this book: Xev Gittler, Bob Escavich, Steve Ruegnitz, Neal Nelson, Bob Adair, and Lisa Pascetta. These individuals made this book better with their comments and suggestions, and I couldn't have done it without them.

Then, in addition to my editor and friends, there were three other technical editors that I would like to thank: Timothy Ritchey, Erik Olson, and Craig Zacker. Their outside perspective was great and their comments were appreciated, adding even more to the quality of this book overall.

The following people provided information on the backup software applications discussed in Chapter 10, *Testing*: Sid Wong of IBM; Ira Simon of Computer Associates International, Inc.; Mike Ivanov, of Seagate; Syncsort, Inc.'s engineering and marketing departments; Ole Fischer and Juergen Ketterer of Hewlett-Packard; Bill Hartman of Veritas Software; the Senior Product Marketing Manager, NT, of Legato; and Ken Peters of Software Moguls.

Thanks also to the production staff of O'Reilly & Associates. Nancy Wolfe Kotary was the production editor and copy editor. Debbie Cunha was the proofreader. Quality assurance was provided by Madeleine Newell, Clairemarie Fisher O'Leary, and Sheryl Avruch. Ruth Okin Rautenberg wrote the index.

Finally, I would like to mention that my entire family, all of my other friends, and my co-workers were very supportive and provided reinforcement. Although I am sick of the question, "How's the book going?", at last I can answer, "It's done!"

1

Backup and Recovery Basics

Generally, backups are looked upon as a necessary evil that someone at your site must be concerned about. If you are reading this book, I bet that someone is you or someone who works for you. Most of the time backups are implemented and then ignored. This is unfortunate, because the backup process safeguards your site's vital data. This is the data that cannot be loaded from diskettes, a CD, or a network install. It is data that is created at your site, by individuals that work for your company.

The vital data may be spreadsheets, word-processing documents, databases, or application software. Remember, this is the guts of your company and what your company depends on to do business or to legally protect themselves. It could be customer information, accounting data, IRS data, or human resources information. This vital data may have taken hours or years to produce, and in some cases may be irreplaceable or extremely difficult to reproduce. If you lose this vital data, it is possible that your company may go out of business immediately, or may later become financially strapped after not being able to produce the information required for a lawsuit.

So why, in so many cases, are backups not given the time and attention they really deserve? I believe it is because it is not a glamourous or sexy task. It happens behind the scenes and is really given attention only when the restores do not work. If the restores fail due to poor backups, then backups are given lots of attention, and this is definitely negative reinforcement.

Furthermore, backups and restores can be quite complex. They involve knowledge of software, hardware, and an in-depth knowledge of your site. You must understand backup and restore software design and features. You must also understand the hardware involved with backups, which includes backup tape and tape library technology. Then, the only way to effectively use the software and hardware is with a careful look at your site. You must know where the vital data is stored, how it is stored, how often it has to be backed up, how long you must keep the backups, and how fast the data must be restored, among other things. Backups and restores do not stand alone in an environment. They are highly integrated and touch upon many different computer systems as well as the computer network.

To help make the task of installing a backup and restore solution at your site a bit easier, this book focuses on the process—a method to the madness. You will have an implementation that is not just thrown together; it will be clearly thought through, your management will understand what you are doing and why you are doing it, and the solution will be easier to extend as your site grows. All of this makes your life easier to manage as a system administrator.

Fundamental Concepts

A Windows NT system consists of four basic parts:

- Windows NT operating system
- Operating system data
- Applications
- User data

In the case of a complete system failure, you would perform all of the steps listed below to completely recover your system. With a partial failure, depending on what was damaged, you might perform a smaller subset of the list:

1. Install the operating system from the original media.
2. Restore the Registry and the WINS databases from your backup tape(s).
3. Restore the applications from your backup tape(s) or from their original media.
4. Recover your data from your backup tape(s).

You do not have to fully understand all of the Windows NT operating system to do effective and proper backups. With a few exceptions (notably the Registry and WINS databases), the operating system does not need to be fully backed up. What you do need to fully understand is the hardware and software surrounding backups as well as some backup and restore concepts you may not have been introduced to before. The following sections introduce you to the backup and restore foundations.

Backups, Archiving, and HSM

There are distinct differences among backups, archiving, and hierarchical storage management (HSM), and these three concepts are generally discussed together. Therefore, this section is provided to clear up the definitions early on. Many commercial software backup and restore products provide all three capabilities, and you should understand the differences to determine what is needed for your site. Keep in mind that the following definitions are general in nature. The exact definitions and the relationships between backups, archiving, and HSM vary from vendor to vendor and product to product, depending on their particular implementation.

Backups

A backup is the process of copying a file or folder to another location or another form of media. The original file or folder is left alone. The backup copy of the file or folder can be restored later if it is removed accidently or the entire computer encounters some sort of cataclysmic disaster, such as a fire or theft. The backup process is configurable to backup portions of a disk or entire disks.

Archiving

Archiving is the automatic or user-initiated process of making a permanent copy of data that is no longer needed regularly, onto tape for long-term storage. The original data optionally can be deleted from the original hard disk to free disk space after it is archived. Archiving is a logical extension to backups, *not* a substitution for backups. An important distinction between the two is that backups usually expire after some period of time, while archives are generally kept for a long time or forever. Sometimes the archiving process (along with deletion) is referred to as grooming or disk grooming.

The advantage of archiving is that the disk space saved on each individual system can be substantial and may reduce the amount of disk space required per workstation or server. The archiving process can be performed on a project basis, where related data from a project can be archived together onto one tape. Grouping the data for archives is a logical way of storing information.

The disadvantage is apparent when an archived file or folder is required. As with the restore process, the archived data must be consciously retrieved from the media on which it was stored, and this can take more time compared with the immediate response a user would get from their hard disk drive. The amount of time to perform the retrieval depends on the location of the required tape. The required tape for the retrieval of the archive may or may not be immediately available.

Hierarchical Storage Management (HSM)

HSM is a process used to conserve disk space or data storage management. Data is manually or automatically migrated from one location to another. The migration, for example, can initially be from a client disk to the server disk and later from the server disk to tape. This migration can also be extended to include moving the data from tape storage to optical storage. HSM is *not* a substitution for backups or archiving.

When the migration is automatic, it is based on a set of policies or rules. The rules may include the location of the file, when it was last accessed, the file size, the file owner, or the amount of free space on the disk. After the file is migrated, a marker or stub is put in place of the file. When the file is accessed at a later time, it is recalled automatically. This is where the distinction between archiving and HSM is made. Archiving is a permanent copy of data and the original data remains on disk or is deleted. HSM is a migration of the data, with the marker or stub left in place to allow for its automatic recall.

The advantage of HSM is that the disk space saved on each individual system can be substantial. When the migrated data is accessed, it is recalled transparently. Also, if configured to do so, HSM can assist administrators with dealing with hard disks becoming too full.

The disadvantage is that it may take substantial time to retrieve data that has been migrated; this is in contrast to the data being on the local hard disk. This is a matter of educating your end users so they understand the HSM policy in place at your site. HSM has been implemented successfully on mainframes, and the users of that particular community are well aware of its implications. The difference between the mainframe and distributed systems is that disk space on the mainframe has been substantially more expensive. Many times, instead of implementing HSM to save disk space, managers of distributed systems prefer just to purchase larger disks.

The best initial approach is to implement a fully functional backup strategy at your site. Your first concern should be to protect the vital data at your site on a day-to-day basis. While you are determining which backup and restore software and hardware best suits your site, don't hesitate to consider the archiving and HSM implementations of the different vendors. However, always remember your first goal should be to get backups operating properly. After the backups are under control, then refocus on the archiving and HSM. Make the archiving and HSM project a follow-up project to the backup and restore project.

Software Introduction

There are three broad categories of backup and restore software available:

Data movement utilities

These are simple programs that move data from a disk to another device such as a tape drive. The intelligence built into these programs is minimal. These utilities do not provide important features such as tape spanning and tape verification.

Simple backup and restore software

The types of software that fall into this class are usually backup and restore programs that are only for use on one system and must be individually configured. These types of packages are good for small businesses or for home use. They do not scale well into larger environments, because they do not support features available in the complex backup software products. They are best suited for the local backups.

The Windows NT Tape Backup Utility (TBU), is an example of simple backup and restore software. This software is shipped with the operating system, so it is essentially free. The TBU is a simple package that is easy to use. Unfortunately, it does not scale well to medium and large backup environments. There are a number of commercial vendors that provide more scalable backup and restore software than the TBU (see Chapter 8, *Commercial Software*).

Comprehensive backup software

Into this class falls a broad range of programs, usually commercial, that provide a wide variety of tape and backup management. These packages generally are designed with Windows NT services, configuration and backup information databases, complete log files, and additional options to provide enhance capabilities.

The comprehensive commercial backup software products provide such features as heterogeneous operating system support, tape management, multiple device control, centralized administration and configuration, network backups, online restore information, and more. These are just some of the features that make this software scalable to medium and large environments.

When comprehensive backup software packages are implemented, it is important to keep in mind the relationship between the backup server and the backup clients. In the context of this book, the term *server* refers to the system receiving the data to be backed up. Additionally, the server system writes the data to tape. The term *client* refers to the systems sending the data to be backed up from their local disk. A client could be a user's desktop system, a file server, a database server, an application server, or the backup server itself.

This book primarily focuses on the comprehensive backup software. It touches briefly on the TBU and does not cover the data movement utilities.

Hardware Introduction

Backups can be performed using many different types of media, such as floppy diskettes, CDs, hard disks, optical disks, or magnetic tape. By far the most popular medium for backups is magnetic tape; this book focuses on tape technology. This popularity is predominately because of the cost of the media, the ease of implementation, and the convenience of physically storing the tapes. For many years, well before distributed computers were invented, the mainframe used magnetic tapes for backups. Since this technology was first used, engineers have constantly been designing faster and more reliable tape drives, as well as magnetic tapes with more capacity and a longer lifespan. Like the rest of the computing industry, it is ever changing for the better.

Below is a brief introduction to tape drives, tape libraries, and other terms that are frequently used. Note that Chapter 9, *Hardware*, has more details.

Tape Drives

The following terms refer to the most popular tape drives and tape media in use today:

4mm/DAT
> This term refers to a commonly used tape drive and tape technology. The DDS-1 standard has the slowest tape drive throughput and the lowest capacity tapes; the DDS-3 standard has the fastest tape drive throughput for DAT tapes and the highest tape capacity.

8mm
> This term refers to a tape drive and tape technology in which there are two different types. The Mammoth drive uses the Advanced Metal Evaporated (AME) tape media technology and the other 8mm tape drives use the Metal Particle (MP) tape media technology.

Advanced Intelligent Tape (AIT)
> This term refers to the newest of the tape drive and tape technologies. The AIT incorporates a new recording format, which makes it incompatible with any other 8mm data cartridges, even though it uses the same AME media and the helical scan recording method.

Digital Linear Tape
> There are multiple Digital Linear Tape models, each with the same physical drive and tape size, but with increased data transfer rates and tape capacities.

The Digital Linear Tape drives are backward-compatible for both reading and writing.

Quarter Inch Cartridge (QIC)

This term refers to a tape and tape drive technology in which there are the minicartridge drive and tape standards (3.5 inches) and the data cartridge drive and tape standards (5.25 inches).

Tape Libraries

To manage medium and large backup implementations, you will typically need one or more tape libraries. These libraries are robotic devices and are often referred to by names such as stacker, autochanger, jukebox, carousel, or silo. All of these terms are generally used interchangeably and are considered the same type of device. The differences is in the physical size of the unit, the number of tape drives in the unit, and the number of tape slots in the unit. Tape libraries all have the following basic components:

Tape drives

The tape drives inside a library are standard tape drives that may have been slightly modified to fit in the library. Tape libraries can hold as few as one tape drive or as many as ten or more drives.

Tape cartridge slots

The tape cartridge slots are where the tape library stores tapes that are not being used by the tape drives. There can be as few as five or as many as hundreds or thousands of slots. To determine how many tape slots your site requires (what size library your site needs) continue reading further in this section.

Robotic arm

The robotic arm in a tape library moves tapes from the tape cartridge slots to the tape drives. The movement of the arm is dictated by commands received from the backup server and the backup software. This drastically reduces the need for human operators to place the tapes in the tape drives.

Entry/exit door

On some tape libraries (especially the larger ones) there is an access port or door used to move tapes in and out of the library. It may support one or more tapes to be added or removed from the library at the same time. This door can be used while the rest of the library is fully functional. If the tape library does not have this component, then the library must be completely opened to add or remove any tapes.

Other Terminology

Here are some terms related to tape drive technologies to give you a quick overview:

Advanced Metal Evaporated (AME)
> This is a type of tape media that is coated with metallic particles. The AME media is composed of 90% to 100% magnetic material, coated with a diamond-like carbon on the recording surface, and lubricated with a protective back coating. These features make the AME media superior to the MP media (described later in this list). The AME media is more reliable because of reduced drive head wear and head contamination, and because the media supports a higher recording density.

Duty cycle
> The duty cycle is the maximum amount of time that a drive should be used within a 24-hour period. For example, a 20% duty cycle means that the drive should be utilized no more than 4 hours and 48 minutes per day (.20 × 24 hours = 4.8 hours).

Helical scan
> This term refers to a recording scheme for tapes in which the method of reading and writing data is achieved by wrapping the tape partially around an angled and rotating tape head. This recording method creates a single helical data track pattern on the tape.

Linear serpentine
> This term refers to a bidirectional recording scheme for tapes in which one track is recorded in one direction and the next track is recorded in the reverse order with a tape head that moves over the tape.

> - Normal linear serpentine tracks are written to tape parallel to the edge of the tape.

> - Symmetrical phase recording (SPR) linear serpentine tracks modify the normal linear serpentine for higher tape capacity. This is achieved by writing to tape in an angled manner on tracks thinner than the normal linear serpentine and with more tracks per tape.

Metal Particle (MP)
> This is a type of tape media that is coated with metallic particles. The MP media is made up of about 45% magnetic material, which is mixed with other additives.

Tape streaming
> This term refers to the speed that the software and other hardware can write data to a tape in a particular tape drive. The tape drives are all rated at maximum speeds, but the ability to actually use those speeds is dependent on

Zhow well a system can stream data to the tape. There are two different tape streaming techniques associated with backups:

Serial backups

There is essentially a one-to-one relationship between the backup client and the backup tape. With serial backups, the client system plays a large role in tape drive utilization. If the client happens to be a small system, it may not be able to drive the tape device on the backup server to the rated speed. This throughput dependency on the backup clients is the disadvantage to this technique. However, the major advantage is that when you need to perform a restore, the data can be removed as fast as the backup server, network, and backup client can perform the restore. There is no extra processing that has to be done to remove the data from the tape.

Multiplexed backups

With multiplexing backups, the backup server can switch between clients as needed and keep the tape drive streaming. So the speed of the backup server or the tape drive is never dependent on the speed of the backup client. Multiplexing's advantage is this ability to keep the tape drive(s) constantly writing. Therefore, the overall throughput of the backup server is based on the processing power of that backup server. The disadvantage of multiplexing backups is that it does have an impact on restore speeds. As the data is restored from a tape, the backup server has to skip portions of the tape to get to the data required for the restore, so restoring from a multiplexed tape requires some processing to determine what portions of the tape are needed for the backup client and the physical skipping through the tape to find the portions of tape to read for the restore. However, it should be noted that the overall cost to your site and your backup window may be minimized by using a parallel implementation, since the amount of data backed up is far more than the amount of data that is restored.

Tape track

Tapes are linear devices by nature. To increase the amount of data that can be written to a tape, the tape drives write data to multiple tracks on a tape. The width of the tape and the angle of the read/write head of the tape drive determine how many tracks are on a tape.

Design Considerations

The size of your site determines the type of backups you will implement. There are two primary design techniques: local backups and networked backups. Both of these techniques are described later, and software and hardware is available to implement either type of backup.

Local Backups

The implementation of local backups is illustrated in Figure 1-1. Note that back-ups are performed on individual systems. Each computer is connected to its own backup device and each computer is separately configured. These individual computers may or may not be connected to a network. The key is that the network or other computers are not required for backups. This is a good way to perform backups in your home or at a small office.

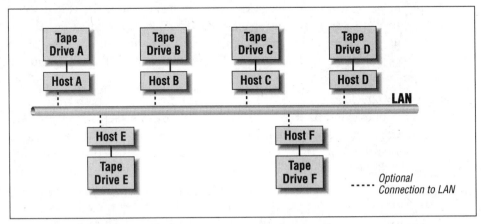

Figure 1-1. Local backup implementation

Advantage

>The Tape Backup Utility (TBU) is packaged with Windows NT and does not have to be purchased separately.

Disadvantages

>The initial capital cost to implement local backups may appear to be relatively low. No network is required, inexpensive tape drives can be installed on each system, and you can choose to use free software. However, an individual tape drive does cost more than a network board and a small network hub. Even with two computers, it is more cost effective to purchase a single tape drive and share that drive over a network. As your environment expands, this disparity grows. So, make sure you do the calculations. The expense of a network and additional third-party backup and restore software may be more cost-effective than using the TBU and installing individual tape drives.

>If you choose this implementation, the backup configuration and tapes are co-located with the corresponding system. In the case of disaster, such as flood, fire, or burglary, the system and corresponding tapes may all be damaged. Therefore, you must move the tapes to another location to ensure your ability to recover after a system or site disaster.

Finally, local backups are not very scalable, because they require systems to be individually configured and the tapes to be independently managed. If your site grows larger, it will require more and more manpower to adequately support.

Networked Backups

Networked backups are implemented by grouping computers as illustrated in Figures 1-2 and 1-3. This implementation is generally referred to as departmental backups or centralized backups. The data is sent over the network to a designated computer where there is a shared tape drive or tape library. The systems performing the backups are called backup servers[*] and the other computers are called backup clients.[†] You enter configuration details and manage your tapes for the backups on each backup server. The backup server(s) can be located in a secure area to reduce accessibility, tampering, or theft. Also, backup configuration and tape management is reduced, because you have relatively few backup server systems to handle.

Figure 1-2 depicts departmental backups. The computers are grouped by LANs, departments, floors, or some other logical grouping. With this implementation, if possible, the backup servers would be installed in a computer equipment room or closet to reduce access and prevent tampering.

Figure 1-3 illustrates centralized backups. With this type of implementation, a larger number of backup clients send their data to a relatively small number of backup servers (versus the departmental backups). Sometimes this strategy also groups computers, but the groups are much larger and designated by business unit, building, or region.

Advantages

With this implementation, your backup server(s) can be located at a completely different site and placed in a machine room with other important systems. There are instances when a backup server located at site A backs up the backup clients at site B and vice versa. Of course this reduces accessibility, tampering, or theft of the backups, but it also provides you with immediate offsite backups. With this implementation, your central operations group can handle the backup configuration and tape management for all backup servers.

---

[*] The backup server can be exclusively used for backups and restores, or it can be a shared resource also used for other purposes.

[†] A backup client can be an individual's desktop system, or it can be a server, such as an SQL server, a print server, or a file server.

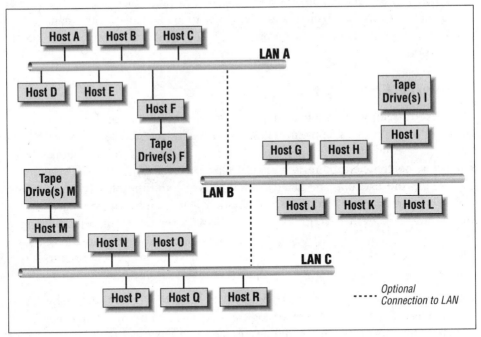

Figure 1-2. Networked backups, departmental implementation

Disadvantages

Your initial capital investment for the networked backups is higher than for the local backups. Some of those costs include the following:

- Even though your site may already have a large network infrastructure in place, the network may need to be expanded to handle the additional load (networked backups will place a significant load on your network infrastructure). You may actually choose to install a dedicated network for backups.

- You are utilizing the network and therefore the TBU software cannot be used. So for this implementation, you have to purchase the appropriate software.

- Purchasing a tape library is a definite requirement for centralized backups and desirable for departmental backups. The cost of tape libraries varies greatly, but is definitely more expensive than individual tape drives.

With the centralized backups, there are a few other costs and considerations involved:

- Your backup server system will be used exclusively for backups.

- You may also require dedicated staff to operate your centralized backup system(s) effectively. This is different from the other implementations where staff members may work part-time on backups and part-time on other projects.

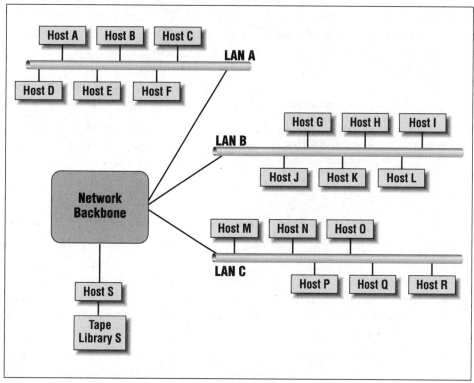

Figure 1-3. Networked backups, centralized implementation

- Be aware that it may be difficult to achieve centralized backups because of the organizational boundaries that are transversed. Experience has shown that a mandate or visible support from your CIO-level management or equivalent is sometimes the only way centralized backups can be successfully implemented.

Design, Efficiency, and Trade-offs

Protecting your vital data is important and the amount of irreplacable data stored on computers is growing by leaps and bounds. This is fueled by the growth of hard disks and corresponding expansion of the amount of data that can be stored on each computer. These technological advances are great, but the number of hours available to back up the data, the *backup window*, is not growing. There are only so many hours in a day and so many hours in a week. So the first part of the dilemma is that over time you will have more data to back up in a set number of hours.

The other part of the dilemma surrounds the fact that your site will execute far more backups than restores. Therefore it may appear at first that the engineering of your solution must primarily focus on completing backups in a timely manner. However, the users are not concerned with how fast the backups are performed; they are concerned with how fast they can restore data. The restores are what they are directly exposed to and use. So while designing your solution it is also important to watch the restore speeds, to keep your customers or users happy.

To add yet another factor into the dilemma, you must look at both single file or folder restores as opposed to restoring an entire hard disk. You have to look at both the frequency of restores and the impact of losing that amount of data:

- The majority of restores are of single files or folders. In this case, someone accidently deletes something that should not have been removed or someone leaves the company and a document they created must be located. However, losing a single file or folder generally does not cause much corporate exposure.

- The minority of restores are of an entire hard disk. This situation may occur if you have a hardware failure and a disk has to be replaced and then rebuilt. In this situation, the corporate exposure and business loss could be potentially quite grave.

Some sites implement local backup because of the efficiency of the local restores. They feel, and rightly so, that the networked backups will have an impact on the restore times. Unfortunately, in larger sites with local backups, the overhead of managing all of the individual tape drives, all of the individual tapes, and all of the individual configuration details becomes overwhelming very quickly. This can cause tapes to be lost or incorrectly marked, as well as configuration errors and incomplete backups. The lack of control with local backups may actually affect the overall restore times (from the time the restore is requested until all data is actually placed back onto the hard disk). With local restores, it is likely that it could take an operator an hour or more to get to the computer requiring the restore (remember that these are larger sites) and find the essential tape(s) for a local restore. This manual process may be slower than with networked backups where a tape library is used. Tape libraries can be large enough to hold many weeks of data, and require no operator intervention once the restore request is placed. The amount of time may be longer to get the data off of the tape with networked restores, but there is generally no manual intervention required for tape(s).

For larger sites, tape libraries are the answer, because most restores are only for files and folders, and the libraries reduce the day-to-day tape management overhead. However, even with this solution, you may want to implement procedures to handle the special case in which an entire disk has to be restored. For example, a disk that is a striped 40 GB disk. You may choose to configure your largest backup clients so that you may take the required tapes out of the backup server's tape library, attach a standalone tape drive to the client, load any appropriate software on the system, and then perform a local restore using the media from the networked backups.

So what do you design your solution for: the frequently performed majority of the restores or the highly visible minority of restores? The answer is that you must consider both throughput rates for your implementation.

As you can see, the dilemma of backup and restores is maintaining a delicate balance between designing the backups efficiently to fit within the allowed backup window without losing sight of how important different types of restore speeds are to the end users and administrators. This is where your engineering skills meet your interpersonal skills. While putting in a great technical backup solution, you must work with your users and administrators to set their expectations for restores.

In addition to a great backup solution, you should consider technology that compliments backups and restores. This is other technology, discussed in Chapter 2, *In Addition to Backups*, that also adds protection to your data. Backups are not everything to data protection; they are just one piece, albeit an important one, in the technological puzzle.

Phased Approach

Properly performed backups, in tandem with properly planned backups, are the key to success. The implementation phases you should consider for the backup and recovery strategy at your site are briefly described in the following sections. Chapters 4 through 12 cover each phase in detail. No matter what size your environment is, you should at least consider all phases covered in this book. Some may be inappropriate for your site, at least initially, but sites do change and grow.

Phase 1: Requirements Definition

There are many requirements that must be considered to properly choose the backup software and hardware to be used. These items include what type of data and how much data is important, how much time you have to do backups, and your restore expectations. This book provides a checklist of items to help you step through your site to determine what is currently in place or planned to be implemented. The site survey helps you ask the right questions as they apply to backups and recovers. Use the items from the checklist that suit your site as the basis of your requirements document. Add any other items appropriate for your site and use the requirements document within your organization to obtain agreement about what is required for the backups and restores. Also within this phase, you should set server and network sizing goals to be used in the Testing Phase.

It is important to keep one concept in mind as you do the site survey and sizing: rarely in the history of computing has the amount of data at a particular site been reduced. The disk capacity grows and the data grows. Disk drives are getting larger and the price is getting lower. It is common for the distributed environment to grow at 100% per year in data storage. With this type of growth, you need to plan for it and not implement a backup solution that you will outgrow immediately. You don't want to underestimate the amount of data to back up, the number of systems to back up, or the size of the backup server. Of course, you need to use common sense, but definitely don't minimize your requirements.

This information is covered in detail in Chapter 4, *Requirements Definition*.

Phase 2: Policy and Politics

The information obtained in the requirements definition phase will also assist you in writing your backup policy as well as planning educational sessions appropriate for your site. A policy statement checklist and a sample backup policy are both provided in this book. The list provides the items that should be included in your backup policy. There is also information that covers the educational aspects of backup and recovery. In a large organization, sometimes the policy and politics are more difficult to overcome than the technical aspects.

This information is covered in detail in Chapter 5, *Policy and Politics*.

Phase 3: Software

After obtaining the site requirements and defining your backup policy statement, the next phase covers the backup and restore software aspects. With respect to software, this book does not cover the data movement utilities described previously. It touches on the simple backup and restore software, such as the TBU which is included with Windows NT operating system. This book primarily focuses on the comprehensive backup software products commercially available in the market.

There are three chapters covering backup and restore software. One chapter (Chapter 6, *Software Features*) is dedicated to a high-level discussion of backup and restore software design and features. It should help you understand basic backup and restore application design architecture, and it also provides a vendor survey. The survey is a list of features you should consider for your site. Another chapter (Chapter 7, *Windows NT Backup Software*) discusses the Windows NT Software, Tape Backup Utility (TBU). Since the TBU has a limited feature set and is not scalable, another chapter (Chapter 8, *Commercial Software*) is dedicated to available commercial backup and restore software. There is a wide range of third-party software that you can purchase. The checklist in this chapter should be reviewed and notes made on what is important to you and your site. The important items can be used to narrow which applications best suit your needs.

Phase 4: Hardware

Like the software, the backup hardware should be customized to your site. This book covers the tape drive hardware, tape library hardware, and backup server hardware. Factors important in purchasing your hardware include the amount of data to be backed up, your backup window, and tape management. The hardware is expensive and a large investment, so make sure that you will not outgrow it too fast.

This information is covered in detail in Chapter 9, *Hardware*.

Phase 5: Testing

Once the hardware platform is chosen and the field of commercial software is narrowed down to three or fewer vendors, the testing can commence. The issues surrounding testing the software and hardware at your site are covered in this book. You should not skip the testing phase, because you will uncover problems and issues that you cannot uncover any other way. The vendors perform as much testing as possible, but remember, your site configuration is not exactly the same as the vendor's quality assurance test lab. Actually, the vendors have a limited test capability compared to all of the technical options available today. There are thousands of different combinations of hardware and software, and no two companies are identical. Each site has different PC hardware platforms, different network components integrated together, and different combinations of installed software. Therefore, testing at your site is important to the success of your backup and restore strategy. During the test phase, you should evaluate the features of the application software as well as the performance of the overall system. The performance results of the onsite testing should be compared to the server and network sizing goals obtained in this book. The comparison of the live testing results to these performance goals will help determine if the system, as a whole, meets your throughput requirements. The features, performance, and pricing information will all help you make the best choice of backup and restore software to purchase for your site.

This information is covered in detail in Chapter 10, *Testing*.

Phase 6: Integration

After testing, it is time to integrate the backup software and backup hardware chosen. Integration may be viewed as a one-time occurrence. However, this may not necessarily be the case. If you are extremely successful with the backup solution you implement, you may be asked to implement your solution at other sites. Also, as your organization grows you will have to expand your backup implementation to support the growth. Proper integration is important and must consider many different aspects of your organization.

This information is covered in detail in Chapter 11, *Integration Hints.*

Phase 7: Administration

Administrative maintenance is required for the life of your backup solution, and this book provides suggestions for what should be done on an ongoing basis. If the administration is not set up well, it will become a burden. There are tasks that must be done occasionally and others that must be done daily. The occasional tasks are commonly overlooked, but are just as important as the daily tasks. You cannot just put the backup solution in place and ignore it; otherwise, you will be caught by surprise down the road.

As you can see, the different phases described above all work together. Each phase feeds vital information into other phases. Understanding the global picture of what needs to be done will make the details that follow easier to comprehend. Now that you understand the global picture, don't get too overwhelmed. This book will take you through one phase at a time.

This information is covered in detail in Chapter 12, *Administration Hints.*

2

In Addition to Backups

It is important to perform proper backups to be able to perform successful restore, but backups are not the only solution to protect your computers and data. There is technology available with Windows NT and from third-party vendors that does not replace the need for backups but does complement backups. These items are briefly covered in this chapter to get you thinking of things above and beyond backups.

System Consistency

Understanding what you have on your system(s) and how it is organized is important for effective and proper backups. In sites with tens, hundreds, or thousands of Windows NT systems, it is vital to have as much consistency in disk layouts between systems, as possible. A consistent disk layout on all of your systems will help in the configuration and maintenance of your backup implementation.

You should place the operating system, applications, and user data in the same location on disk for each computer you install and configure. If you have the luxury of multiple disk drives, then separate the data across the drives. If possible, it is recommended that the user data be kept separate from the operating system or applications. This type of preparation will make your life in the backup business easier.

Disaster Recovery

Disaster recovery and backup and recovery are related topics. Disaster recovery involves preparation for and procedures to take in the event of a disaster. Disaster recovery is a huge world in and of itself. Backup and recovery constitute just the data recovery component of disaster recovery.

Disaster recovery arrangements and tactics may include but are by no means limited to the following:

Alternative location

You must consider defining a different operational location that must be contracted for or set aside before a disaster occurs. You may choose to lease an additional building, or for large organizations that span multiple sites, you may set up each site to support vital portions of the other site. The site itself must be prepared.

Alternative power sources

You can gain access to different power sources in many different ways. If possible, you may want to obtain electricity from different companies, through a different power grid, into your building. Also, you may want a generator installed at your site. However, depending on your business needs, your requirements may not be as stringent, so uninterruptible power supplies may be all that are needed.

Alternative hardware

The hardware requirements will vary greatly, based on your business requirements. Your site may have a contract with a third party to provide the hardware in case of an emergency. At the time of the disaster it would be set up and made available. You may have requirements to have the hardware on hot standby and actually up and running at the alternative site. Besides determining the availability of the hardware, you need to have a comprehensive understanding of what hardware is minimally required in a disaster scenario, so unnecessary hardware can be eliminated during this time frame.

Alternative network

Like all of the previous items, there are several varieties of alternative networks that can be put in place. If your Internet connection is vital for business, multiple connections through different Internet service providers can be established. If you have multiple sites, you may want each Internet connection to feed into a different site. Don't forget to feed an Internet connection to the alternative location if it is required. The network between multiple sites must also be considered. You may want to have multiple connections between sites in addition to having them through different long haul carriers. Also, the local area network must be considered for the alternative site.

Alternative data source

Some data is vital in the event of a disaster. For instance, you may need human resource data to determine the number and names of employees in the event of a building being destroyed, in addition to the data required to continue operating, if it is required. You may choose to use other technology to keep a mirrored hot backup copy of portions of the data at an alternative site. At a minimum, you must ensure that copies of the backup tapes are sent offsite. The tapes are a slow medium from which to perform a restore, but that may be adequate and cost-beneficial for an entire site or for parts of a site.

During the planning of the backup implementation, the group in your organization responsible for disaster recover should be involved with your work. They may have requirements that you can easily implement with planning. This is in contrast to waiting until after your implementation and the finding their requirements difficult, or perhaps impossible, to integrate.

Uninterruptible Power Supply (UPS)

At some sites, the server systems are located in an equipment room or data center that is equipped with a generator and battery banks. The generator can provide backup power for hours, or sometimes days, to all of the equipment located in the equipment room. With many hours and sometimes days to handle the power outage, your servers can be shut down gracefully by hand, protecting your data. The UPS option discussed here is not for that kind of support.

At sites without generator support, it is common to have important systems connected to a UPS. The UPS has a battery that provides power to the connected computer in the event of a power outage. Usually the life of this battery is less than an hour. The UPS is connected to the incoming power and the computer is then connected to the UPS. The older UPS units have no additional connection to the computer they protect. Newer UPS units support a COM port connection between the UPS and the supported system.

With only a power connection between the UPS and the computer, if the UPS senses a power outage, it will continue to provide power to the attached computer for the life of its battery. The UPS may start beeping to alert everyone that it is the sole source of power to the computer. It is the administrator's responsibility to go to that computer and gracefully shut it down to prevent loss of data. This may be a problem if the power outage is widespread and the administrator has a lot of computers to shut down. If the computer and UPS are located in a closet or in another building, the beeping may not be heard by the administrator. The UPS may run out of power, causing the attached system to crash, potentially losing or corrupting data.

The new UPS units support a COM connection to the attached computer, so when the power goes out, the UPS notifies the computer via the COM port that the power is being supplied by the UPS and has a limited battery life. The Windows NT operating system has support for this type of UPS and is completely configurable. The configuration includes the ability to have a file executed before the system is gracefully shut down. The configuration is done through the *Control Panel* UPS icon.

TIP   Before purchasing a UPS, check with the Windows NT hardware
                 compatibility guide to verify operating system-level support.

The UPS support can be added to any Windows NT server or workstation. Generally they are used for server support to prevent loss of data or data corruption in the event of a power outage. However, if a user is working on a spreadsheet or document on their desktop workstation and the power goes out, the work they performed since their last save will be lost (unless the package being used supports an automatic save capability).

Windows NT requires some housekeeping (for example, synchronizing information in memory with what is on the hard disk) to be done before a system is shut down. When this housekeeping does not occur, data is likely to be lost or damaged. Therefore, the UPS is a complementary technology to backups, because it helps protect data from becoming corrupted due to an unexpected power outage.

Advanced Disk Techniques

There are also a number of techniques available to protect against disk failure.

Disk Mirroring

Windows NT supports disk mirroring, which is commonly referred to as RAID 1 (Redundant Array of Independent Drives level 1). This technique maintains a second hard drive containing an exact data replication of the first drive. When changes are made to the primary drive, the secondary (mirrored) drive is updated. To support disk mirroring, you are required to have a second hard drive installed. So there is a cost associated with this type of reliability. The second hard drive cannot be smaller than the primary drive, and if the secondary drive is larger, the additional disk space is wasted.

Disk mirroring is configured through the Windows NT Disk Administrator. Select Start → Programs → Administrative Tools → Disk Administrator.

If the operating system detects that a file or sector is corrupted on the primary drive, the secondary drive is accessed to obtain the information. If you plan on implementing disk mirroring, make sure that the backup software you choose can support this type of technology and can perform backups appropriately.

Disk Duplexing

This technique is the same as disk mirroring, but a second disk controller is used for the secondary disk drive. This protects against disk failure or controller failure.

Disk Striping

Windows NT supports disk striping, which is commonly referred to as RAID 0. RAID 0 requires a set of drives for implementation; Windows NT supports from 3 to 32 drives for disk striping. The drives are used together and the data is spread between the drives. This technique writes data in stripes across disk partitions in the set of drives (the size of the stripe is the striping factor). A partition of the same size is selected for each disk.

Disk striping can be implemented with or without parity. When disk striping is implemented with parity it is referred to as RAID 3 or RAID 5. RAID 3 is striping with dedicated parity and RAID 5 is striping with distributed parity. Windows NT implements RAID 5. If you implement striping with parity, when one drive is lost, the data on that drive can be reproduced based on the information from the parity stripe and what is remaining on the good drives.

With RAID 5, there is one additional stripe added to the data, known as the parity stripe. The parity stripes are spread among all of the drives. The parity stripe is calculated by an Exclusive OR (XOR) of all data stripes. If one stripe is lost or corrupted, the remaining stripes can be subtracted (with XOR) from the parity stripe, and the result is the missing or damaged stripe. Disk striping decreases access time to the data on disk and disk striping with parity provides additional measures to ensure data is not lost.

Disk striping is configured through the Windows NT Disk Administrator. Select Start → Programs → Administrative Tools → Disk Administrator. Disk striping can also be part of a hardware solution where the hard disk is configured directly for striping. The advantage of hardware striping is that you will obtain faster access speeds in contrast to the software solution.

If the operating system or disk hardware detects that a file or sector is corrupted and you have implemented disk striping with parity, the data can be reconstructed if necessary. If you plan on implementing disk striping, make sure that the backup software you chose can support this type of technology and can perform backups appropriately.

Virus Protection

Computer viruses are pervasive and can cause grave damage to your computers. They can infect your computers by being passed on diskettes or in attachments to your email. A computer virus is a program that spreads itself to other programs or macro files and can destroy or corrupt the software and data on your computer. Unfortunately, there are individuals in the world with lots of time on their hands to develop these annoying pieces of software.

Windows NT is not shipped with virus protection software. There are third-party vendors that provide this type of functionality.

If you implement backups without virus protection software, you may be backing up viruses without realizing it is happening. This could lead to restores that contain viruses. Therefore, the virus protection software is a great complement to backups. You need to eliminate the viruses before backups occur.

Network Security

In the past few years, the use of the Internet has exploded. The Internet includes networks in over 100 countries, with over one million computers, and over 10 million users. With the enormous growth of the Internet, there are many advantages gained from using it, but there can be many disadvantages, too. It is important to recognize this and protect your data from network intrusions.

Windows NT is not shipped with firewall software or any type of network filtering software. Third-party vendors can provide this type of functionality. Properly implemented network security helps reduce the vulnerability of the computers connected to the network. Protection of this type is also a great complement to backups.

3

Special Windows NT Considerations

There are unique backup and restore characteristics of Windows NT. All Windows NT servers and workstations store configuration information in the Registry. Servers mapping NetBIOS to TCP/IP with WINS have a backup requirement for the WINS database. No matter what size site you have, you must have a basic understanding of these Windows NT characteristics.

Registry

The Registry is vital to Windows NT's operations. Some parts of the Registry are in use by system resources at all times. Special utilities, designed with these facts in mind, must be used to ensure that the Registry data is backed up properly.

Windows Internet Name Service (WINS)

The WINS database stores some information in the Registry, so that information is naturally taken care of by backing up the Registry. However, not all of the WINS information is stored in the Registry; there is a separate WINS database. The WINS manager provides the ability to automatically backup the WINS database to another location on disk; you should verify that this is configured properly.

Another consideration is what you should *not* back up in Windows NT. It may seem counterintuitive, but it is just as important as what you should backup. Things that are automatically recreated if they are no longer present, as well as things that can be recreated by other means (besides a tape restore) should not be backed up. By not backing up what is not needed for a restore, you save money by using fewer backup tapes and reduce the amount of time required to perform your backups.

Registry

The Windows NT Registry is at the core of Windows NT's operations. It was designed to supersede the *.INI* files (*WIN.INI* and *SYSTEM.INI* files) and other configuration files (*CONFIG.SYS* and *AUTOEXEC.BAT*) used in Windows 3.x. As noted above, there is a Registry on every Windows NT workstation and server. This section provides a high-level introduction to the Registry. However, you should note that most backup software products backup the Registry without you having to be aware of the exact file names listed below.

The Registry is a hierarchical database. This database is used when the system boots and while the system is running. It contains essential configuration information for such things as users accounts, applications, system tools, hardware, device drivers, and network protocols. The Registry is automatically changed and updated as users, passwords, software, and hardware are added and removed from your system. It is can also be changed manually using the *regedt32* program.

WARNING   Be extremely careful when using the *regedt32* program. Incorrect changes made to the Registry could make your system inoperable. The Registry editor is not an end-user tool and should be used only by a knowledgeable systems administrator.

The Registry's hierarchical tree starts with the root keys. Each root key contains keys, subkeys, and values. A hive is the combination of a key, subkeys, and values. In Windows NT version 4.x, there are five root keys:

HKEY_CURRENT_USER
> This root key contains all information pertaining to the user currently logged into the system and is referred to as the user's profile. It includes the user's folders, screen colors, and Control Panel settings. This root key is a subkey of HKEY_USERS.

HKEY_CLASSES_ROOT
> This root key is a shortcut to the HKEY_LOCAL_MACHINE\Software\Classes subkey. This part of the Registry is used by the Windows NT Explorer and the Object Linking and Embedding (OLE) to ensure the correct application is used when a file is opened.

HKEY_CURRENT_CONFIG
> This root key is used when the system is started up and contains the hardware profile.

HKEY_USERS
> This root key contains all user profiles for this system.

HKEY_LOCAL_MACHINE

> This root key is used by Windows NT for numerous functions such as the security accounts management, software configuration and installation, and hardware configuration and installation.

The five root keys access six Registry hives, which consist of database files. The following table gives the hive names and the names of the Windows NT files associated with each hive:

Hive	Files
HKEY_LOCAL_MACHINE\SAM	*SAM* *SAM.LOG*
HKEY_LOCAL_MACHINE\SECURITY	*SECURITY* *SECURITY.LOG*
HKEY_LOCAL_MACHINE\SOFTWARE	*SOFTWARE* *SOFTWARE.LOG*
HKEY_LOCAL_MACHINE\SYSTEM	*SYSTEM* *SYSTEM.LOG*
HKEY_CURRENT_USER	*USER###* *USER###.LOG* *ADMIN###* *ADMIN###.LOG*
HKEY_USERS\DEFAULT	*DEFAULT* *DEFAULT.LOG*

Notice that there is not a one-to-one correlation between the number of root keys and hives. The relationship between the two is too complex to cover in this book. What is important here is that you get a feel for the contents of the Registry, not its complex underlying architecture.

As shown in the previous table, each hive is stored on the hard drive as a file and has a corresponding *.LOG* file. These files are located in either the *System-Root\system32\config* or *SystemRoot\profiles\username* folders.* However, the information stored in these folders is what your system uses to initialize your computer. After your system is running, the hive files on the hard disk are considered inactive. The active portion of the Registry is in memory and used by Windows NT to run the system. The hive files on disk get updated when the system is gracefully shut down or rebooted. Backup programs must be cognizant of this behavior and not just back up the inactive hive files on the disk. The hive files on your disk must be synchronized with the changes in your systems memory before a backup can be considered current.

---

* *SystemRoot* is the directory where Windows NT was installed, and by default is *C:\winnt*.

The Emergency Repair Disk and the Repair Disk Utility

The emergency repair disk (ERD) is a diskette that you create for your computer that has the information required to repair the Registry. If the Registry on your computer becomes corrupted or unusable, you can use the ERD to get back a functional copy of the Registry (there are examples later of when this may happen). Once the ERD is initially created, use the repair disk utility (*RDISK.EXE*) to keep the ERD updated.*

As a site expands, it becomes just about impossible to maintain an ERD for every computer. It is hard to automate the process of updating the ERD, so this maintenance is not practical. The information in this section is included for completeness.

If they are used at all, the ERD and *RDISK* should be used as a complement to backups of the Registry. The *RDISK* utility and the Windows NT manual pages both state that these are *not* backup tools. The *RDISK* utility is used to create or update the ERD, and the ERD is used with the Windows NT setup diskettes to allow you to use the repair process available.

The ERD contains copies of the *AUTOEXEC.NT* and *CONFIG.NT* files and the Registry database files. It can be used only on the system where it was created. The Registry database files on the ERD are listed here (the underscore next to the name indicates the file is compressed):

system._
Database file for system configuration information

security._
Database file for system security information

sam._
Database file for the Security Accounts Manager (SAM) information

software._
Database file for software configuration information

default._
Database file for the system default information

*ntuser.da_*
Database file for user information

---

* The ERD can be created when the Windows NT server or workstation software is installed, or at a later time by using the *RDISK.EXE* utility. The *RDISK.EXE* utility is located in the *SystemRoot\system32* folder. You also have to remember to update the ERD (using *RDISK*) if you make any hardware or software changes to a system.

If you did not create an ERD when you installed your system(s), you should create one for each system as soon as possible. To do so, under the Windows NT Start button, select the Run... option and enter the command RDISK. There is an option to create the ERD. This option will format a diskette and then copy the appropriate information to it.

Once the ERD is created, you must update it when changes are made to your system. These system changes include adding or removing a user, changing administrator or user passwords, adding or removing an application, or making any hardware alterations. To do this, run the *RDISK* utility and select the option to update the ERD. This option will first save the current Registry configuration information from memory to your system hard disk. It will then remove what is currently on the ERD by formatting the diskette and then copy the appropriate information to the diskette.

During the time you are actually updating the ERD, you are left vulnerable; it is only for a few minutes, but it is worth mentioning. The *RDISK* utility formats your previous ERD and then copies new information to the diskette. At this very moment, you are without an ERD. If this is potentially a problem at your site, you may want to have two ERDs per system and rotate them as changes are made. This way you can have the most current one being created, and the previous one is still available in case of failure during the *RDISK* update process.

There are other reasons that you should have a current ERD and an ERD that is one version back. For example, let's say you installed some new hardware and then ran *RDISK*. After a few days, you may find an application that does not work properly with the new hardware. With an ERD that is one version back, the older ERD can be used in the repair process, and you can restore your system to the state it was in before the hardware installation. Another example is that if you change the administrator's password and then diligently run *RDISK*, you may realize a week later that you forgot the new password. Once again, the ERD that is one version back can be used for the repair process.

To restore or repair the Registry from the ERD, you must have access to the Windows NT original setup diskettes or the setup diskettes that are created when Windows NT is installed. You boot from the first setup diskette, insert the second diskette when prompted, and then proceed to the selection to repair a damaged system's Windows NT. During the original installation, if you specified a floppyless installation, then you won't have the setup diskettes. In this case, to restore from the Registry on the ERD, boot from the original installation CD and proceed to repair a damaged NT system.

Registry Backup and Recovery Options

The following two options are recommended backup and restore techniques. These options are fairly easy to use and the software discussed in this section does take into consideration the Registry unique characteristics:

Windows NT Tape Backup Utility (TBU)

Backups of the Registry are done with the TBU by making a specific choice in the Backup Information dialog box. This dialog box is displayed when the Backup option is chosen from the Operations menu within the TBU. By default, the Registry backup option is not selected; you have to consciously make this selection.

The TBU allows backups of the Registry only along with the backups of some other file or folder. The TBU has no option to back up just the Registry.

A restore of the Registry using the Windows NT TBU is accomplished by selecting the correct option in the Restore Information dialog box. After the restore of the Registry, the computer must be rebooted for the restored information to take effect.

Commercial backup and recovery software

All commercial software products have the ability to back up the Registry. Some key features to consider are the ability to have the Registry backed up automatically with scheduled backup and the ability to back up or restore only the Registry if required.

The following three options are *not* recommended backup and restore techniques. They are only being covered in the interest of thoroughness. None of these options are easy to use, and they have a lot of steps to take into consideration.

WARNING   Each of the following backup and restore options has a number of gotchas that can lead to simple human error.

Windows NT Resource Kit Utilities

The Microsoft NT Resource Kit must be purchased separately from the base operating system. This kit contains two utilities that can be used to backup and restore the Registry. The *REGBACK.EXE* utility is for backups and the *REGREST.EXE* utility is for restores. One advantage of these utilities is that the backups are made to disk as opposed to tape. If the Registry becomes corrupted and *REGBACK* was used, it is easy to restore the Registry with *REGREST.* However, one disadvantage is the backup with *REGBACK* is an additional administrative step that has to be done manually or has to be automated. Another possible disadvantage is that the Resource Kit has to be purchased separately and the Resource Kit Utilities are not really well supported.

The *REGBACK* utility backs up the Registry database files to a specified floppy or hard disk directory location (for example: REGBACK C:\RBUDIR). This directory is the only parameter specified when using this utility. If the location specified contains previously backed up database files, the utility will not copy over existing files. A message will appear that states the save failed.

The *REGREST* utility requires two parameters (for example: REGREST C:\RBUDIR C:\OLDREG). The first parameter is the name of the directory where the *REGBACK* backup exists. This folder has to be on the same volume as the current Registry database files. If the *REGBACK* directory was on another volume or a floppy diskette, then the backed up files must be copied to the same volume as the current Registry before the *REGREST* command will work. The second parameter is the location of where to copy the replaced Registry information. The end of the restore process includes removing the restore's source directory (in this case *C:\RBUDIR*). If you want to keep this folder, you must make a copy.

You can use the *REGBACK* utility to back up your registry to a floppy diskette. If the database files are too large to fit on one floppy diskette, you can use *REGBACK* to back up the Registry to a hard disk location and then use the 16-bit MS-DOS–based *BACKUP* utility to back up to the floppy (this utility handles the spanning of floppy diskettes). To restore the database files, you would use *RESTORE* to restore the files from the floppy diskettes to the hard disk and then the *REGREST* utility to restore the Registry from the hard disk file.

Copying the Registry

It is possible to make a copy of the Registry database files as a backup option. This is done by booting another operating system and copying the files in *SystemRoot\system32\config* or *SystemRoot\profiles\username* folders to another location. If your Registry hives are located on a FAT file system, you can boot from an MS-DOS floppy and then perform the copy. If your Registry hives are located on an NTFS file system, you can boot from a Windows NT bootable diskette and then perform the copy. Note that because you are running a different operating system or another instance of Windows NT, the Registry database files on your hard disk are not used, and therefore contain all the correct information.

The Registry editor

The Registry editor *REGEDT32.EXE* provides the ability to save a key. To perform this type of backup, bring up the *REDEDT32* utility. This is done by clicking on the Windows NT Start button, selecting the Run... option, and then just typing in REDEDT32. When the Registry editor is running, click on the Registry menu option and choose the Save Key... option. Follow the instructions to perform the backup.

The restore of the Registry is also accomplished through the *REDEDT32* utility. When the Registry editor is running, choose Registry → Restore....

WINS Database

The WINS server provides dynamic computer name registration, IP address to Net-BIOS name resolution, and vice versa. This service provides backwards compatibility for Windows 3.x or Windows for Workgroups systems that are WINS client–enabled. These clients can use the Windows NT WINS server, which helps with the migration to Windows NT. As noted earlier, the Windows NT servers, which are configured to be WINS servers, have a WINS database. The WINS clients have software to interface with the WINS servers, but the database is only located on the servers.

There are entries in the Registry for the WINS server. These entries are not discussed here, but they are naturally protected with the backup of the Registry itself. The WINS database, which is separate from the Registry, is stored in the *SystemRoot\system32\wins* folder. There are four database files:

WINS.MDB
> The actual database file that contains all of the WINS information

SYSTEM.MDB
> The schema of the database

JET.LOG
> The transaction log of the database

WINSTMP.MDB
> A temporary file

During the installation and configuration of the WINS server software, there are two backup options:

- The first option is in the WINS Server Configuration menu and is labeled Backup On Termination. By default, this option is not selected. If this option is selected, the WINS database will be backed up automatically when the WINS Manager is stopped (an exception to this is when the system is shut down gracefully).

- The other option is also encountered in the WINS Server Configuration menu. This option is the Database Backup Path. Note that the path provided with this option cannot be a network path. When the path is specified, the WINS server automatically performs a full backup of the database every 24 hours.

After the WINS server is installed and configured, maintenance is performed through the WINS manager. The WINS manager has a backup option, too. Within the WINS manager, select Mappings → Backup Database. The Select Backup Directory window will appear. Note, once again, that in this window a network path cannot be specified. An important option within the window to note is the Perform Incremental Backup option (at the bottom of the window). If it is enabled, the backup performed will contain only the changes within the database from the last full backup of the database. Of course, you must perform a full backup before this option can be successfully used.

The backup copy of the WINS database is restored automatically, if, upon startup, WINS finds the current database is corrupted. When WINS finds the database corrupted, an automatic recovery is performed from the specified pathname. Additionally, a manual restore can be performed. Within the WINS manager, Mappings → Restore Database is used to perform the manual restore.

To make the most effective use of disk space with respect to the WINS database and its backup, it is important to perform other maintenance measures. These measures include scavenging and compacting the WINS database.

Scavenging is the process by which the database is purged of old entries. During the WINS installation process, the scavenging can be scheduled to occur automatically. There is also an administrative command that can be executed to have the scavenging performed as required.

Compacting is the process by which the database is condensed to remove empty space. Compacting a database helps with performance in addition to reducing disk space requirements. This process is accomplished by stopping the WINS services (there are two services: WINS client and Windows Internet Name Service), running the *COMPACT.EXE* program (located in the *SystemRoot\system32* folder), and then restarting the WINS services.

Parts of Windows NT Not to Back Up

There are certain folders and files in Windows NT that should not be backed up. You may not be concerned about the cost of the tapes, but the time required to perform the backups can be precious. As your site gets larger and the data to back up grows, the amount of time to back up all of the clients will increase. Intelligently and deliberately skipping folders and files during backups is an important time saving consideration.

For example, say you are performing networked backups and backing up all of NT on the clients. Let's also say you have a five-hour window in which to perform backups. You may meet this backup window comfortably for a while, until your site grows. Now you realize your backups are taking about six hours and you are no longer within the backup window. You may find that if you skip backing up portions of NT, it is possible you could stay under the five-hour backup window. The amount of data skipped per client may not be large, but with lots of clients, the total amount of data to skip adds up and you can save time to performing backups. In this example, if you continued to back up all of NT, you would have to purchase an additional backup server. By skipping portions of NT, you can potentially eliminate or at least postpone the purchase of the next backup server.

The folders and files not to back up are listed here with the rationale of why the backup is not required (*X* indicates that these files are located on each drive in your system):

X:\pagefile.sys or other paging files

These files compose the Windows NT virtual memory paging file and are dynamically recreated if they do not exist when Windows NT is booted. You can have multiple copies of this file located on multiple drives.

X:\Temp or other temporary folders

These are any folders that are created as an interim storage location for files. The system one is *C:\Temp*, but there may be others. The location may vary between applications and should be investigated. The contents of the folders should not be backed up, but the folder itself should be.

X:\Recycler or other recycler folders

These are any folders that are used to store removed files or folders temporarily. They are the folders used by the recycle bin. The contents of the folders should not be backed up, but the folder itself should be.

4

Requirements Definition

As you consider the implementation of any backup procedures, the first phase is site survey. Adequately backing up your data requires that you know what is being backed up and how it is being backed up. Every site is different, but this chapter includes a checklist that can be used to assist you. The checklist or site survey helps you evaluate possible aspects of your particular site that affect backups.

The results of the survey will guide you in appropriately sizing the backup system(s) required for your site and assist you in determining if your network infrastructure is adequate for the additional load. The survey also assists in determining what software and hardware to use for your backup server, as well as helping you to perform testing.

Site Survey

This section covers the questions about your environment. The questions are grouped by site, network, data, and cost considerations. After each question, the rationale for the question is provided. These questions should be asked not only about the current environment, but also with respect to any future engineering changes that may be planned for your site.

Of course, not all questions are applicable to every environment, but they will provide food for thought. It is important not to become frustrated during this phase. Distributed environments, by their nature, can create obstacles (such as organizational boundaries) in obtaining the information. However, any information you can collect is better than guessing, so be persistent and don't give up.

Site Considerations

Q: Do you require a particular operating system for your backup server?

This question is most important for large sites that implement the networked backups. Lots of data has to be received by the backup server from hundreds of backup clients. Therefore, the operating system on the server is an important consideration. In a strictly NT environment, the server will be Windows NT–based. This makes administration and maintenance of the backup system easier to handle.

However, even at sites with only NT, you may still want to consider a different backup server operating system. You can purchase more powerful hardware that runs Unix, as opposed to NT. These platforms have faster CPUs, can support more CPUs, and are able to support more memory. Also, the larger server architectures that run Unix are designed with faster backplanes than the architectures that support NT. Of course, this may change in the future.

Environments that choose to have a heterogeneous environment for backups have to coordinate support of their backup server, possibly, by various groups. If a Unix backup server is chosen to back up Windows NT clients, a good working relationship has to be formed between the administrators of each environment to have a successful backup implementation. Of course, tight coordination must be made for the initial installation and configuration of the backup server system. Then, after the initial installation and configuration of the backup server, there are subsequent backup application and operating system patches and hardware upgrades that have to be coordinated on an ongoing basis.

Q: What operating systems are the clients running?

You should investigate how the other operating system environments are performing backups. There may be Unix, Novell, Macintosh, or OS/2 backups performed by other groups within your organization. There is no technical reason that these backups cannot be combined. It is possible to have a centralized backup solution that handles most, if not all, of the client operating systems at your site.

There are advantages and disadvantages to combining the Windows NT backup environment with other environments. The advantages are a consolidated backup infrastructure to support with common tapes, tape drives, backup servers, and software. This can reduce costs. The major disadvantage is that politics may become involved when crossing organizational boundaries.

If a heterogeneous environment is chosen for backups, it is important to have a good set of policies and procedures in place for the backups and restores. Service loads and policies should be documented and formally implemented across the various organizational boundaries. This will help assure compliance and continuity.

Q: Are you constrained to use legacy hardware for the backup server system?

This is a question for sites that implement networked backups. The size of the backup server does have an impact on the amount of time it takes to complete the backups and how quickly restores can be accomplished. Aspects of the backup server that make an impact are the amount of memory, CPU speed, and type of interface boards that are in the server. During the backup process, the backup server must read the data in from the clients across the network, process the data, write it to tape, and catalogue where it resides on tape. During the data restoration, the process is reversed. These processes utilize many different aspects of the backup server.

It is highly recommended that testing be performed before implementation to make sure that the size of your backup server is adequate to meet the backup window available. During the testing process, the backup server should be monitored to determine whether bottlenecks occur on the server. If you find bottlenecks, you can make upgrades to the backup server. Other bottlenecks, such as the client system, the network, or the tape drive are potentially out of your control.

You should investigate what existing purchasing and maintenance hardware contracts exist within your company. Often, it is easier to get additional equipment or support from the existing contracts, and savings may be realized from company-wide contracts. There may be technical reasons why this hardware is not adequate for the backup server, but the option should be explored.

Q: On what hardware platforms are your backup clients running?

You need to know what mix of hardware platforms your backup clients are using. This could include, but is not limited to, Intel, Alpha, MIPS, or Power/PC (you may have some legacy systems to consider). Some sites require PC purchases be made through a central group at your site. If this is the case, you may be able to ask this central group what hardware platforms were purchased. Some sites only allow certain types of PC hardware to be purchased, and in this case the answer may be simple. However, in most sites, PCs are bought by all different groups and each group purchases what they want or what they are familiar with. In this case, you may have to go from PC to PC or group to group to find the answer.

Q: *Will you be using tape drive technology that already exists at your site on the*
     backup server?

The tape drive speed directly affects the length of your backup window. Tape
drives are rated from 500 KB/s all the way up to 5 MB/s and much higher.
There is a big difference and many choices to make.

Maintenance and tape support of the tape drive should be a consideration. It
should not be the sole reason for choosing the tape technology, but it should
be considered. If there is a contract already in place at your site for purchasing tape drives or tapes, like the backup server hardware, that should be
investigated.

With local backups, the tape drives are individually installed on each system,
and sizing the tape drive to the system is important. However, your objective
for the project may also influence what is done.

If the object of the project is to keep the capital expense of the project as low
as possible, then different types of drives sized for different systems may be
the answer for you. Smaller systems cannot drive the faster tape devices to
their rated speeds. It is a waste of capital funds to purchase the faster tape
drives for these slower systems. The disadvantage of this approach is that different tape media have to be purchased for the life of the backup drives and
different maintenance contracts have to be used for each type of drive. This
does increase the total cost of ownership.

If your objective for the project is to implement a solution that is the lowest
total cost of ownership, then the same tape drives should be used for all systems. In this case, a single type of drive is chosen that fits the *average* type of
system. That means that in some cases the drive will be too fast for some systems and too slow for other systems. The initial capital cost is higher, but the
maintenance part is easier. All of the drives use the same tapes, which can be
purchased in bulk, and you only have to deal with maintenance of one type
of equipment.

For networked backup implementations, there are interesting aspects of tape
drive speed that should be mentioned. The backup software plays an important role with respect to how fast the tape hardware can be driven. The
design of the software determines if the package can take full advantage of
the tape drive's rated speed. Testing the software at your site is very
important.

Q: *Will the backup server system be co-located with the backup clients?*

This particular question is not pertinent for local backups. For smaller sites
that implement networked backups, most of the time, the backup server is co-
located with the clients. This is because they share the same network, and

there are limitations on that segment. The server may be located in a different room, such as an equipment room or data center, and possibly on a different floor, but usually the server and clients are located at the same physical building.

With the large sites, there are usually multiple locations. Frequently, the backup server is located at a different site than the clients. This type of configuration provides immediate offsite backups. If the site with the clients has a disaster, backups will be safe at the other site. One major consideration for this implementation is the network capacity between the sites. With newer tape technology utilized with servers that can drive the tape devices at the rated speeds, the network may become the bottleneck. When planning for your backups, you need to consider the network bandwidth available and determine if the remaining bandwidth is enough to support the backups. It may be necessary to install new networks to support your backup project.

Q: Will the backup server be managed by the same individuals who manage the clients, or will these be different groups of people?

Some sites have an operational staff whose job includes managing the backups. These sites may also have a separate systems administration staff handle other aspects of the computers. This most commonly occurs at large sites. If this is how your site is structured, it is important that the two groups communicate during each phase while implementing backups.

There should be a good working relationship established between the two groups. The operational staff is responsible for making sure that the backups are accomplished on a day-to-day basis. The administration staff is responsible for their own group of systems. If the administrator needs to recover a system from a hard disk failure or even a single file due to an accidental deletion, they will be depending on proper backups to accomplish this recovery. If the operational staff fails to make sure the backups are successful, this mistake directly affects the administrator's ability to perform the requested recovery.

Q: What is the priority of backups compared to other batch jobs that may be running, and does your site require some job scheduling integration between backups and other batch jobs?

In most cases, backups run during the night and on weekends. There is a chance that the backup processing may affect other batch jobs also running at night. Another factor is that the batch jobs may be producing output that should be promptly backed up. So it may be ideal to start the backups after a particular batch job completes. This type of situation warrants integration between the scheduling of the batch job and the scheduling of the backups.

If a tight integration between the batch jobs and the backups is not necessary, an easy solution is to begin the backups well after all batch jobs complete. As long as the backups complete, it really does not matter if they start at 8:00 P.M. or 1:00 A.M.

However, at large sites with hundreds or thousands of computers to back up, this may not be enough. Therefore, your site might require an automated job scheduler that can be integrated with batch processing and backups. This type of technology is just beginning to emerge in the Windows NT area and should become more widely available with time.

Q: What are the company's plans for additional systems over the next 12 to 24 months?

At any size site, you want to plan for what will be added to the site over the next 12 to 24 months. You will need to know how many systems will be added to the site, the disk sizes of these new systems, and if any hard drive upgrades will be done for existing computers. All of this information is required for capacity planning. This information may be hard to obtain, but you should try to estimate this.

Q: If the solution may be used at international sites within your organization, will there be data saved in other languages that needs to be backed up?

Filenames in other languages are sometimes saved with a different number of bits to support that particular character set. Since the backup software saves filenames and other information about files, the backup software has to support those other character sets. Basically, the software package must be international. If it is possible that your backup solution may be deployed to international sites, support for the extended character set must be considered.

Q: What restore speeds are required at your site?

The requirements for the expected restore speed are needed for implementing a backup solution at any size site. Most of the time, the answer to this question is "As fast as possible." However, faster restores are more expensive. Also, it is important to juggle the backup speed and the restore speed requirements. Configuration changes can be made to some extent to help with restore speeds; however, these same changes can reduce the backup throughput. A middle ground must be found.

From an engineering perspective, the amount of data backed up far outweighs the amount of data ever restored. Therefore, the backup speeds are more important than the restore speeds. However, from the operational perspective, the restore speeds are what is seen by the operational staff and what is most important. These differing perspectives should be considered carefully.

The restore speeds should be defined and fully tested when the software and hardware you choose for your site is installed and running. If needed, comparative testing can be done between the local restore speed and the network restore speed. If this type of testing is done, do not forget to include the time it takes to retrieve the required tape to perform the restore.

Q: Can the distributed backups be integrated into the mainframe backups?

It is now technically possible to perform backups and restores using portions of the mainframe (MVS/VM) environment. In these solutions, the distributed environment can either send their backup data to the mainframe, or the distributed environment can share large tape libraries with the mainframe. These libraries are large-scale robotic devices, sometimes referred to as tape silos. This type of backup paradigm is breaking new ground. Traditionally the mainframe and distributed environments have kept their distance from one another. However, as it relates to backups, this gap can be bridged.

There are products available today that allow for distributed backups to be performed through the MVS/VM operating systems. The data is sent from a backup server on the distributed side over an SNA or TCP/IP network connection to the mainframe. The mainframe then backs up the data that was written to disks. This is less than optimal if your site has a medium or large Windows NT population, because of the quantity of data that has to be transferred. As the data is processed by the mainframe, there is substantial overhead on the mainframe, and this solution can be quite costly. However, if the backup data for your Windows NT systems is relatively small, you may want to consider this option.

There are other products available today that allow for the mainframe and the distributed backup servers to share a large tape library or silo. These libraries can hold thousands of tapes. The mainframe utilizes a set of preconfigured tapes and tape drives in the tape library, and the distributed backup servers utilize a different set of preconfigured tapes and tape drives. The robotic arm movements within the library are controlled by a separate system. Library requests, such as tape mounts, are sent to the separate library control system. For tape drive reads and writes, both the mainframe and distributed servers are directly connected to their own tape drives. The read and write data is sent directly to the tape drive, not passed through another system. This prevents the mainframe from being a data courier for the distributed environment, thus minimizing mainframe overhead.

Both of these solutions centralize the tape management aspect of backups to one location. Tape management considerations become less of an issue, because usually, the mainframe group is organized with a support staff 24 hours a day, 7 days a week, and mainframe backups are a well-established operational process. Although there are efficiencies to be realized and a great deal of knowledge transferred between the mainframe and distributed operational groups under these scenarios, organizational boundaries must be crossed that can potentially introduce seemingly insurmountable political turf issues.

This book will not go into further detail related to the solutions just discussed. These solutions were mentioned to be considered for your site. However, this book will concentrate on distributed backups in the distributed environment.

Q: What regulatory or company policy issues and concerns should be integrated into the backup implementation?

Contact your company's disaster recovery team, compliance department, and legal department to let them know what you are doing with your backup project. They will most likely have concerns, questions, and issues for you to consider. Getting their input early in the process will help guide you in the right direction.

For example, one responsibility of the legal department is to protect the corporation in the event of a lawsuit. In this vein, any data that is accessible on disk or on backup tapes may be subpoenaed. The corporate attorneys may be concerned about exposure if email messages were subpoenaed. In this example, the corporation may wish not to backup any email messages or institute a small window for retaining email messages. The small window may be for a one-week period with the tapes being reused at the end of the week. So, no email that is over a week old would be on tape backups. This is one example where the legal department may have very specific requirements relating to the backups.

Network Considerations

Q: Can the backup server system support a CDDI, FDDI, fast Ethernet, or ATM connections?

The amount of data required for backup at your site and the size of the nightly backup window available will determine how fast your backup server must run. For example, these calculations may require that your backup server support 100 MB/s network speeds. This is a consideration to be made with the networked backup implementation.

Q: What kind of networks are the clients using?

The speed of the network between the backup server and the backup client is an important consideration for networked backup implementations. Sometimes, all of the systems to be backed up are co-located with the backup server and on the same network. Sometimes, the systems to be backed up are remotely located and will be backed up over 56 KB or 256 KB lines. Most likely, the backup client systems are a combination of fast and slow network connections.

If your site has a combination of network speeds, there is an important feature to consider on the backup server software: serial versus multiplexed backup support.

If you have many slow network connections and you implement serial backups, the backup server may be waiting on data from the backup client because of the low network throughput. With multiplexed backups, the backup server will sense no data coming from one particular backup client and switch to another. This keeps backups running on the backup server as well as the backup server's tape drives streaming, because they are not waiting on the backup clients. For example, let's say your site is multiplexing the data on the backup server, the backup server is on a 100 MB/s backbone, and the backup clients are on many different 10 MB/s networks. For this example, the backup client's slower network will not become a bottleneck. Since the backup server is multiplexed and on a faster network than the clients, the server can switch between the different clients to keep the tape streaming on the backup server.

Some larger sites opt to install 100 MB/s networks between the backup server and some of the backup clients. This network is in addition to the existing networks. The backup network can be installed to support all of the backup clients, the most important backup clients, or the larger backup clients. This separate network keeps all of the backup data off the daily production networks. This type of implementation also helps with restores, because they are done across the backup network without affecting the production network. However, this high-speed network is not used during the day, when backups are not running.

Q: What are the current network speeds and traffic load at your site?

It is important to know this information in order to determine whether additional network capacity is required for the networked backup implementations. To engineer a backup solution properly at medium and large sites, you need to determine whether additional network capacity is required before the solution is put into production. The last thing you want to do is just wait to see whether the network breaks.

Data Considerations

Q: Where is the vital, irreplaceable data located at your site?

Different sites store their data in different locations. The term data is a broad term that includes, but is not limited to, such items as spreadsheets, word processing documents, databases, or applications. Vital, irreplaceable data refers to data that cannot be loaded via diskette, CD, or a network install.

Determining where your vital data is located is important, especially for the networked backup implementations. Backing up data that can be obtained by other means wastes tape, and ultimately, time. The time factor is an issue for both the backup and restore. With the backups, if you are backing up non-vital data on each backup client, then the more backup clients you have, the more the data you are backing up that is not necessary. As you can see, a small amount of non-vital data across a large number of backup clients equals a large amount of non-vital data. The tapes' cost may not be very important to your site, but the amount of time to back up the data is a factor. Remember that you only have so many hours to back up the data. With restores, it can be slow to use tape technology to recover a backup client completely from a raw, new disk. It is faster to restore what you can from CD or via a network install and then restore the vital data from the tape backup server.

Some of the irreplaceable data at a site is located in users' home directories. In general, there are two different ways to configure the location of home directories. The first configuration is with the home directories located on each user's desktop workstation. The second configuration is with the home directories located on a server system. With either configuration, the servers (for example, file servers, database servers, or application servers) have to be fully backed up. Usually, the servers have special custom configurations and changes that can be difficult or time-consuming to reproduce.

If home directories are on a user's desktop, you need to determine if the entire workstation or just the home directories need to be backed up. You need to back up only home directories, unless the workstation has had special configuration changes. The rationale for this is that the basic operating system and applications located on the user's workstation can probably be rebuilt from other media besides backup tape. The information in the user's home directories cannot be reproduced, and therefore should be backed up. With this type of configuration, it is important that the home directories on each workstation are in the same location. This makes configuring the backup server easier and minimizes ongoing configuration management. Remember, the servers still need to be backed up, even though home directories are on user workstations.

If the home directories are located on servers, this may eliminate the need to back up the desktop workstations. In this type of configuration, usually the workstations have only the operating system and perhaps the applications installed on their disk(s). If this is the case, the workstations can be completely rebuilt by diskette, CD, or another networked system, thus eliminating the need to have them backed up.

Determining the exact location of vital data at your site is important, and can get rather complicated. For example, some mail applications store user mail files in the application directory. A conscious decision has to be made to back up this data or not. Besides determining where your home directories are stored, you should document each application at your site and determine where those applications store vital data. This may be a long process, so yet another approach is to back up all data and pay the overhead for the extra tape storage costs.

Q: How many workstations and servers do you have at your site with vital data?

These numbers are really important for sizing your backups. Every computer that is designated to be backed up (Windows NT workstation or server) is referred to as a backup client. A backup client is broadly defined as a system with vital data that cannot be reproduced by any other means. If your site has vital data on workstations and servers, then the number of backup clients is the sum of these two types of systems. If your site has no vital data on your workstations and the workstations will not be backed up, then the number of backup clients can be narrowed to the number of servers.

If an exact number of backup clients cannot be obtained, then an educated guess must be made to the best of your abilities. When using an imprecise count, you may want to pad this number, just slightly, in case you are a bit off. This helps in the event that you make an error, and also helps with unplanned growth that may occur between the time you start planning backups until the backups are fully implemented. Based on my experience and that of others, you should pad between 10% and 25%. For example, assume you have 50 servers at your site to be backed up. For planning purposes, you may want to use the number of 55 to 60 servers. Keep in mind that sites are not reducing the number of computers or the amount of data. So using a larger number will help assure you do not underestimate your backup requirements, and if it is a bit high, you have some room for future growth.

Commercial backup software usually has licensing costs associated with each backup server and the number of backup clients per backup server. So, you need to have a good idea of the number of backup clients you have at your site to help budget for your solution.

Q: How much data has to be backed up?

Once you know where your vital data is located and how many backup clients you have, you need to calculate the total amount of data to be backed up. If an exhaustive survey cannot be done due to time and resource constraints, an estimation is better than nothing at all. You have to have some gauge to help you size your backup requirements.

For example, in the case where home directories are on users' workstations, you may survey 20 users' desktops and determine that the average amount of home directory space is 500 MB. If your site has a total of 130 workstations, then the estimated total disk backups required for workstations would be 65 GB. At this same site, you may survey 5 servers and determine that the average amount of disk space is 5 GB. If your site has a total of 17 servers, then the estimated total disk backups for servers would be 85 GB. The entire site requirements would be adding together 65 GB and 85 GB, which totals to 150 GB total disk backups for the entire site.

Q: Does the data to be backed up reside on a "special" partition?

Examples of applications that create and manage special partitions are Microsoft Exchange, Lotus Notes, or Microsoft SQL Server. Generally these applications are installed on Windows NT servers, and that is where their special partitions reside.

The current off-the-shelf backup software, in general, backs up only standard operating system file types, such as NTFS or FAT. With this in mind, you have these options:

- Purchase a backup utility (available from some database vendors) for the product.

- Purchase an additional piece of software, provided by your backup software vendor, that backs up the special partitions at your site.

- Purchase separate software, from a vendor other than your backup software vendor, that specializes in backing up these types of disk partitions.

- Implement an intermediate step before backups are done. It is sometimes possible that the applications mentioned previously have the option of *dumping* their data from their special partition into a standard file type. Once the data is in a standard file format (NTFS or FAT) it can be backed up by your backup software. This option does require twice as much disk space be allocated for the data: the disk space for the special partition and disk space for the *dumped* data. Also, the reassembly time for restores is longer due to the additional steps involved.

The type of special partitions needs to be determined, so the appropriate backup software or an alternative approach can be used for backups. It is a matter of determining what is available and how you want to integrate it into your site and backup scheme.

Q: Can the databases that are backed up become inaccessible during backup windows, or are they required to be accessible at all times?

Some sites have databases that cannot be brought down without a large loss of revenue to the company. Since backups are a maintenance task and happen every day, a solution must be implemented under which the database is backed up but not brought down. In this situation, whatever solution you implement must be able to provide backups of an active database.

Some backup vendors do have special modules to provide backups of active databases. It depends on the which database application you have installed at your site and which backup vendor you choose.

Q: What backup schedule is required for your site?

The type of vital data you have at your site and the rate of change of that data will determine the backup schedule you implement at your site. The schedules or types of backups can be broken into three general areas: full backups, incremental backups, and differential backups. The following descriptions provide a general description of each and may vary slightly from backup vendor to backup vendor:

Full backups

Full backups back up all files and folders that are on the disk. It is possible to perform full backups each night. This type of schedule is easy to implement, but you waste tapes and time. Not all data changes everyday, so with a full backup schedule everyday, you would be backing up unchanged data each day. At medium and large sites, the extra tapes it would take to perform full backups everyday could become very expensive. Not to mention, you may not have enough time each night to perform the full backups. At small sites, this would require far fewer tapes and less time, so this may be acceptable.

Incremental backups

Incremental backups back up files and folders that have changed since the last incremental backup or the last full backup. So if a full backup is performed on the weekend, then an incremental backup on Monday would back up what changed since the full backup over the weekend. An incremental backup on Tuesday would back up what changed since the incremental on Monday. The incremental backup on Wednesday would backup what changed since the incremental on Tuesday, and so on. A full recover performed on a Thursday would require the full backup from the weekend and the incremental backups for Monday, Tuesday, and Wednesday. The advantage to incremental backups is that the backups utilize minimal tape capacity to get the job done. One disadvantage is that the recovers may require many tapes (depending on which day of the week the recovery is performed).

Differential backups

Differential backups back up the files and folders that have changed since the last full backup. So if a full backup is performed on the weekend, then a differential backup on Monday would back up what changed since the full backup over the weekend. Based on my experience, the backup on Monday would be about 10% of the full backup. A differential backup on Tuesday would back up what changed since the full backup over the weekend. The Tuesday differential backup would be a bit over 10% of the full backup, but just about all of the data will be the same data that changed on Monday. Studies have shown that, for the most part, the same files and folders are accessed everyday; it is generally not the case that users open different files and folder from one day to the next. The differential backup on Wednesday would back up what changed since the full backup over the weekend and so on. The Wednesday differential backup would be more than the Tuesday differential backup, but generally the same data is backed up, once again. A full recover performed on a Thursday morning would require the full backup from the weekend and the differential backup from Wednesday. The advantage to differential backups is that the recovers involve fewer tapes than the incremental backups (depending on which day of the week the recover is performed). Using fewer tapes can make a restore from a differential backup schedule easier than with an incremental backup schedule. The disadvantage is that differential backups utilize more tape capacity to get the job done versus the incremental backups.

Q: Can tapes at your site be rotated and reused at predetermined intervals?

Your individual site's requirements will determine what your tape rotation policy is, or if you rotate tapes at all. An example of a tape rotation policy may be that tapes from incremental or differential backups are reused every four weeks (basically once a month), but the full backup tapes are not rotated and reused. This would mean that the data on the incremental or differential tapes over four weeks old can no longer be retrieved. If some data was created but then removed between two full backups, after four weeks you could no longer retrieve that data from backups.

If you have a fairly stable environment and stable data with low turnover of employees, your site may be a good candidate for reusing tapes. The reason the employee turnover rate is important is because of the backups of employee-generated data. If some employees are only there for a short period of time, you may want to make sure your tape retention and rotation policy takes this into consideration. Their accounts and the contents of their home directory may be removed when they depart. I have seen a situation in which a former employee's data was required from six months previously. In this case, the full and differential tapes for that home directory had to be acquired from the backups for just before their account and home directory was removed. If you have a high rate of change and employee turnover, you may want to think twice before instituting a tape rotation policy that is too strict.

So reusing tapes is a good way to save money on the recurring cost associated with tapes. However, you should ensure that the tapes you reuse are not going to cause problems with restores.

Cost Considerations

Q: How will the initial capital cost for the backup project be funded?

For local backups, there is a one-to-one correlation among the number of tape devices, software licenses, and computers. Therefore, the capital cost of implementing local backups can be attached to the cost of purchasing the computer up front or charged back to each department.

If you implement networked backups and the computers are grouped by department, then the capital costs are easy to determine. All costs associated with the backup server are charged back to the department that server supports. It is similar to local backups, because there is a fairly tight correlation between the backup clients and backup servers.

For the networked backups that not grouped by departments, it is not quite as easy. The total cost of the more centrally located system must first be determined. Then it must be distributed equitably among all backup clients, based on the predicted amount of data that backup client will back up. Once a cost of backups is determined for each backup client, this charge must be summarized for each department.

At some sites, one particular department or group within the organization is tasked with implementing the backups. This group usually has its own budget for the backup project, and the initial capital costs are absorbed by this group.

Q: *How will you sell upgrades and increased capacity for the backup infrastructure to the individuals who will fund the backup project?*

Your organization's backup requirements will probably increase once the initial backup infrastructure is installed. Hard disks in existing systems may be upgraded. These disks are getting bigger and the price per megabyte is getting smaller. Every time you turn around the standard disk size shipped is larger. Also, the number of systems within your organization is likely to keep growing. So those additional systems also need to be backed up.

In the distributed environment, available disk space will eventually be used and the data on those disks need to be backed up. Consider implementing a chargeback system. This would add an additional tariff to every new disk or new system purchased. This money would be used to fund upgrades to the backup infrastructure.

Sizing Backups

The most frequently asked questions, with respect to sizing backups, are what size backup server(s) is required and whether a specific network can handle the additional load. This section will help you answer these questions for your site.

Backup Server Sizing

When determining the server size required to handle your site, the unit of measurement best suited for this purpose is GB/h (gigabytes per hour). You may wonder why you don't use GB/s (gigabytes per second) or MB/s (megabytes per second) as the metric. The problem with per-second measurements is that they are too precise for this purpose. With medium and large sites, the backup server is handling gigabytes and sometimes terabytes of data. Additionally, when backups are running, the backup server is handling network traffic, communicating with each backup client, interfacing with the database associated with the backup server software, and writing to tape. Using the GB/h measurement allows you to calculate the flow of this large quantity of data, taking into consideration trends and overhead processing on the backup server to obtain the actual throughput required. With GB/h, you step back from the problem so that you can see how your overall system is behaving.

The GB/h calculation for the backup server is the aggregate throughput. If the backup server is configured with three tape drives all writing simultaneously, the GB/h would be for all three drives combined. If the backup server has two tape drives, the GB/h would be for the throughput for both drives working together.

For the following sizing estimation procedure, I have assumed that full backups are performed on the weekends. I also assumed that during the weekdays (at night) differentials are performed. The differential is assumed to back up anything on the backup client that had changed since the last full backup. For example, on Saturday through Sunday full backups are done. On Monday night, anything that had changed on Monday would be backed up. On Tuesday night, anything that had changed on Monday and Tuesday would be backed up. On Wednesday night, anything that had changed on Monday, Tuesday, or Wednesday would be backed up. This would go through Friday night. Then, starting Saturday, the full backups would begin and the cycle would start again.

This is a common schedule implementation. If a restore must occur on a Thursday, it requires only the tape(s) used for the full backup the previous weekend, and then the tape(s) used for the differential on Wednesday night. Also, experience has shown that the majority of data changed on a day-to-day basis is the same data Monday through Friday. For this reason, Friday night backups are not five times the size of the differential backup performed on Monday night. You might see Friday night backups twice the size of the differential backups performed on Monday night.

Sizing steps

Server sizing is the process of determining how fast your backup server or group of backup servers must perform to meet the backup window requirements with the amount of data you have at your site. The sizing provides a throughput goal that must be achieved for your backup implementation to be successful.

Once the backup software and hardware is chosen for your implementation, tests at your site must be done. During the testing, the sizing throughput value you calculate from the following steps can be used as your objective. The testing will reveal the actual throughput you can achieve, and can be compared to the calculated goal. If necessary, changes can be made to increase the throughput.

The server sizing equation is as follows:

$$GB/h = \frac{total\_workstation\_data + total\_server\_data}{backup\_time\_window}$$

This equation should be calculated in two different ways:

- Calculate the GB/h required for full backups. In this case, the equation is used as shown and the *backup_time_window* variable is the total number of hours you have available for full backups.

- Calculate the GB/h required for differential backups. For this case, you multiply the numerator by 15% and change the *backup_time_window* variable to the appropriate time allotted for the differential backups.

The larger value of the last two calculations indicates the throughput that the server or group of servers must be able to obtain to be able to complete backups in the time frame desired. Remember, this is the throughput the backup server must achieve to perform the backups including all the overhead processing on the backup server(s). This throughput value should be increased 10% to 25% to account for possible errors in calculating the total number of backup client hosts, the amount of vital data at your site, or growth in the number of computers within your company between the time you start planning the backups until the system is fully implemented.

The variables in the previous equation are defined as follows:

- The variable *total_workstatation_data* is zero, if you do not have vital data on your workstations.

    If a comprehensive disk space survey of all Windows NT workstations was performed, this variable is the sum of all vital data to be backed up on user desktops.

    If an estimated disk space survey was performed for the Windows NT workstations, this variable must be calculated by multiplying the average amount of vital data to be backed up on workstations by the total number of workstations at your site.

- The variable *total_server_data* is the sum of all vital data to be backed up on servers, if a comprehensive disk space survey of all Windows NT servers was performed.

    If an estimated disk space survey was performed for the Windows NT servers, this variable must be calculated by multiplying the average amount of vital data to be backed up on servers by the total number of servers at your site.

- The *backup_time_window* variable is the number of hours available to accomplish backups at your site. You might want to figure this number with the full expectation that backup server maintenance might need to be performed on the weekends when you generally perform full backups. This type of maintenance would include such tasks as operating system patches, upgrades, or tape drive hardware maintenance.

Server sizing example

For this example, say that your company, Genorff Engineering Inc. (GEI), wants to determine the backup server size. GEI has a total of 200 Windows NT workstations to back up, each having an average of 100 MB of vital data. GEI also has a total of 10 Windows NT servers, each having an average of 6 GB of vital data. On the weekends, GEI has a 17-hour window (8:00 A.M. Saturday to 1:00 P.M. on

Sunday) to perform full backups. On the weeknights, GEI has a 5-hour window (11:00 P.M. to 4:00 A.M.) to perform differential backups.

Let's go through the earlier equation for this example for *full backups*:

$$GB/h = \frac{20 \text{ GB} + 60 \text{ GB}}{17 \text{ hours}} = 4.71 \text{ GB/h (approximately)}$$

Now let's go through the equation outlined earlier for this example for *differential backups*:

$$GB/h = \frac{(20 \text{ GB} + 60 \text{ GB}) \times .15}{5 \text{ hours}} = 2.4 \text{ GB/h}$$

Based on these calculations, GEI requires a backup server or a group of backup servers that must be able to support an aggregate of 4.71 GB/h (the larger of the two calculated values) to be able to meet all stated requirements. For planning purposes, you should increase that value by 10% to 25%. So the aggregate value of 4.71 GB/h realistically would actually be between 5.18 GB/h and 5.89 GB/h.

The value you just calculated will be used during the testing phase, described in Chapter 10, *Testing*. You now know the performance you must attain to have a successful backup implementation.

Server sizing quick reference matrices

For your server sizing, quick reference matrices are provided (see Tables 4-1, 4-2, and 4-3 at the end of this chapter). Down the right side of the matrix, choose the value that most closely matches the total amount of vital data you have at your site. This is the sum of variables *total_workstatation_data* and *total_server_data*. Then go across the top of the matrix to find the number of hours you have available for backups, and you can quickly see the total number of GB/h or MB/h your server must be able to attain to complete your backups. This value is used for testing as described in Chapter 10.

When reviewing the matrices, you may note some very large GB/h performance values that must be obtained by the backup server. You may feel these values are unrealistic, but you must consider two factors. First, you may have to have multiple backup servers to get that type of performance. So the value would be the total of all of your backup servers added together. Second, you may have to implement your backups with a Unix backup server versus an NT backup server. It is well known that NT version 4.0 does not have an optimal TCP/IP network stack. This will change with subsequent versions, but for now the performance is lagging.

The tables are split into blocks of 12 hours. Since the weekends have far more than 12 hours available for backups, the matrices were extended. Note that the final matrix only goes up to 36 hours. Yes, there are 48 hours in a weekend, but do not forget to leave time on the weekends for maintenance activities such as maintaining the tape library and tape drives, disk drives, and the server itself. Also, there is maintenance of the software, such as the operating system and backup software for installation and configuration of patches and upgrades. It is easy to forget to schedule time for this type of support activity.

Network Sizing

During the implementation of backups, you may have a concern regarding the current network's ability to handle the additional load. When determining network sizing, the best suited measurement is MB/s, which is different than with server sizing. Networks do not average their data movement over an hour. Networks have to be sized to handle spikes in data transfer and are best suited to be quantified with the smaller metric.

During your initial planning, you can use the value you acquired in your server sizing exercise to help with network sizing. This is a good starting throughput value to give you an idea of the network traffic to expect. However, you do need to record throughput spikes you see during your onsite testing, using the software and hardware you have chosen. The network must have the ability to handle the spikes without causing the network to break.

The network traffic that will occur between the backup servers and the backup clients should be calculated. In most cases, the backup clients will be located on multiple subnets, so the network load will naturally be distributed between those subnets. The area of most concern is the network to which the backup server or group of backup servers is directly connected and any long haul network that may exist between the backup server and the clients. For sites with existing networks, you must determine if the addition of the network backups will be too much of a burden on the infrastructure and if new networks should be installed.

Network sizing based on server sizing

This section lists the steps to take to calculate the network size required for your site, based on the server sizing. Remember this value must be rechecked once you know what throughput spikes you experience based on your site testing and integration!

The network sizing equation is:

$$\text{bits/second} = \left(\frac{server\_speed \text{ GB/h}}{3600 \text{ seconds/hour}}\right) \times 8 \text{ bits/byte}$$

The variable *server_speed* is the larger of the two GB/h values calculated for the server speed in the previous section. This variable is divided by 3600, because there are 3600 seconds in an hour. Then that value is multiplied by 8, because of the 8 bits per byte.

The value calculated with this equation is what your network must be able to handle *at a minimum*. The value will probably be higher in order to handle network spikes (this is reiterated because of its importance).

Network sizing example

For this example, the same company as in the server sizing example will be used, Genorff Engineering Inc. (GEI). GEI has determined that they need to be able to handle 2.4 GB/h during the weekdays and 4.71 GB/h during the weekends to complete their backups in the required window. Based on these values, the estimated network throughput requirements can be calculated.

$$\text{bits/second} = \left(\frac{4.71 \text{ GB/h}}{3600 \text{ seconds/hour}}\right) \times 8 \text{ bits/byte} = 10.48 \text{ MB/s}$$

The results indicate that the GEI network must be able to handle an additional 10.48 MB/s, as a minimum, between the backup server and the backup clients. (The maximum is determined by what spikes are seen in throughput speeds during the test phase and finally your integration phase.)

Remember that the 10.48 MB/s is usually distributed between the clients, and therefore the load will be distributed across multiple subnets. The network on which the backup server is located must handle the entire 10.48 MB/s. If the backup clients are in a different location than the backup servers, the wide area network between the two sites must also handle the 10.48 MB/s.

Network sizing quick reference matrix

For your network sizing, a quick reference matrix is provided (see Table 4-4 at the end of this chapter). In the matrix, find the server speed that most closely matches the one you determined was required in the previous section. Based on this value, you can see what the network requirements will be for your backup server or if you need multiple backup servers. So if you can obtain the server speed required, you now know what stress this type of server performance will place on your network. Based on your current network utilization and using the value you got from the following matrix, you can determine what type of network upgrade may be required for the backup implementation. Some of the values in the matrix may seem excessive, but for full backups at some larger sites, it is not out of the question.

This was stated earlier, but is worth covering again. The network speed obtained from the matrix is the required speed of the backup server network. Remember that you can configure the backup software to back up data from clients that are across multiple subnets. Therefore you can distribute the network load for the backups across multiple slower networks where the backup clients are located.

If you can truly drive the backups at the required speeds (obviously with a very high-powered backup server) and you are using the latest in tape technology, you may be able to overpower a 100 MB/s network. In this situation, you might want to consider other network technology, or put multiple backup servers on multiple 100 MB/s networks. This may happen at extremely large sites that have the performance requirement and lots of backup clients. (Most sites will not fall into this category.)

Table 4-1. Server(s) Sizing Matrix: 3 to 12 Hours

Total Vital Data to Back Up	Number of Hours Available to Complete Backups									
	3 hrs	4 hrs	5 hrs	6 hrs	7 hrs	8 hrs	9 hrs	10 hrs	11 hrs	12 hrs
5 GB	1.7 GB/h	1.25 GB/h	1 GB/h	833 MB/h	714 MB/h	625 MB/h	555 MB/h	500 MB/h	455 MB/h	417 MB/h
10 GB	3.3 GB/h	2.5 GB/h	2 GB/h	1.7 GB/h	1.43 GB/h	1.25 GB/h	1.1 GB/h	1 GB/h	909 MB/h	833 MB/h
15 GB	5 GB/h	3.75 GB/h	3 GB/h	2.5 GB/h	2.14 GB/h	1.87 GB/h	1.67 GB/h	1.5 GB/h	1.36 GB/h	1.25 GB/h
20 GB	6.6 GB/h	5 GB/h	4 GB/h	3.33 GB/h	2.86 GB/h	2.5 GB/h	2.22 GB/h	2 GB/h	1.82 GB/h	1.67 GB/h
25 GB	8.3 GB/h	6.25 GB/h	5 GB/h	4.17 GB/h	3.57 GB/h	3.13 GB/h	2.78 GB/h	2.5 GB/h	2.27 GB/h	2.08 GB/h
30 GB	10 GB/h	7.5 GB/h	6 GB/h	5 GB/h	4.28 GB/h	3.75 GB/h	3.33 GB/h	3 GB/h	2.73 GB/h	2.5 GB/h
35 GB	11.7 GB/h	8.75 GB/h	7 GB/h	5.83 GB/h	5 GB/h	4.38 GB/h	3.89 GB/h	3.5 GB/h	3.18 GB/h	2.92 GB/h
40 GB	13.3 GB/h	10 GB/h	8 GB/h	6.67 GB/h	5.71 GB/h	5 GB/h	4.44 GB/h	4 GB/h	3.64 GB/h	3.33 GB/h
45 GB	15 GB/h	11.3 GB/h	9 GB/h	7.5 GB/h	6.43 GB/h	5.63 GB/h	5 GB/h	4.5 GB/h	4.09 GB/h	3.75 GB/h
50 GB	16,7 GB/h	12.5 GB/h	10 GB/h	8.33 GB/h	7.14 GB/h	6.25 GB/h	5.55 GB/h	5 GB/h	4.54 GB/h	4.17 GB/h
55 GB	18.3 GB/h	13.8 GB/h	11 GB/h	9.17 GB/h	7.86 GB/h	6.87 GB/h	6.11 GB/h	5.5 GB/h	5 GB/h	4.58 GB/h
60 GB	20 GB/h	15 GB/h	12 GB/h	10 GB/h	8.57 GB/h	7.5 GB/h	6.67 GB/h	6 GB/h	5.45 GB/h	5 GB/h
65 GB	21.7 GB/h	16.3 GB/h	13 GB/h	10.8 GB/h	9.28 GB/h	8.13 GB/h	7.22 GB/h	6.5 GB/h	5.9 GB/h	5.42 GB/h
70 GB	23.3 GB/h	17.5 GB/h	14 GB/h	11.7 GB/h	10 GB/h	8.75 GB/h	7.78 GB/h	7 GB/h	6.36 GB/h	5.83 GB/h
75 GB	25 GB/h	18.8 GB/h	15 GB/h	12.5 GB/h	10.7 GB/h	9.37 GB/h	8.33 GB/h	7.5 GB/h	6.82 GB/h	6.25 GB/h
80 GB	26.7 GB/h	20 GB/h	16 GB/h	13.3 GB/h	11.4 GB/h	10 GB/h	8.89 GB/h	8 GB/h	7.27 GB/h	6.67 GB/h
85 GB	28.3 GB/h	21.3 GB/h	17 GB/h	14.2 GB/h	12.1 GB/h	10.6 GB/h	9.44 GB/h	8.5 GB/h	7.73 GB/h	7.08 GB/h
90 GB	30 GB/h	22.5 GB/h	18 GB/h	15 GB/h	12.9 GB/h	11.3 GB/h	10 GB/h	9 GB/h	8.12 GB/h	7.5 GB/h
95 GB	31.6 GB/h	23.8 GB/h	31.7 GB/h	15.8 GB/h	13.6 GB/h	11.9 GB/h	10.6 GB/h	9.5 GB/h	8.64 GB/h	7.92 GB/h
100 GB	33.3 GB/h	25 GB/h	20 GB/h	16.7 GB/h	14.3 GB/h	12.5 GB/h	11.1 GB/h	10 GB/h	9.09 GB/h	8.33 GB/h
110 GB	36.7 GB/h	27.5 GB/h	22 GB/h	18.3 GB/h	15.7 GB/h	13.8 GB/h	12.2 GB/h	11 GB/h	10 GB/h	9.17 GB/h
120 GB	40 GB/h	30 GB/h	24 GB/h	20 GB/h	17.1 GB/h	15 GB/h	13.3 GB/h	12 GB/h	10.9 GB/h	10 GB/h
130 GB	43.3 GB/h	32.5 GB/h	26 GB/h	21.7 GB/h	18.6 GB/h	16.2 GB/h	14.4 GB/h	13 GB/h	11.8 GB/h	10.8 GB/h

Table 4-1. Server(s) Sizing Matrix: 3 to 12 Hours (continued)

Total Vital Data to Back Up	Number of Hours Available to Complete Backups									
	3 hrs	4 hrs	5 hrs	6 hrs	7 hrs	8 hrs	9 hrs	10 hrs	11 hrs	12 hrs
140 GB	46.7 GB/h	35 GB/h	28 GB/h	23.3 GB/h	20 GB/h	17.5 GB/h	15.5 GB/h	14 GB/h	12.7 GB/h	11.7 GB/h
150 GB	50 GB/h	37.5 GB/h	30 GB/h	25 GB/h	21.4 GB/h	18.8 GB/h	16.7 GB/h	15 GB/h	15.2 GB/h	12.5 GB/h
160 GB	53.3 GB/h	37.5 GB/h	32 GB/h	26.7 GB/h	22.9 GB/h	20 GB/h	17.8 GB/h	16 GB/h	14.5 GB/h	13.3 GB/h

Table 4-2. Server(s) Sizing Matrix: 13 to 24 Hours

Total Vital Data to Back Up	Number of Hours Available to Complete Backups											
	13 hrs	14 hrs	15 hrs	16 hrs	17 hrs	18 hrs	19 hrs	20 hrs	21 hrs	22 hrs	23 hrs	24 hrs
5 GB	385 MB/h	357 MB/h	333 MB/h	312 MB/h	294 MB/h	278 MB/h	263 MB/h	250 MB/h	238 MB/h	227 MB/h	217 MB/h	208 MB/h
10 GB	769 MB/h	714 MB/h	667 MB/h	625 MB/h	588 MB/h	555 MB/h	526 MB/h	500 MB/h	476 MB/h	454 MB/h	435 MB/h	417 MB/h
15 GB	1.15 GB/h	1.07 GB/h	1 GB/h	937 MB/h	882 MB/h	833 MB/h	789 MB/h	750 MB/h	714 MB/h	682 MB/h	652 MB/h	625 MB/h
20 GB	1.54 GB/h	1.43 GB/h	1.33 GB/h	1.25 GB/h	1.18 GB/h	1.11 GB/h	1.05 GB/h	1 GB/h	952 MB/h	909 MB/h	869 MB/h	833 MB/h
25 GB	1.92 GB/h	1.43 GB/h	1.67 GB/h	1.56 GB/h	1.47 GB/h	1.39 GB/h	1.32 GB/h	1.25 GB/h	1.19 GB/h	1.14 GB/h	1.09 GB/h	1.04 GB/h
30 GB	2.31 GB/h	2.14 GB/h	2 GB/h	1.88 GB/h	1.76 GB/h	1.67 GB/h	1.58 GB/h	1.5 GB/h	1.43 GB/h	1.36 GB/h	1.3 GB/h	1.25 GB/h
35 GB	2.69 GB/h	2.5GB/h	2.33 GB/h	2.19 GB/h	2.06 GB/h	1.94 GB/h	1.84 GB/h	1.75 GB/h	1.67 GB/h	1.59 GB/h	1.52 GB/h	1.46 GB/h
40 GB	3.08 GB/h	2.86 GB/h	2.67 GB/h	2.5 GB/h	2.35 GB/h	2.22 GB/h	2.11 GB/h	2 GB/h	1.9 GB/h	1.82 GB/h	1.74 GB/h	1.67 GB/h
45 GB	3.46 GB/h	3.21 GB/h	3 GB/h	2.81 GB/h	2.65 GB/h	2.5 GB/h	2.37 GB/h	2.25 GB/h	2.14 GB/h	2.04 GB/h	1.96 GB/h	1.87 GB/h
50 GB	3.85 GB/h	3.57 GB/h	3.33 GB/h	3.13 GB/h	2.94 GB/h	2.78 GB/h	2.63 GB/h	2.5 GB/h	2.38 GB/h	2.27 GB/h	2.17 GB/h	2.08 GB/h
55 GB	4.23 GB/h	3.93 GB/h	3.67 GB/h	3.44 GB/h	3.24 GB/h	3.06 GB/h	2.89 GB/h	2.75 GB/h	2.62 GB/h	2.5 GB/h	2.39 GB/h	2.29 GB/h
60 GB	4.62 GB/h	4.28 GB/h	4 GB/h	3.75 GB/h	3.53 GB/h	3.33 GB/h	3.16 GB/h	3 GB/h	2.86 GB/h	2.73 GB/h	2.61 GB/h	2.5 GB/h
65 GB	5 GB/h	4.64 GB/h	4.33 GB/h	4.06 GB/h	3.82 GB/h	3.61 GB/h	3.42 GB/h	3.25 GB/h	3.09 GB/h	2.95 GB/h	2.83 GB/h	2.71 GB/h
70 GB	5.38 GB/h	5 GB/h	4.67 GB/h	4.38 GB/h	4.12 GB/h	3.89 GB/h	3.68 GB/h	3.5 GB/h	3.33 GB/h	3.18 GB/h	3.04 GB/h	2.92 GB/h

Table 4-2. Server(s) Sizing Matrix: 13 to 24 Hours (continued)

Total Vital Data to Back Up	Number of Hours Available to Complete Backups											
	13 hrs	14 hrs	15 hrs	16 hrs	17 hrs	18 hrs	19 hrs	20 hrs	21 hrs	22 hrs	23 hrs	24 hrs
75 GB	5.77 GB/h	5.36 GB/h	5 GB/h	4.69 GB/h	4.41 GB/h	4.17 GB/h	3.95 GB/h	3.75 GB/h	3.57 GB/h	3.41 GB/h	3.26 GB/h	3.13 GB/h
80 GB	6.15 GB/h	5.71 GB/h	5.33 GB/h	5 GB/h	4.71 GB/h	4.44 GB/h	4.21 GB/h	4 GB/h	3.81 GB/h	3.64 GB/h	3.48 GB/h	3.33 GB/h
85 GB	6.54 GB/h	6.07 GB/h	5.67 GB/h	5.31 GB/h	5 GB/h	4.72 GB/h	4.47 GB/h	4.25 GB/h	4.05 GB/h	3.86 GB/h	3.69 GB/h	3.54 GB/h
90 GB	6.92 GB/h	6.43 GB/h	6 GB/h	5.63 GB/h	5.29 GB/h	5 GB/h	4.74 GB/h	4.5 GB/h	4.28 GB/h	4.09 GB/h	3.91 GB/h	3.75 GB/h
95 GB	7.31 GB/h	6.78 GB/h	6.33 GB/h	5.94 GB/h	5.59 GB/h	5.28 GB/h	5 GB/h	4.75 GB/h	4.52 GB/h	4.32 GB/h	4.13 GB/h	3.96 GB/h
100 GB	7.69 GB/h	7.14 GB/h	6.67 GB/h	6.25 GB/h	5.88 GB/h	5.56 GB/h	5.26 GB/h	5 GB/h	4.76 GB/h	4.55 GB/h	4.35 GB/h	4.17 GB/h
110 GB	8.46 GB/h	7.86 GB/h	7.33 GB/h	6.88 GB/h	6.47 GB/h	6.11 GB/h	5.79 GB/h	5.5 GB/h	5.24 GB/h	5 GB/h	4.78 GB/h	4.58 GB/h
120 GB	9.23 GB/h	8.57 GB/h	8 GB/h	7.5 GB/h	7.06 GB/h	6.67 GB/h	6.32 GB/h	6 GB/h	5.71 GB/h	5.45 GB/h	5.22 GB/h	5 GB/h
130 GB	10 GB/h	9.28 GB/h	8.67 GB/h	8.13 GB/h	7.65 GB/h	7.22 GB/h	6.84 GB/h	6.5 GB/h	6.19 GB/h	5.91 GB/h	5.65 GB/h	5.42 GB/h
140 GB	10.8 GB/h	10 GB/h	9.33 GB/h	8.75 GB/h	8.24 GB/h	7.78 GB/h	7.37 GB/h	7 GB/h	6.67 GB/h	6.36 GB/h	6.09 GB/h	5.83 GB/h
150 GB	11.5 GB/h	10.7 GB/h	10 GB/h	9.38 GB/h	8.82 GB/h	8.33 GB/h	7.89 GB/h	7.5 GB/h	7.14 GB/h	6.82 GB/h	6.52 GB/h	6.25 GB/h
160 GB	12.3 GB/h	11.4 GB/h	10.7 GB/h	10 GB/h	9.41 GB/h	8.89 GB/h	8.42 GB/h	8 GB/h	7.62 GB/h	7.27 GB/h	6.96 GB/h	6.67 GB/h

Table 4-3. Server(s) Sizing Matrix: 25 to 36 Hours

Total Vital Data to Backup	Number of Hours Available to Complete Backups											
	25 hrs	26 hrs	27 hrs	28 hrs	29 hrs	30 hrs	31 hrs	32 hrs	33 hrs	34 hrs	35 hrs	36 hrs
5 GB	200 MB/h	192 MB/h	185 MB/h	178 MB/h	172 MB/h	167 MB/h	161 MB/h	156 MB/h	152 MB/h	147 MB/h	143 MB/h	139 MB/h
10 GB	400 MB/h	385 MB/h	370 MB/h	357 MB/h	345 MB/h	333 MB/h	323 MB/h	313 MB/h	303 MB/h	294 MB/h	286 MB/h	278 MB/h
15 GB	600 MB/h	577 MB/h	556 MB/h	536 MB/h	517 MB/h	500 MB/h	484 MB/h	469 MB/h	455 MB/h	441 MB/h	429 MB/h	417 MB/h
20 GB	800 MB/h	769 MB/h	741 MB/h	714 MB/h	690 MB/h	667 MB/h	645 MB/h	625 MB/h	606 MB/h	588 MB/h	571 MB/h	555 MB/h
25 GB	1 GB/h	962 MB/h	926 MB/h	893 MB/h	862 MB/h	833 MB/h	806 MB/h	781 MB/h	758 MB/h	735 MB/h	714 MB/h	694 MB/h

Table 4-3. Server(s) Sizing Matrix: 25 to 36 Hours (continued)

Total Vital Data to Backup	Number of Hours Available to Complete Backups											
	25 hrs	26 hrs	27 hrs	28 hrs	29 hrs	30 hrs	31 hrs	32 hrs	33 hrs	34 hrs	35 hrs	36 hrs
30 GB	1.2 GB/h	1.15 GB/h	1.11 GB/h	1.07 GB/h	1.03 GB/h	1 GB/h	968 MB/h	938 MB/h	909 MB/h	882 MB/h	857 MB/h	833 MB/h
35 GB	1.4 GB/h	1.35 GB/h	1.3 GB/h	1.25 GB/h	1.21 GB/h	1.17 GB/h	1.13 GB/h	1.09 GB/h	1.06 GB/h	1.03 GB/h	1 GB/h	972 MB/h
40 GB	1.6 GB/h	1.54 GB/h	1.48 GB/h	1.43 GB/h	1.38 GB/h	1.33 GB/h	1.29 GB/h	1.25 GB/h	1.21 GB/h	1.18 GB/h	1.14 GB/h	1.11 GB/h
45 GB	1.8 GB/h	1.73 GB/h	1.67 GB/h	1.61 GB/h	1.55 GB/h	1.5 GB/h	1.45 GB/h	1.41 GB/h	1.36 GB/h	1.32 GB/h	1.29 GB/h	1.25 GB/h
50 GB	2 GB/h	1.92 GB/h	1.85 GB/h	1.79 GB/h	1.72 GB/h	1.67 GB/h	1.61 GB/h	1.56 GB/h	1.51 GB/h	1.47 GB/h	1.43 GB/h	1.39 GB/h
55 GB	2.2 GB/h	2.12 GB/h	2.04 GB/h	1.96 GB/h	1.89 GB/h	1.83 GB/h	1.77 GB/h	1.72 GB/h	1.67 GB/h	1.62 GB/h	1.57 GB/h	1.53 GB/h
60 GB	2.4 GB/h	2.31 GB/h	2.22 GB/h	2.14 GB/h	2.07 GB/h	2 GB/h	1.94 GB/h	1.88 GB/h	1.82 GB/h	1.76 GB/h	1.71 GB/h	1.67 GB/h
65 GB	2.6 GB/h	2.5 GB/h	2.41 GB/h	2.32 GB/h	2.24 GB/h	2.17 GB/h	2.09 GB/h	2.03 GB/h	1.97 GB/h	1.91 GB/h	1.86 GB/h	1.81 GB/h
70 GB	2.8 GB/h	2.69 GB/h	2.59 GB/h	2.5 GB/h	2.41 GB/h	2.33 GB/h	2.26 GB/h	2.19 GB/h	2.12 GB/h	2.06 GB/h	2 GB/h	1.94 GB/h
75 GB	3 GB/h	2.88 GB/h	2.78 GB/h	2.68 GB/h	2.59 GB/h	2.5 GB/h	2.42 GB/h	2.34 GB/h	2.27 GB/h	2.21 GB/h	2.14 GB/h	2.08 GB/h
80 GB	3.2 GB/h	3.08 GB/h	2.96 GB/h	2.86 GB/h	2.76 GB/h	2.67 GB/h	2.58 GB/h	2.5 GB/h	2.42 GB/h	2.35 GB/h	2.29 GB/h	2.22 GB/h
85 GB	3.4 GB/h	3.27 GB/h	3.15 GB/h	3.04 GB/h	2.93 GB/h	2.83 GB/h	2.74 GB/h	2.66 GB/h	2.58 GB/h	2.5 GB/h	2.43 GB/h	2.36 GB/h
90 GB	3.6 GB/h	3.46 GB/h	3.33 GB/h	3.21 GB/h	3.1 GB/h	3 GB/h	2.9 GB/h	2.81 GB/h	2.73 GB/h	2.65 GB/h	2.57 GB/h	2.5 GB/h
95 GB	3.8 GB/h	3.65 GB/h	3.52 GB/h	3.39 GB/h	3.28 GB/h	3.17 GB/h	3.06 GB/h	2.97 GB/h	2.88 GB/h	2.79 GB/h	2.71 GB/h	2.64 GB/h
100 GB	4 GB/h	3.85 GB/h	3.7 GB/h	3.57 GB/h	3.45 GB/h	3.33 GB/h	3.23 GB/h	3.12 GB/h	3.03 GB/h	2.94 GB/h	2.86 GB/h	2.78 GB/h
110 GB	4.4 GB/h	4.23 GB/h	4.07 GB/h	3.93 GB/h	3.79 GB/h	3.67 GB/h	3.55 GB/h	3.44 GB/h	3.33 GB/h	3.24 GB/h	3.14 GB/h	3.06 GB/h
120 GB	4.8 GB/h	4.62 GB/h	4.44 GB/h	4.29 GB/h	4.14 GB/h	4 GB/h	3.87 GB/h	3.75 GB/h	3.64 GB/h	3.53 GB/h	3.43 GB/h	3.33 GB/h
130 GB	5.2 GB/h	5 GB/h	4.81 GB/h	4.64 GB/h	4.48 GB/h	4.33 GB/h	4.19 GB/h	4.06 GB/h	3.94 GB/h	3.82 GB/h	3.71 GB/h	3.61 GB/h
140 GB	5.6 GB/h	5.38 GB/h	5.18 GB/h	5 GB/h	4.83 GB/h	4.67 GB/h	4.52 GB/h	4.38 GB/h	4.24 GB/h	4.12 GB/h	4 GB/h	3.89 GB/h
150 GB	6 GB/h	5.77 GB/h	5.56 GB/h	5.36 GB/h	5.17 GB/h	5 GB/h	4.84 GB/h	4.69 GB/h	4.55 GB/h	4.41 GB/h	4.29 GB/h	4.17 GB/h
160 GB	6.4 GB/h	6.15 GB/h	5.92 GB/h	5.71 GB/h	5.52 GB/h	5.33 GB/h	5.16 GB/h	5 GB/h	4.85 GB/h	4.71 GB/h	4.57 GB/h	4.44 GB/h

Table 4-4. Network Sizing Matrix

Server Speed Required	Backup Server Network Required
100 MB/h	.22 MB/s
125 MB/h	.28 MB/s
150 MB/h	.33 MB/s
175 MB/h	.39 MB/s
200 MB/h	.44 MB/s
225 MB/h	.5 MB/s
250 MB/h	.56 MB/s
275 MB/h	.61 MB/s
300 MB/h	.67 MB/s
325 MB/h	.72 MB/s
350 MB/h	.78 MB/s
375 MB/h	.83 MB/s
400 MB/h	.89 MB/s
425 MB/h	.94 MB/s
450 MB/h	1 MB/s
475 MB/h	1.06 MB/s
500 MB/h	1.11 MB/s
525 MB/h	1.17 MB/s
550 MB/h	1.22 MB/s
575 MB/h	1.28 MB/s
600 MB/h	1.44 MB/s
625 MB/h	1.39 MB/s
650 MB/h	1.44 MB/s
675 MB/h	1.5 MB/s
700 MB/h	1.56 MB/s
725 MB/h	1.61 MB/s
750 MB/h	1.67 MB/s
775 MB/h	1.72 MB/s
800 MB/h	1.78 MB/s
825 MB/h	1.83 MB/s
850 MB/h	1.89 MB/s
875 MB/h	1.94 MB/s
900 MB/h	2 MB/s
925 MB/h	2.06 MB/s
950 MB/h	2.11 MB/s
975 MB/h	2.17 MB/s

Table 4-4. Network Sizing Matrix (continued)

Server Speed Required	Backup Server Network Required
1 GB/h	2.22 MB/s
1.25 GB/h	2.78 MB/s
1.5 GB/h	3.33 MB/s
1.75 GB/h	3.89 MB/s
2 GB/h	4.44 MB/s
2.25 GB/h	5 MB/s
2.5 GB/h	5.56 MB/s
2.75 GB/h	6.11 MB/s
3 GB/h	6.67 MB/s
3.25 GB/h	7.22 MB/s
3.5 GB/h	7.78 MB/s
3.75 GB/h	8.33 MB/s
4 GB/h	8.89 MB/s
4.25 GB/h	9.44 MB/s
4.5 GB/h	10 MB/s
4.75 GB/h	10.56 MB/s
5 GB/h	11.1 MB/s
5.25 GB/h	11.67 MB/s
5.5 GB/h	12.2 MB/s
5.75 GB/h	12.78 MB/s
6 GB/h	13.33 MB/s
6.25 GB/h	13.89 MB/s
6.5 GB/h	14.44 MB/s
6.75 GB/h	15 MB/s
7 GB/h	15.56 MB/s
7.25 GB/h	16.11 MB/s
7.5 GB/h	16.67 MB/s
7.75 GB/h	17.22 MB/s
8 GB/h	17.78 MB/s
8.25 GB/h	18.33 MB/s
8.5 GB/h	18.89 MB/s
8.75 GB/h	19.44 MB/s
9 GB/h	20 MB/s
9.25 GB/h	20.56 MB/s
9.5 GB/h	21.11 MB/s
9.75 GB/h	21.67 MB/s

Table 4-4. Network Sizing Matrix (continued)

Server Speed Required	Backup Server Network Required
10 GB/h	22.22 MB/s
10.25 GB/h	22.78 MB/s
10.5 GB/h	23.33 MB/s
10.75 GB/h	23.89 MB/s
11 GB/h	24.44 MB/s
11.25 GB/h	25 MB/s
11.5 GB/h	25.56 MB/s
11.75 GB/h	26.11 MB/s
12 GB/h	26.67 MB/s
12.25 GB/h	27.22 MB/s
12.5 GB/h	27.78 MB/s
12.75 GB/h	28.33 MB/s
13 GB/h	28.89 MB/s
13.25 GB/h	29.44 MB/s
13.5 GB/h	30 MB/s
13.75 GB/h	30.56 MB/s
14 GB/h	31.11 MB/s
14.25 GB/h	31.67 MB/s
14.5 GB/h	32.22 MB/s
14.75 GB/h	32.78 MB/s
15 GB/h	33.33 MB/s
15.25 GB/h	33.89 MB/s
15.5 GB/h	34.44 MB/s
15.75 GB/h	35 MB/s
16 GB/h	35.56 MB/s
16.25 GB/h	36.11 MB/s
16.5 GB/h	36.67 MB/s
16.75 GB/h	37.22 MB/s
17 GB/h	37.78 MB/s
17.25 GB/h	38.33 MB/s
17.5 GB/h	38.89 MB/s
17.75 GB/h	39.44 MB/s
18 GB/h	40 MB/s
18.25 GB/h	40.56 MB/s
18.5 GB/h	41.11 MB/s
18.75 GB/h	41.67 MB/s

Table 4-4. Network Sizing Matrix (continued)

Server Speed Required	Backup Server Network Required
19 GB/h	42.22 MB/s
19.25 GB/h	42.78 MB/s
19.5 GB/h	43.33 MB/s
19.75 GB/h	43.89 MB/s
20 GB/h	44.44 MB/s
20.25 GB/h	45 MB/s
20.5 GB/h	45.56 MB/s
20.75 GB/h	46.11 MB/s
21 GB/h	46.67 MB/s
21.25 GB/h	47.22 MB/s
21.5 GB/h	47.78 MB/s
21.75 GB/h	48.33 MB/s
22 GB/h	48.89 MB/s
22.25 GB/h	49.44 MB/s
22.5 GB/h	50 MB/s
22.75 GB/h	50.56 MB/s
23 GB/h	51.11 MB/s
23.25 GB/h	51.67 MB/s
23.5 GB/h	52.22 MB/s
23.75 GB/h	52.78 MB/s
24 GB/h	53.33 MB/s
24.25 GB/h	53.89 MB/s
24.5 GB/h	54.44 MB/s
24.75 GB/h	55 MB/s
25 GB/h	55.56 MB/s
25.25 GB/h	56.11 MB/s
25.5 GB/h	56.67 MB/s
25.75 GB/h	57.22 MB/s
26 GB/h	57.78 MB/s
26.25 GB/h	58.33 MB/s
26.5 GB/h	58.89 MB/s
26.75 GB/h	59.44 MB/s
27 GB/h	60 MB/s
27.25 GB/h	60.56 MB/s
27.5 GB/h	61.11 MB/s
27.75 GB/h	61.67 MB/s

Table 4-4. Network Sizing Matrix (continued)

Server Speed Required	Backup Server Network Required
28 GB/h	62.22 MB/s
28.25 GB/h	62.78 MB/s
28.5 GB/h	63.33 MB/s
28.75 GB/h	63.89 MB/s
29 GB/h	64.44 MB/s
29.25 GB/h	65 MB/s
29.5 GB/h	65.56 MB/s
29.75 GB/h	66.11 MB/s
30 GB/h	66.67 MB/s
30.25 GB/h	67.22 MB/s
30.5 GB/h	67.78 MB/s
30.75 GB/h	68.33 MB/s

5

In this chapter:
- *Policy Statement*
- *Education*
- *Charge Back*

Policy and Politics

Backups and restores are not strictly technical in nature. Backup projects fail or are ineffective more frequently due to political or organizational issues than technical problems. This chapter covers the nontechnical aspects of implementing a backup implementation. Taking the items listed in this chapter into consideration in the early phases of planning will improve your project's chances of acceptance and success.

Policy Statement

Without question, the most important component to understand, and understand early, is your backup policy. The policy statement and the educational sessions mentioned below go hand in hand. The policy includes not only what data will be backed up and how often, but what data will *not* be backed up and why it is omitted from the backups. The backup policy can be difficult to accomplish but is very important to achieve.

This is where the compliance and legal departments, as well as senior management, should be enlisted. When they are involved from the beginning, you will cement a relationship that will help with future audits and upgrades of the backup and recovery system and process. Also, schedule the audits from the beginning (for example, every six months) to review the backup system performance and growth. Basically, you must build an alliance to assure ongoing compliance and efficiency.

The backup policy statement should be a living document. It should be flexible and should change as required by site changes. When changes are made, don't forget to notify all managers, system administrators, and end users about the changes and pass out the new statement. Actually, this statement is a good candidate for your internal corporate web site. As the document changes, email notifications can be sent out with just highlights of the changes made to the statement. The email can reference the actual document located in a web page where everyone can read it as required.

The following is a checklist of items to consider including in your backup policy. The list is not in order of importance. The importance of each item is determined on a site-by-site basis.

Q: What systems will be backed up?

The systems to be backed up are determined by your site survey. These are the computers that contain vital data. The raw number of backup clients isn't enough information for your policy statement. The specific groups of the backup clients or specific functions of particular backup clients must be stated so that there is no miscommunication or confusion. You don't want to state specific backup clients by name, because specific computer names are difficult to track as your site grows. For example, it is easier to state that all servers in the accounting and payroll departments will be backed up instead of each backup client's name.

Q: What data will be backed up?

This is the vital data identified in the site survey. What will be backed up should be well defined and specifically stated in the policy, so that there is no possibility of confusion at a later time. When identifying what data will be backed up, you may want to define it as the type of data, not every specific file or folder name. For example, all home directories on the systems will be backed up.

Q: What backup schedule or policy will be implemented?

You should state specifically when full backups will be performed. Additionally, you should discuss whether incremental backups or differential backups will be performed and at what intervals. This will set the appropriate restore expectations of the user community and help define the recurring tape costs. The number of tapes required for a particular restore affects the restore speed. The number of tapes to perform a backup affects the ongoing costs of tapes for your site.

Q: What will be the policy for building and updating Emergency Repair Disks?

For sites that do build and update the ERDs, you should document what the policy will be for these diskettes. You should state clearly that they do need to be created upon system installation (it may be obvious, but worth stating) and when they should be updated. Decide whether they should be updated only when changes are made to the systems, or on a regular schedule, such as once a month.

Q: What data will not be backed up?

Stating what will not be backed up may seem excessive. You may be inclined to state that if it isn't in the list of what is backed up, it is not backed up. However, when someone sees a list of what isn't backed up, it sometimes triggers a question or concern. The whole idea of the policy statement is to be thorough, and, in doing so, you should include a list of what is not backed up as well as what is backed up.

Q: What is the tape rotation policy for the backup tapes?

How tapes are rotated and reused should be well defined. This will set expectations for what can be restored. Let's say full backups are performed weekly and incremental backups are performed on weekdays. It may seem logical that after eight weeks, the incremental tapes are rotated and reused. This means that any data older than eight weeks that was created during the week and then removed during that same week may not be restorable. Data older than eight weeks that was backed up during the full backup on the weekends will be available for a restore.

Q: How long will the backup tapes be kept onsite?

At most sites, backup tapes are kept locally for some amount of time and then moved offsite to a warehouse. There may be legal or compliance issues involved with defining how long the tapes stay onsite. For example, backup data may be required by your company to be placed in an offsite location immediately because of disaster recovery reasons. If you are implementing networked backup, your backup server may not be co-located with your backup clients. If the tapes and backup clients are not physically at the same site, the length of time the tapes remain at the same site as the backup server may be longer. These issues should be defined up front.

Q: What is the expected restore response for backup tapes kept onsite?

This information is a factor of how long the tapes are kept onsite. For example, you may decide that the tapes are kept locally for only four months. In this case, the backup policy may be that for restores of information less than four months old, the expected response time will be some number of minutes or hours. The number of minutes or hours for these types of restores depends on whether you have a tape library and the size and responsiveness of your staff. Generally, the networked backups are implemented with a tape library, and the local backup implementation rarely uses tape libraries.

If you do not have a tape library, the restore response value is very site-dependent. The restore request must be received by the staff responsible for the backups and restores. If the restore request is for data from the previous night, then the tape required may still be in the tape drive and the restore can be started immediately. If the request is for a previous night's backup, then the tape must be acquired and physically loaded into the tape drive. This is all based on human intervention and is definitely site-dependent.

If you have a tape library, then you first need to determine how much data is kept in the library. To calculate this value, refer to Chapter 9, *Hardware*. For example, if the library contains two months' worth of backup data, then the restore window for the past two months is all handled by the library mounting the appropriate tape. In this case, no human intervention is required for restore requests that go back two months, and the response time for that restore window may be determined to be under five minutes. For restore requests for data beyond that period of time, human intervention is required to locate the tape and then place it in the tape library.

Q: At what offsite location will the backup tapes be kept for long-term storage?

You may be using a company that specializes in long-term storage of tapes, and your company may already have defined this location. Generally, larger sites do use this type of service. If you do, then you should coordinate for additional storage at this site. If you do not, you may want to consider finding an alternative location.

If cost is an issue with long-term storage, you may be able to set up an exchange program with another group within your company. This can only be done if the other group is not located in your building. It is most desirable if a lockable cabinet or a safe can be purchased and placed in the other group's building and vice versa. Then, at well-defined intervals, tapes can be exchanged to provide offsite or long-term storage. The tape retrieval process also should be outlined, to prevent possible misunderstandings.

Q: How long will the backup tapes be retained in long-term storage?

This is another part of the backup policy that must be coordinated with your legal and compliance departments, as well as senior management. Different backup data at your site may carry different requirements for how long tapes are retained.

The answer to this question should also help determine what type of tape drive hardware you purchase. Each type of tape media has a different shelf life, or the number of years the backup tape can remain on a shelf and still be used for a successful restore. You must know how long your company wants to keep tapes to help you determine the best tape technology for your site.

Q: What is the expected restore response for backup tapes in long-term storage?

Once the tapes are moved offsite, the restore response time is defined differently. It could take anywhere from one hour to two days to retrieve the required tape(s). This should be stated clearly in the policy statement to keep everyone's expectations in check.

Using the previous example, once tapes are four months old, they are taken offsite. To add to that example, let's say the retrieval of offsite tapes takes a maximum of 24 hours. That means the backup policy states that any recovers over four months old will be handled in no sooner than 24 hours. It may be desirable to provide a window of 24 to 26 hours to allow for any unpredictable events, in this sample case.

Q: When will backup tapes completely expire, and what will happen to the tapes, once they have completely expired?

At some point, the tapes are considered completely expired. Don't forget, that they should be held for the length of time required by your legal and compliance departments. After that required time frame, there should be procedures to retire the tapes. Some sites may require that these tapes be degaussed and destroyed. These steps might need to done in a very specific manner or by specific individuals. It might or might not be feasible to reuse these tapes. These issues must be considered and the procedures written down for everyone to comprehend the procedures involved.

Q: Who manages systems that are backed up, and who is responsible for the restores?

It should be clear in the backup policy who is responsible for the backups and who is responsible for the restores. This might or might not be the same group of individuals (generally, it is the same group). This responsibility may be delegated to a group or an individual on a department-by-department basis, or may be delegated on a company-wide basis. The exact group for backups and restores must be well defined. You may want to set up one email alias at your site for the backup group or individual and another email alias for the restore group or individual. That way, mail can be sent to the alias in the event that there is a new host to backup, a problem with a backup, or a restore request. The aliases are easy to manage, and if the individuals change, the aliases themselves stay the same.

Each of the items listed can actually form a section of your backup policy. There may also be other sections, depending on your site.

Education

Education is an important aspect to having your backup strategy accepted by managers, administrators, and users. Everyone must understand what is being backed up, how often the backups are done, and what the restore policies are. It is also helpful to inform everyone about any issues that result from your legal or compliance department's requirements. If some procedure or policy seems weird to people, it is often easier to accept if they understand the source of the requirement in question.

With local or networked backups (possibly more so with networked backups), it is common to have the backups supported, managed, and monitored centrally by one group. This can be difficult for some people to accept and can cause people to become uneasy for a number of reasons:

- The apprehension could be as simple as human nature. In the distributed environment, everyone has become accustomed to having things close, so that they can easily touch and feel the hardware. To overcome this issue, education is your best bet. The more everyone understands, the better chance you have an accepted and successful backup strategy.

- Some people may be uncomfortable because they think central support may jeopardize the security of the data being backed up. The data may be secretive or confidential and should only be accessible to a few individuals. To overcome this issue, the answer may be to encrypt data on the backup clients before it is sent to the backup server. The backup software must be able to support this feature.

Education planning sessions are beneficial. You should have different sessions, with each one targeted for the particular people attending the session. For example, you may have a planning session for management, another for system administrators, and a different one for end users. Each person has a different perspective and will have different types of questions.

The management planning session may concentrate on what documentation they feel is necessary with respect to the backup infrastructure. The management's focus is centered on reports that provide information on trends and cost issues surrounding backups and restores. The planning session may be based on consolidating what information is important for the monthly reports. Such items might include changes and trends in the following areas: the amount of data backed up, the number of backup clients, the amount of time it takes to perform backups, the restore speeds, the number of restores, successful and unsuccessful backups and restores, or the software or hardware maintenance costs.

The system administrators' session may concentrate on procedural items and more of the details of how the backups are configured. The system administrators need to know what backup and restore policies are implemented. This includes what data is backed up and how often the data is backed up (backup schedule). They should know where the different backup client programs reside, what they would be used for, and how to use them. The administrators should know what configuration options they can implement locally on their backup clients without involving the backup server. They may also be interested in a general overview of the backup server hardware and software.

The end user session may focus on policy issues and restore issues. The end users generally will need only high-level information about backups. They need to know what is backed up (as it relates to end users) and the backup schedule. They also need to know how to perform a restore.

The planning sessions should be customized for your site. You should provide everyone with as much information as possible. The better the backup environment is understood, the better it can be utilized, and the more advocates you will have behind your implementation.

Charge Back

Properly performing backups is a very important and ongoing project. As the backups are being implemented, a decision has to be made on how to proceed. Hard disk size is continually growing and new systems are always being purchased. Backups cannot be put in place and then ignored. The infrastructure must be upgraded to handle additional capacity, and the funds for this must come from somewhere. Determining where the funds are coming from in advance helps assure continuity of funding.*

With the local backup implementation, whoever owns the system has the responsibility of purchasing upgrades for the backups or purchasing a tape drive with the new system.

With departmental network backup implementations, obviously the logical collection of backup clients is by department, and the entire cost of the backup infrastructure is the departments' responsibility.

With the large, centralized, networked backups, the backup infrastructure supports many different departments within the organization. How to divide the cost of upgrades and additional capacity can be difficult. One option for large sites is to institute a charge back policy. Every time a new system or disk is purchased, a tariff is applied and then set aside for backup support. This could be a set charge per MB of disk space. It would best be coordinated through your purchasing and accounting departments.

---

* This topic was also briefly mentioned in the site survey in Chapter 4, *Requirements Definition*, with the question "How will you sell upgrades and increased capacity for the backup infrastructure to the individuals who will fund the backup project?"

6

Software Features

Now that you have defined your requirements and policies, you should examine the various software and hardware capabilities available to help implement your backups. This chapter provides a broad picture of the backup and restore software concepts. No specific software packages are mentioned, only software design characteristics and features. The first section discusses different backup and restore software with respect to its design. The second section provides a checklist of important features you should review. You should formulate your vendor survey after you decide which features are appropriate for your environment. Chapter 7, *Windows NT Backup Software*, and Chapter 8, *Commercial Software*, provide details on specific backup and restore applications.

Software Design Characteristics

The high-level design characteristics of comprehensive commercial backup software include the following:

Services

> The backup and restore software is generally supported by multiple services running (background jobs) on both the backup servers and backup clients. These can be seen in the Control Panel→Services icon. For the most part, these services are automatically put in place when the application software is installed and are set to start at bootup.

Configuration information

> Usually a configuration file or database is located on the backup server. This file or database holds all of the information needed by the backup software. This includes what will be backed up, when it will be backed up, the level of backup, security information for backups and restores, tape drive and library

information, backup exceptions, backup priorities, and any other pertinent information required to perform backups and restores.

Backup information

The comprehensive backup software packages frequently have a database or databases that hold information about what was backed up, which client performed the backup, which tape has the backup data, and where it is located on the tape. This database or group of databases may also contain even more detailed information about the data backed up, such as last change date, size, and owner. This information is located on the backup server and is used for reports or client restores. When you execute a restore, the online database(s) is accessed. The information about what was backed up is easily acquired, which in turn makes the restore process simple, fast, and flexible. With relatively little effort, the restore program allows you to browse around from day to day until you decide what really should be recovered. The less-sophisticated backup programs do not have such databases. This information must be read in from tape before the restore can be done. This approach can be cumbersome, time-consuming, and is not scalable.

Log files

The comprehensive software packages definitely have one or (more likely) multiple log files. The log files are for troubleshooting and helping you understand what was done and when it was completed. In some instances these log files are located only on the backup server. In other cases, they are located on the backup server and the backup clients. There are pros and cons to both approaches. Of course, if your site is large, it is easier to manage the logs if they are compressed on the backup server.

Special options

These are add-on features that can be purchased in addition to the basic backup and restore software. Sometimes these include support for backing up SQL Server partitions, backing up Microsoft Exchange, use of tape libraries (robotic devices sometimes called autochangers), enhanced monitoring features, or integration into Simple Network Monitoring Protocol (SNMP). Most medium and large sites require some of these options. Like purchasing a car, it is nice to know up front which features are standard, which are optional, and which are unavailable.

Some of the comprehensive backup and restore software vendors have implemented their software such that the backup servers have no (or limited) knowledge, of other backup servers. In general, this means that each backup server has its own configuration information, backup information, and set of log files. Each backup server is administrated and monitored separately.

Other vendors have a more integrated approach to master and slave backup server relationships. This means that the configuration information, backup information, and log files are integrated and shared between backup server systems in some manner, which is vendor-dependent. Generally, there is a master administration and monitoring console for watching over the entire environment. Some vendors integrate failover capability with this type of design. If one backup server is not available, another takes over the backup or restore. This can be a big benefit if you are implementing networked backups.

The design characteristics listed previously provide a generic view of the backup packages to help you understand the big picture. Of course, each part of the design may be referred to using different, vendor specific terminology. Chapter 8 describes various vendor applications and their design characteristics in more detail.

Vendor Survey

Many vendors provide backup software for the distributed environment, and it is important to choose one that fits your requirements. It is not the intent of this book to recommend a backup and recovery software vendor. The intention of this book is to help you think about the different features available in backup and restore software so that nothing is overlooked. There are many different features, and not all features are in all software packages. Also, you may not require all features at your site.

After going through the feature checklist, the features deemed important to your site can be used to narrow down what commercial applications best suit your needs. You should narrow down your search results to no more than three software packages. It is too complex and not cost-effective to compare and contrast more than three applications during the test phase. This chapter covers only the generic features. The detailed applications and each of their features are covered in Chapter 8.

As you consider each feature in the following checklist to determine which are relevant to your site, remember to take into account future computer growth and systems engineering changes that may be planned for your site. The list is grouped into considerations of site, administration and configuration, data, tape, documentation, customer support, and others.

Some of the following questions are similar to the ones found in the section "Site Survey" in Chapter 4, *Requirements Definition*. The reasons for this repetition are first, that your site survey must determine a particular requirement exists at your location, and second, that you must ask if a corresponding feature exists in the backup and restore application software. Another distinction between the two surveys is that some of the results from the site survey were used in backup server and network sizing and in the policy statement.

In contrast, the vendor survey concentrates on application features. Those features discussed here are used in a matrix in Chapter 8 to help you compare and contrast the vendors based on features. The occasional duplication you find between the site survey and the vendor survey was done intentionally to cover all bases.

Backup Server Considerations

Q: On what versions of Windows NT does the backup server software run?

In a strictly NT environment, it is assumed that the server will be Windows NT–based. This makes administration and maintenance of the backup system easier to handle. You need to know the Windows NT version and service pack number that the backup server software was actually validated to run under so that you can make informed decisions. If you are running version x with service pack y, make sure that the server backup software you consider has been validated by the vendor with the same NT version and service pack you are running at your site. Don't let the vendor tell you that they are sure it will run even though they have not validated it themselves.

Q: On what other operating systems does the backup server software run?

Your current plans may be to have a homogeneous Windows NT backup server and client environment. However, if you find your server throughput requirements are not being met by the Windows NT operating system or the hardware available, you may decide that you need a different server configuration. This is especially true for the large network backup implementations where performance and throughput requirements can be very high. It is technically possible and often desirable to have a Unix backup server supporting Windows NT backup clients.

Q: Is the backup server software designed to be multithreaded?

Windows NT is designed to support multiple CPUs. Multithreading has to be designed into the application software to take advantage of this Windows NT design enhancement. The ability to multithread can greatly enhance performance on the backup server and is important for networked backup implementations.

Q: Is the backup server software to perform any failover to an alternate server in the event of a server failure?

Some sites require the backup server to be highly available. If your site is one of these, then the backup and restore software should meet this need. You should be aware of the following aspects of failover:

- How the failure of the backup server is detected

- How the tasks being performed by the backup server that fails are transferred to an alternative backup server

- What occurs when the unavailable backup server becomes usable again

- How the software handles the configuration and backup information in the event of a server failure

Different implementations of server failover may be better suited to your site. The details of how the vendor handles the failover should be investigated.

Q: What are the minimum and suggested backup server hardware requirements to support the product?

This consideration is most important for the local backup implementations. The networked backup implementations generally have as the backup server one of the more powerful systems in their environment. In the case of the local backups, every computer that has to be backed up must have the minimum hardware requirements for the chosen software. At a minimum, this includes the supported CPU platform, memory, operating system version, operating system patches (service packs), and hard disk requirements for the application.

Q: What installation media is the product shipped on for the backup server?

The local backup implementation should be very concerned with the media of the backup and restore software. If the media is shipped in only the CD format, every computer that needs the software must have a CD drive or a CD drive must be moved between systems. If your site is mixed, some computers may have CD drives and some may only have floppy drives. For these sites, the vendor should be asked if they can provide both media because it makes your initial installation process go smoother and helps make recovery from the bare hard disk easier.

Backup Client Considerations

Q: What backup client operating systems are supported by the product?

Once again, your current plan may be to back up and restore only Windows NT client systems. However, if your backup implementation is successful, you may be asked to back up some other operating system, such as NetWare 4.1 NDS, NetWare 3.1x, Solaris, SunOS, HP-UX, IRIX, Digital Unix, AIX, SCO, Windows 95, Windows 3.x, DOS, VINES, Macintosh, OS/2, or any other desktop operating system, using the same backup server. It is technically possible to have a Novell or Macintosh back up clients using a Windows NT backup server; you should consider this option.

Q: What installation media is the product shipped on for the backup clients?

If you decided not to do a network installation, you should investigate the media the backup client software is shipped on. Every backup client has to be able to read that kind of media to make your installation go smoothly. If the media is shipped in the CD format only, every computer that needs the software must have a CD drive or a CD drive must be moved between systems. If your site is mixed, some computers may have CD drives and some may have only floppy drives. For these sites, the vendor should be asked if they can provide both media types, because it makes your initial installation process smoother and makes recovery from the bare hard disk easier.

Site Considerations

Q: Does your site require the backup client software to be integrated into an automatic software distribution mechanism, such as Microsoft System Management Servers (SMS)?

In the distributed environment, the management of application distribution is difficult, but vital. The backup client software fits into this category. If your site has implemented a distribution mechanism, such as SMS, you need to make sure that the backup software can be disseminated using this capability. The client backup software affects many hosts at your site and should not have to be treated as a special case.

Q: If your site has no automatic software distribution mechanism, does the backup software provide this functionality?

For sites with no other mechanism for distributing the backup client software, it would be beneficial if the backup software vendor had that capability. This feature is useful during the initial installation of the product, as well as when new versions of backup client software are released. It saves your staff from having to visit every backup client to install the new software individually on each system.

Q: Does the backup software provide support for backing up and restoring special partitions?

(The support of special partitions was also addressed in the site survey.) This support is usually part of the options available from the backup and restore software vendor. It may also be supported by another vendor. You should consider, at a minimum, special disk partitions for SQL servers and Exchange servers at your site. Make sure you can back up and restore the specific versions of these products you have at your site.

Q: Does the product support network installs?

For medium and large sites, network installation is very important. This is where the software is placed on a server that is accessible by all backup clients. Instead of having to have a CD or floppy to perform the installation of the backup software, you point to the network location of the software and perform the installation from there. Many software packages provide this feature, and so should the backup server and client software.

Q: Does the software support use of a read-only file system for the client binaries?

You may have a site where the client binaries will be stored centrally on a read-only file system. These types of file systems might include a read-only NTFS share partition, a read-only NFS-mounted partition, or you may be using Transarc's Distributed File System (DFS) or Andrew File System (AFS) in a read-only configuration. If your site supports any of these types of implementation, you must make sure that the backup and restore application allows the client binaries to be used in this manner. There are backup and restore applications that do support this paradigm, and it may be a determining factor as to which vendor fits your needs.

If you have your backup and restore software installed on a read-only file system and running on the backup clients, you must be able to run this software without having to write permissions back to the source of the binaries. In general, you should check whether there are any application-specific restrictions.

One specific example of a problem with read-only file systems is when the log files must be written to the same location where the backup and restore binaries are located. You must make sure to determine whether there are log files on the client machines. If so, verify that the location of the log files can be configured to a different location from the read-only file system. Don't assume that having a read-and-write file system will solve this problem. All the clients are accessing the same location on these servers. This would mean that all clients would be writing to the same log file on the server. This introduces potential problems with log file permissions and ownership as well as open file contention among all of your backup clients: the log files may become useless or the application may not run properly.

Administrative and Configuration Considerations

Q: What information is stored in the backup database for each individual file?

When the backups occur, information is stored in a backup database. Such information includes what was backed up, what tapes were involved with the backup, and where on the tapes the data is actually located. Additional details about the files may also be included, ownership, permissions, or modification date or time. The more data you have backed up on the files, the easier it is to determine what should be restored. However, the more information you have about each file, the larger the backup database will be. You should ask the vendors you are considering for your site for the exact information contained in the backup database.

Q: *What is the amount of disk space required for the backup database (on the backup server) for an average backup client?*

This value is important for planning the hard disk requirements on the backup server. Unfortunately, it is a difficult number to obtain, because the *average* backup client is hard to define. Items that affect the backup database size for each client are the number of files backed up, the size of the files backed up, and the amount of file-specific information the application records. You should try to acquire as much estimate information as possible from the vendors. The estimate usually can be obtained in the number of KB stored in the backup data per file.

Keep in mind that having smaller disk requirements for the backup database might or might not be good for your site. The smaller the backup database, the smaller the amount of information that is kept online for each file backed up. You should find the balance between what file information is required to do quick, successful restores and how large the backup database will grow. The goal is to find the correct data to restore, then perform the restore. The alternative is restoring data because you think it is the right data and then having to restore different data because your first attempt resulted in a useless restore.

Q: *What type of backup restarts can be done on the backup server?*

At sites that implement networked backups, you will find that being able to stop and restart backups from the point at which they were stopped is an important consideration. You do not want to have to restart backups from the beginning because you waste time and tapes. The backup servers at medium and large sites are handling lots of hosts and data. The impact of this feature is greater at the larger sites. You may need to stop a backup for an emergency situation, such as a very important restore or a crisis—for example, a disk failure on the backup server.

In a worst-case scenario, an emergency may occur that requires you to stop the backup server when you are performing a full backup. This may happen when 80% of your full backups have already been completed. It is crucial to be able to keep that 80% of data backed up, stop the backups, and then restart the backups having to finish only the remaining 20%.

Another example is when your site schedules a power outage over the weekend. It is very advantageous to have the option to do some backups before the power goes out and the remaining backups once the power and all of your backup clients are back on the air. This flexibility is important.

Q: What type of backup retry can be done by the backup server?

If an error occurs when a backup is initiated by the backup server to the backup client, it is important that the backup software automatically retry that particular connection. The number of retries and the interval time to wait until the retry is executed should be configurable.

Q: How are the backups initiated?

In most sites, it is necessary to have both server- and client-initiated backups. The server initiated backups are used on a night-to-night basis to get the back-ups accomplished. This keeps the administration of this daily process to one system or set of systems. For medium and large sites, it is too difficult to main-tain nightly backups by having them started from each individual system. The client initiated backups are useful when an individual (end user, programmer, or system administrator) wants to perform an ad hoc backup in addition to the nightly scheduled backups. This individual may have made major changes to something on their system and would like to safeguard it immediately, as opposed to waiting until the scheduled backup occurs.

Q: Can end users initiate restores?

In some sites, it may be desirable to have end users able to restore some files on their own. This relieves the administration staff from some of the restore work. The backup software package must have appropriate permissioning on the restores so that the end user can restore only his or her own file(s).

Q: Can remote restores be performed?

It may be desirable for a host, *clientA*, to be able to restore data for the host *clientB*, but have all the restore data be sent to *clientB*. This is known as a remote restore. The administrative staff should not have to visit a user's desk-top to perform a restore. The staff member should be able to perform the restore (with all the appropriate permissions set up properly) from the admin-istrator's desktop. For sites that are very spread out, this feature becomes a time-saver.

Q: Can cross restores be performed?

In this type of situation, let's say *hostA* used to be backed up by a backup server. For some reason, *hostA* was decommissioned and is no longer in exist-ence. However, a restore request is required from the backup data from hostA. The data from this restore must be located on hostB. This type of restore may sound complicated, but is realistic; it can be referred to as a *cross restore* of *hostA*'s data to *hostB*. The staff member should be able to perform the restore (with all the appropriate permissions set up properly) from the administrator's desktop, which is hostC. For sites that are very spread out, this feature becomes a time-saver.

Q: Does the backup software allow for wildcards or regular expressions to be used for backups?

Some sort of ability to do backups based on wildcards or regular expressions is important. This feature would be part of the backup software itself. There will be cases in which you will want to specify that you don't care what disks are configured on a system, as long as all of them are backed up. Another case is where you want items backed up based on a regular expression. As sites grow, it becomes more difficult to know the configuration of every system on the network. It is at this point where you may find that the ability to back up based on wildcards or regular expressions is an important feature.

Q: Does the backup software allow for wildcards or regular expressions to be used for restores?

Like wildcards or regular expressions for backups, this ability for restores is another nice feature to have, and can save time (this would be a feature in the backup software). Not having to select items individually to be restored can make the restore that much faster and less prone to error.

Q: Does the application provide GUI access and command-line access?

Both types of access to the software are important. Obviously, when you are co-located with the backup system, the GUI access is fast and easy to use. However, using a GUI from a remote location may be very slow or not work at all. Backups generally run at night and on the weekends, and remote access may be necessary to administrate or perform restores of a system from home using a modem connection. Also, the GUI is not conducive to scripting. It may be desirable to script certain functions in Perl, for example. You may find a need to take the reports generated by the backup product and reformat them into a layout that fits into your site's reporting requirements. You need command-line access to add this kind of functionality to your backup environment.

It is important to grasp the difference between which tasks can be accomplished with GUI access and which can be accomplished on the command line. The most desirable situation is that *everything* you can do from within the GUI can also be done on the command line. You should not assume that everything from the GUI can be done via the command line. You should specifically ask the software vendor if everything available from the GUI interface is also available from the command-line interface, or if the command-line interface is only a subset of the GUI interface.

Q: Is the configuration information on the backup server printable?

It is nice to have the ability to print the configuration information for individual clients being backed up or for all clients being backed up. At times, it is easier to review the entire list to look for anomalies or problems as opposed to looking at just one backup client at a time.

Q: Is it possible to do host grouping? If so, how are the hosts ordered within the group for backups?

At large sites, in particular, it is convenient to be able to configure the backup server software with groups of similar hosts. Depending on how the vendor implements host grouping, this feature could reduce administrative tasks. These tasks would be done on a group-by-group basis, as opposed to a host-by-host basis. If the backups are started by groups, you need to know how the hosts are ordered within that group.

If the software product does provide host grouping, you need to know how the hosts within the groups are ordered for backups. The absolute worst way to have hosts grouped is by Internet (IP) address. That means that all hosts on one subnet will be backed up, and then another subnet will be backed up, and so on. If your backup server is configured with multiple tape drives or multiplexing onto a tape drive, then multiple hosts will be backed up at the same time. If the hosts are ordered by IP addresses, then one subnet could get pounded by multiple backup clients being backed up at the same time. Chances are good that the subnet on which those backup clients are located is a 10 MB/s network, and that network could easily become the bottleneck on the backup server.

Another bad way to order hosts within a group is alphabetically, because a common naming convention is to list hostnames by specific group or department followed by a number. For example, the servers in the accounting department might be named *acct1*, *acct2*, *acct3*, and *acct4*. The servers in the payroll department might be named *pay1*, *pay2*, and *pay3*. If the host ordering is alphabetical, the accounting department's hosts will be backed up, then the payroll department's hosts would be backed up. If the accounting department's hosts are on the same subnet and the payroll's department hosts are on another subnet (say each are a 10 MB/s network), then there is a strong possibility that the network might become the bottleneck.

Another way to order hosts within a group is by reverse IP address. This is far kinder to the subnets on which the hosts are located. For example, let's say you have seven hosts to back up on three subnets, and the backup clients and their host IP addresses are the following:

> *hostAA*, 2.5.7.1
> *hostAB*, 2.5.7.2
> *hostBA*, 2.5.8.1
> *hostBB*, 2.5.8.2
> *hostBC*, 2.5.8.3
> *hostCA*, 2.5.9.1
> *hostCB*, 2.5.9.2

When the hosts are ordered by reverse IP address, they are backed up in the following order:

> *hostAA*, 2.5.7.1
> *hostBA*, 2.5.8.1
> *hostCA*, 2.5.9.1
> *hostAB*, 2.5.7.2
> *hostBB*, 2.5.8.2
> *hostCB*, 2.5.9.2
> *hostBC*, 2.5.8.3

This spreads the backups across multiple subnets at the same time. As you can see, this is far more scalable for larger sites.

One other approach to host ordering is the ability to custom-order the hosts as you desire. For the larger sites, it is nice to have the default ordering be reverse IP address ordering with the ability to override that ordering with a custom configuration.

Q: Can you specify the priority of each host for backups?

Having the ability to prioritize the order in which hosts are backed up is very important. When backups start, the backup server creates some sort of queue that consists of a list of clients to be backed up. The order of the hosts in this queue is set by precedence or priorities applied to the backup clients. There might be a mission-critical host or group of hosts for your site. Having the ability to prioritize backups allows you to back up specified clients before other backup clients.

There are multiple ways to set backup client precedence. One way is through manual configuration. With this method, you can set the priority for each client independently as you see fit. Another way is to have the precedence set by the order in which you enter the backup clients into the backup software during your configuration. Having precedence set by the order you enter the backup clients into the software during your configuration is not a very flexible or scalable approach to this problem.

For example, say that you have 20 hosts already configured into your backup software, and six months later you get in a new important server that needs to be backed up first, before all other backup clients. If the order of the backup clients is set by how they were configured and entered, then in this example you would have to add the new host and then reenter all of the 20 other backup clients to change the priority. With more hosts, this really becomes an impossible task.

More important is your ability during backups to add a backup client with a very high priority. With the addition of the high-priority backup client, the backup server software should automatically change its backup queue to reflect the new high-priority backup client. For example, you may want a particular backup client to perform a database dump and then start its own backups. This backup client might be extremely important, and you might want it to be backed up before any other backup clients. You should be able to set the priority of this database backup client higher than that of any other client, so that the backup server will back it up next, no matter what other clients are in the backup server's queue for backups.

Q: Can the product support multilevel backups?

It is important to be able to perform multiple levels of backups. Most commonly, these are referred to as full backups, incremental backups, or differential backups. Full backups back up all files and folders that are on the disk. An incremental backup is one that backs up files and folders that have changed since the last incremental backup or the last full backup. A differential backup will back up the files and folders that have changed since the last full backup. These options are very important for you to be able to configure the backup software to suit your environment.

Q: Can the product support calendar-based backup scheduling?

Calendar-based backups are extremely nice to have, and, at some sites, are absolutely necessary. With calendar-based backups you can add exceptions based on date. For example, you may choose not to perform backups on holidays. You could go through the calendar on your backup server and skip backups altogether for each holiday. This task becomes more difficult and possibly more confusing if you do not have calendar-based backups. Anything confusing introduces a greater likelihood of human error.

Q: Can the configuration information on the backup server be entered in bulk?

This is an extremely desirable feature for larger sites. If you have to support hundreds of backup clients, it is time-consuming and conducive to human error to enter numerous backup clients manually one at a time. The bulk entry would enter a group or list of backup clients at one time, as opposed to entering each backup client individually.

If the product does not directly support bulk entry, the next best option is to be able to write the scripts or programs to do the bulk entry yourself. This would be accomplished by having command-line access to all the appropriate commands to configure backup clients on your backup server.

Q: Does the backup server software provide the ability to have backup exceptions?

If an entire folder or file system is specified for backup, it is desirable to have the backup server able to be configured not to back up a particular file or folder. If it is configured on the backup server, it is nice to apply this exception to all clients backed up by that server. For example, you may want to exclude the *pagefile.sys* swap files from your backup clients. Therefore, it would make sense to configure this on the backup server for all backup clients, and not have to go to each backup client to add this to the configuration of those backup clients.

Q: Does the product support client-based backup exceptions?

While it is important to have server-based exceptions that cover all backup clients, it is also helpful to have client-based exceptions. There may be client-specific things that don't require backups, such as a database dump. An administrator may choose to have multiple copies of a database dump available on disk in the folders named *dbdump1, dbdump2, dbdump3* (where *dbdump1* is the most current copy). However, it might be a waste of tape to back up every one of the copies. Therefore, that administrator should have the option of specifying that the backup server not back up the folders *dbdump2* and *dbdump3*.

If the backup exclusion list is located on the backup clients, it should be in some location other than where the backup and restore binaries are located. When using a centrally managed filesystem share or mount for the backup and restore binaries (where all backup clients get their binaries from the same location), the same backup exclusion list would be used for every backup client. When changes are made to the backup exclusion file on the centrally managed server, these changes affect all backup clients. You should be aware of this type of situation, because it does not provide any flexibility for client-specific backup exclusions.

Monitoring, Reporting, and Logging Considerations

Q: Can the backup server be configured to send arbitrary commands, such as pages and/or email notifications to individuals?

There are events that occur on a backup server requiring human intervention. Events such as inserting a tape required for a restore, or a backup failure might require immediate attention from an operational staff member. It is convenient to have the option within the backup server software to have these events automatically trigger notifications in the form of arbitrary commands. These commands can be specified when you configure your backup server. At some sites, email may be an appropriate way to notify individuals, while other sites may have an automated paging capability. It is important to understand what type of notifications can be sent from the backup server software. The most flexible option is the ability to send any command you choose when a notification is required.

Q: What monitoring is provided for the backup server?

Every backup and restore software vendor provides monitoring of some sort. Determining what type of monitoring is right for your site is important. This is monitoring in addition to log files, and the level of monitoring varies from product to product. The monitoring may be as detailed as displaying the status of each and every file or folder backed up from the backup client. The monitoring may be high-level monitoring and provide you a window with the progress of the backup clients that contains no details. This is basically just when a backup client starts or finishes.

Sites with local backup implementation and smaller sites implementing networked backups may prefer the granularity of the detailed monitoring, which reports each file and folder backed up from the clients and the progress of those files and folders. The details might provide a better picture of what is happening when backups or restores occur.

Medium and large sites with networked backup implementations may prefer high-level monitoring for the overall progress of backups and restores. For large sites, being responsible for hundreds of backup clients and monitoring individual files and folders of each backup client becomes overwhelming.

Any amount of monitoring will cause system overhead, but eliminating monitoring is not advised. What is needed is a happy medium. The monitoring should not adversely affect backup server system performance, but in the event of failures, you need enough information to troubleshoot and correct the failures.

Q: Does the product have tape drive monitoring?

Another important aspect of monitoring, with respect to backups, is monitoring of tape devices. Depending on your site's requirements, this feature may or may not be needed, but it should be considered. While the backups are running, if the tape drives are writing, you know immediately that backups are active. If you can monitor tape drives, you can also see if the drives are being driven at their rated specifications.

For example, if you can monitor your tape drive, you may find that you are obtaining a rate of about 800 KB/s. If your tape drive is rated for 1.5 MB/s, you may wonder why you are not getting this rated throughput. Configuration changes may make the tape drive write faster, or there may be a bottleneck on your backup server that should be identified.

The backup software may supply only total time and total KBs backed up as part of its reporting mechanism. You might feel that this is adequate because you can take the total KBs backed up, divide it by the total time required to back up the data, and determine the KB/s you are achieving with your tape drives. If you have multiple tape drives, you would then divide the KB/s you calculated by the number of tape drives. There is one major flaw with this approach. The KB/s rate you calculated is the tape drive throughput plus the overhead involved with backups. The overhead includes the time it takes to start up the backups, the time it takes to switch between backup clients, the time it takes to process the backup server's databases, and, if you are using a tape library, the time to load the tape drives. Therefore, the calculated KB/s is lower than the throughput you are actually obtaining on your tape drives. If you can monitor the actual tape drive throughput, you are literally watching the drive's throughput and not the throughput plus the backup software overhead.

Q: Does the product have central monitoring capability for all backup servers?

Monitoring of the backup server(s) at your site can be accomplished in many different ways. As described later, you can have SNMP monitoring. However, if that is not available or not planned for your site, you need monitoring capability for the backup software itself, at a minimum. The backup software vendors generally provide this type of capability. If you have more than one backup server for your site, it is helpful if the backup server monitoring capability can watch all of those servers.

Q: Does the product have remote monitoring capability?

Since backups typically run at night and on weekends, it is important to be able to monitor the backups over a slower network connection, such as a home modem connection. In this type of situation, response time when using a GUI may be unacceptable. Therefore, you should ask the vendor if they have a different interface that may allow you to monitor the backup server without having to use the GUI. An alternative to this is if you can run the GUI on your home computer but point to the backup server for the monitoring information. In this case, the monitoring data is the only data going over the modem connection, not the entire GUI.

Q: Is Simple Network Management Protocol (SNMP) supported?

SNMP is a de facto standard for systems software or hardware monitoring in the distributed computing environment. SNMP has a manager side and an agent side. The manager is where administrators can control and watch the environment. The agents are what is actually being managed by the manager and providing input to the manager. Agents can be located on any of following types of hardware or software:

- Network components, such as bridges, hubs, or routers
- Computer systems, such as workstations or servers
- Hardware components, such as tape libraries or modem nests
- Software packages, such as shrink-wrapped off-the-shelf backup and restore software or your site's custom software

There are two types of manager/agent SNMP implementations:

Traps
> The SNMP agent can be implemented to trap events and send notifications to the manager.

Polling
> The SNMP agent can be implemented in a manner that allows the manager to poll the agent as the manager sees fit. For the manager to poll an SNMP agent, the agent must have a defined management information base (MIB). The MIB is a standard way to store information that can be retrieved or polled by the SNMP manager. The agent's MIB is compiled into the manager, and then the MIB is queried by the manager as needed to determine the health and welfare of the agent.

If you have currently implemented a systems monitoring application at your site or you think there is a possibility that there will be an implementation at your site, you need to make sure that the backup software supports SNMP monitoring. Backup software is very complex with interactions with the clients, network, disk drive, and tape drive(s). Therefore, it is a perfect candidate for monitoring to keep track of all these moving pieces.

Don't let a software vendor tell you that they have SNMP support without understanding if it involves only traps or both traps and polling. Initially, the traps may be enough for your systems monitoring, but as your monitoring environment grows and becomes more sophisticated, you will want the ability to poll your backup server software agent. Also, if the vendor provides only traps, make sure that the traps are configurable and not set values. The vendor can not possibly have set the trap values appropriately for every site; you should be able to set them and tune them for your specific site.

There is a big advantage to using SNMP for your monitoring needs. The manager in the SNMP environment can be gathering information from all types of agents. The manager then, depending on the implementation of the manager software, would be able to do correlation of the different agents to help isolate problems. For example, you may have agents on your routers, bridges, backup server software, and Windows NT operating system. When there is a problem (remember that the definition of what is considered a problem is configurable), you use the manager to determine if it is a router, bridge, backup server software, or the NT platform problem. The manager will tell you immediately what is not causing the problem and may even tell you immediately what is the problem. This type of cross-platform, cross-hardware, and cross-software correlation is invaluable, especially in large site environments. It eliminates the need for a monitoring system for the network, another for the NT systems themselves, and then yet another for the backup server software.

Q: What support is provided for the log files?

At medium and large sites where many backup clients are supported, the log files associated with the backups can become quite large. For troubleshooting and daily monitoring, it is important to determine how the log files are handled and exactly where they are located. Every message that can be found in a log file should be fully documented in the vendor's manuals. Additionally, there are third-party log watching software packages available, which need to be configured to trigger on certain messages.

Q: Where are the log files located?

Different backup software keeps the logs on either the backup server, backup clients, or on both. The larger your environment (the more backup clients at your site), the more difficult it becomes to manage the log files on the backup clients. The hard disk space on those backup clients must be monitored to make sure that you don't fill your client disks and cause other problems. Also, the log files themselves have to be rolled over, so that the logs don't grow without bounds. It is all technically possible to handle; just something to consider if the backup software has backup logs on the clients.

Q: What reporting mechanisms are available with the product?

For the backup server, what is reported, how it is formatted and consolidated, and how it is distributed are all important considerations. Every site has different reporting requirements, and it is impossible for the software vendors to meet all of these needs. You may find a backup and restore vendor whose report generator fits your site requirements, but generally, this does not happen.

Your site may require that the output from the backup vendor's software be fed into a program, written at your site, to reformat, consolidate, or split up the information to fit your management's needs. You'll need to know if the report format is published and how it is distributed from your backup server. It is also important that the vendor knows that you are doing this custom work, so that as report formats from their product change, they can notify you, and you can make adjustments in your site specific software.

Another aspect of reporting is the capability to do ad hoc reporting. The ability to query the backup server and obtain an old report is important. Management will inevitably request backup reports on a moment's notice, and you should be able to obtain the information they need.

Data Considerations

Q: Is data compression implemented on the client or server system, and is it configurable?

Depending on the backup software, data compression can be performed on the backup client or the backup server. Of course, the best option is to be able to configure the compression to occur where it best suites your site. Keep in mind that you do not really gain anything by performing compression on both the backup client and the backup server, because you don't gain anything compressing data that has already been compressed.

Data compression on the backup client or backup server saves time and money. By using compression, the amount of time and tape required to back up a specific amount of data is reduced. The type of data you are compressing and the backup software's compression algorithm determines the compression ratio you are able to achieve. By using compression, you may reduce the space consumed on a tape anywhere from 33% to 66%.

By compressing data on the backup client before it is backed up, you can also substantially reduce the overall network bandwidth used to perform backups. However, you should always remember that the compression on the client takes CPU and memory resources from the backup client. If the backup client is performing other batch jobs, compression could affect those batch jobs. If your site is concerned about network traffic and backups have to be done over slow network connections or compete with other network traffic, client-side compression may be your best solution. Once the data is compressed on the client, there is less data to move across the network.

Compression on the backup server is achieved by having compression tape drives or by having a compression algorithm run on the backup server. Sometimes the most effective compression is done by the backup tape drive because it is performed by hardware, not software.

The compression question is very site-specific. Where it is performed is a matter of what client, network, and server issues you are most concerned with in your environment. Some basic guidelines are:

- If you want the least impact on a backup client, perform server-side compression.

- If you have processing power that you can utilize on the backup clients, use client-side compression.

- If you have problems or issues with network traffic and performance, use client-side compression (assuming that you have the processing power on the backup client).

Q: Does the product provide multi-language support?

Some applications, such as word processors or spreadsheets, support internationalization, or the ability to store files and folders in languages other than English. Different languages usually have different character sets. The different character sets take varying numbers of bits to store the characters. Backups deal with file and folder names on the systems they are backing up. Therefore, the backup software must support internationalization to be able to back up the file and folder names stored in these different languages.

If your company is international and shares technical solutions among sites, a successful backup solution may be used at one of your international sites. Of course, the possibility of this happening might be remote initially, but successful backup implementations are prime candidates for expanding or duplicating for other sites. Basically, if your company is international in nature, this should be a required feature.

Q: Can the product back up open files?

Even though backups are generally performed at night when most individuals at your company are not working, there is always a chance that a person or application is using a file or folder in some manner and it has been left open (in use). The more computers you are backing up, the greater the chance that this will occur. Also, some shops (manufacturers, for example) are open 24 hours a day, and therefore files will be open and in use at night. It is important to make sure that the backup product can back up open files.

Q: Can the product perform hot database backups?

A backup of an active database is not a trivial task. In order to back up an active database as transactions are being performed against it, the backup has to back up not only the database data itself, but also must handle the transactions in some manner.

At some sites, the database can be shut down, so that it is no longer active. In this situation, no transactions against the database can occur and the data within the database can be backed up without any transaction contention. After the backup is completed, the database would be restarted and open for business. This is a clean way to perform database backups, but it is not practical.

Another approach is to perform a dump of the database into a regular file; the dump can occur while the database is active. Then you back up the dump file, as opposed to taking the data directly from the database itself. This is a valid approach, but should be performed with one warning: make sure that the database dump that is backed up is a complete dump, not a partial one. It is a timing issue to make sure that backups are not performed while the dump is occurring. If this happens, the dump data is not valid, and without valid backups, you cannot have successful restores. The backup must be performed after the dump has completed. One other planning note regarding this approach is that you must have additional disk space, above and beyond the database disk space, to store the dump file. The larger the database, the larger the necessary temporary disk space for the dump file.

It takes special software to back up active databases. You should ask the vendor if they have this software available or if it is software that can be purchased from a third-party vendor. Either way, it will be an additional cost that should definitely be considered.

Q: Can the product perform pre- and/or postprocessing?

There are times when you might like to perform some other operation before and/or after the backup occurs. For example, you may want to shut down a database before the backup, back it up, and then restart the database after the backup completes. Another example is that you may want to verify that a database dump has finished before starting a backup. As you can see, this feature can be very valuable.

If a software vendor supports this type of feature, it is important to understand how it is implemented:

- The most flexible implementation is to have the preprocessing and postprocessing available on a file-by-file basis. This is extremely granular and provides you with the ability to perform any required processing for specific files.

- Another approach is to have the preprocessing and postprocessing available on a backup client basis. With this approach, you can customize the processing on a client-by-client basis.

- Another implementation may be to perform processing before all of the backup clients start and then again after they all finish. This is not very flexible, because one dependency in the preprocessing may keep backups of all clients from occurring.

- Yet another implementation is host grouping, each group consisting of one or more clients. Preprocessing occurs before the client host group backup begins, and postprocessing after they complete.

If the software vendor does implement pre- and/or postprocessing, you should compare their implementation of this feature with your requirements to see if there is a good match.

Security Considerations

Q: What is the method of granting permissions for recovers?

There are a couple of different possible implementations of security for recovers. One approach is to grant permission for the restore based on a user's logon ID and comparing that with the owner of the data that was backed up. If the two match, then the recover can occur. Of course, the override to this implementation would be if the logon ID is administrator or a user's logon ID that was part of the administrator's group. If the override occurs, the data is recovered.

Another approach is to grant permissions based on a user's logon ID and the hostname where the recover is being performed. If the logon ID matches the owner of the data that was backed up and the hostname of where the recover is being performed matches the configuration information on the backup server, then the recover can be done. In this case, the administrator on one backup client is not considered the same as the administrator on another backup client. This is helpful for environments in which the administrators are different on different backup clients.

Both of these implementations use the user's logon ID as a key to granting permissions for restores. In a heterogeneous environment where a backup server is backing up different types of backup clients, it is important to control user names across the different platforms. For example, say you have a backup server backing up both Unix and NT systems. If you have a user ID *fsmith* in the Unix environment, you should not have a user ID *fsmith* in the NT environment (unless they are the same individual). Otherwise, the Unix *fsmith* might be able to recover the files for the NT *fsmith*, and vice versa.*

---

* Heterogeneous backup environments amplify the need for cross-platform user ID management.

Q: *What is the security mechanism between the backup clients and the backup server when backups are performed?*

The backup clients have to talk to the backup server to perform backups as well as restores. How this is done should be investigated. A common approach is for the backup software to have a defined network port that is used to establish communications. Another approach is to have the backup clients trust the backup server and allow access. You should understand exactly what authentication is used between the backup server and its clients.

Q: *What user management authentication is provided for the administration and configuration of the backup server?*

For accountability, it is best if users log on as themselves (as opposed to *administrator*) to perform tasks on the backup server. When the support staff logs onto the backup server as *administrator*, there is no way to know which individual logged in. Therefore, it is more secure to have the administrators log in as themselves to perform all tasks on the backup server. With this type of implementation, the backup server software determines which individual user accounts are authorized to make changes, based on configuration information within the backup server software.

Q: *Does the product support data encryption before backups are performed?*

If your data will be backed up over a public network that other individuals may have access to, encryption is a good way to protect your data. This feature provides encryption on the backup client before the data is passed over the network to the backup server. During the restore process, the data is passed from the backup server to the backup client encrypted and is then decrypted on the backup client before the data is written to the hard disk.

Tape Considerations

Q: *What tape drives are supported by the backup server software?*

You should ensure that the tape devices your site currently has or is planning on purchasing are supported by the backup product. The most popular drives and media are:

- 4mm/Digital Analog Tape (DAT)
- 8mm/Exabyte
- Quarter Inch Cartridge (QIC)
- Digital Linear Tape (DLT)

A detailed description of each of these drive and media types is provided in Chapter 9, *Hardware.*

Q: What format does the backup software use on the tapes?

Every product takes a different approach to the type of tape format used to write to the media. There are advantages and disadvantages to each implementation:

- Some products write to tape in well-defined standard formats that can be read independently of the backup software itself. This is a major advantage. One of these formats is the GNU tar format.* If the software product writes to a tape using this format, you can then read that tape without the backup software product with the GNU tar program. The disadvantage to this approach is that tar has been around the industry for a long time and is not optimized for the current tape technology. Therefore, it may be difficult to achieve the performance required using this tape format.

- Some products write to tape with a modified standard format. The standard formats were designed to write to tapes serially, not in a multiplexed fashion (see the following discussion on multiplexing to tapes). In cases where a site has a requirement for tape multiplexing, the software vendor may modify the standard format to perform the multiplexing. This approach does speed up backups and that is its major advantage. The disadvantage is that as with a proprietary tape format, you have to use software from the backup vendor to read the tape's contents: you cannot use programs associated with the standard formats.

- Some products write to tape with a proprietary format. In this case, whether the tape is written to serially or multiplexed, the tape format is proprietary. You always have to have the backup vendor's software or a portion of the software to read the contents of the tape. This is the major disadvantage to this approach. The advantage is that these formats are highly optimized to write and read tapes as fast as possible.

Keep in mind that a software vendor may have chosen a combination of these tape formats.

Q: Are tape libraries supported by the backup server software?

At sites that implement networked backups, a tape library will be used. The tape libraries automate the process of putting tapes in tape drives when the backup and restore software requires a particular tape. They can be small or very large. Chapter 9 has a complete section discussing tape libraries and

---

* There is a group of public domain GNU programs such as GNU tar, GNU C, GNU C++, or GNU emacs (just to name a few) that are very popular in the Unix environment. These programs have been ported to Windows NT. GNU is a recursive acronym that stands for "GNU's not Unix." One of the GNU programs is *tar,* which stands for tape archive. Tar has been around the Unix industry since Unix was developed and is considered one of the standard formats for tapes and floppy diskettes.

how to size a tape library for your site. Some common features of a library are the following:

Hot-swappable drives

This feature allows tape drives to be changed while the other drives are still in use, so that the repair of one tape drive does not affect the entire tape library.

Software drive locking

This feature disables one or more of the tape drives. One important reason for this feature is to allow hot swapping of tape drives. Once a tape drive is known or suspected to be bad, you'll want to be able to lock it (so the backup software does not use it) until it is repaired or replaced.

Entry/exit door

This feature allows tapes to be removed or added to the tape library without having to open the main door to the library.

Bar code label

This label has a standard bar code on it so that the optical arm on the tape library arm mechanism can read the bar code and retrieve the correct tape. The bar coding also should be supported by the backup software, so that the software refers to the tapes by their bar code number.

Cleaning tapes

Tape drives all need to be cleaned periodically and the tape library and backup software have to have the ability to support cleaning tapes. These are special tapes that will have a different bar code label attached.

Just because the hardware has one of these options, it does not automatically mean that you can use that feature. If the tape library supports these features, the backup software still must support these features as well. Each of the library features are discussed in detail in Chapter 8.

Initially, tape libraries cost more than individual tape drives. The cost savings a tape library provides is through reduced manpower and reduced operator (human) error. With individual tape drives, every tape request has to be satisfied by a human putting the correct tape in the drive. With libraries, if they are sized correctly, the majority of tape requests will be satisfied by the tape library itself. If you are considering a backup implementation with tape libraries, you need to know whether the backup software provides support for the libraries and for which libraries.

Q: *Is it possible to have media grouped within tape libraries?*

If you decide to implement a backup solution with a large backup library, sometimes it is beneficial to allow the media in the library to be grouped. The grouping generally is done to keep together data that expires at the same rate.

For example, you could have within a tape library a group of tapes that contains only email data. For legal reasons, this data might be required to be overwritten or expired weekly. If these tapes are part of a particular group of tapes, it is easier to configure that group of tapes to expire every week. You could have another group of tapes that are configured to expire after seven years for other data. If the email data was stored on tapes with other data, it would be more difficult to manage the tapes.

Q: Can you lock a tape drive or a tape slot, so that the backup software does not use it?

If you are experiencing problems with a tape drive that is attached to the backup server, it is important to have the ability to lock that drive. It is also important to have the ability to lock a tape slot, so that the backup software does not use that particular tape. The tape slot is where a tape library stores tapes that are not being read or written to by a tape drive. There can be any number of reasons that this locking feature might be needed. A bad tape drive or bad tape are the most common reasons.

Q: Does the backup software allow you to replenish a tape library?

In an operational environment, it is important to be able to replenish a tape library. This is the process of taking old tapes out of the library and putting in new ones. Believe it or not, not all software products have this capability. If this feature is not available and you do use a tape library, you will eventually write procedures or a script to perform this function. At certain intervals, the tape library will require older tapes to be removed from the tape library, so that new tapes can be put in. Restores are more often required on most recently backed-up data, which is why the older tapes are removed from the library to make room for new tapes.

Q: What is the maximum number of tape drives supported by the software?

There may be a limitation to the number of tape devices the software can use simultaneously. If there is such a restriction, you should find out in advance.

Q: What tape drive controllers (usually SCSI) are supported?

Backup software has to support many different hardware components in order to operate. One of those pieces is the tape drive controllers. The tape drive controllers are purchased apart from the tape drives themselves, so you need to verify that each piece is certified and has been tested by the backup software vendor. It is very frustrating to purchase hardware and then find out afterwards that there is an incompatibility with the software.

Q: Can the product support tape RAID?

Tape RAID is a fairly new development for backup software vendors. This technique allows backups and restores to be performed across multiple tape drives at the same time, which makes the process of writing to tape a parallel process. With this technique, a portion of the backup data is sent to as many tapes as you configure for your tape RAID. Without the RAID support the backup data is written to one tape drive serially; you still can have multiple tape drives, but each tape drive is written to serially.

The benefit to this technique is that it is extremely fast. As data is backed up, it is written across multiple tapes at the same time. This may be the right answer for your site if you have one large backup client that has a limited backup window. You could attach multiple tape drives to this large system to implement a tape RAID backup solution and reduce the backup window required.

The disadvantage to the tape RAID technique is that the multiple tape drives and tapes that perform the backup are also needed to perform a restore. If you have a centralized network backup implementation, tape RAID may not be practical. Using multiple tape drives and tapes for a restore means that those drives and tapes are not available for other restores. If a second restore requires the same tapes, the second restore has to wait for the first restore to complete. Even with serial backups, you risk the chance of one tape being needed for multiple restores, but the odds increase when you implement tape RAID.

The ability to use this technique is backup software vendor–dependent; not all software packages support tape RAID. Also, this technique is site-dependent. Tape RAID requires multiple tape drives and tapes to perform backups that could possibly be performed with one tape drive and one tape. The extra hardware resources might not be available or might be too costly.

Q: Does the product support tape retensioning?

Tape retensioning is the ability to keep the tape tight within its external case. To best utilize tapes for backups, the tapes should be retensioned before use. This feature is usually performed automatically. However, you should have the option of performing it manually as well.

Q: Does the backup software provide tape integrity checks or tape verification?

Tape integrity verifies that the data placed on the tape is valid. If the data is not on the tape, then the backup is useless, so tape verification can be very important. If the product does provide tape integrity checks, it is important to understand how this is configured. You need to know if it is implemented on a host-by-host basis, by groups of hosts, or based on an entire backup session. How the tape verification is performed is a vendor-specific implementation; each vendor does it differently. If the vendor provides this feature, ask how they perform the validation of the tapes as they are written.

You may choose to have tape verification for some backup clients and not for others. Tape verification will slow down backups, because after the tape is written, the integrity of the data on the tape has to be checked. The amount of throughput performance you lose when doing tape verification will depend on the backup product.

Tape reliability is getting better and better with the new tape technologies. However, you should make a cognizant decision to use tape verification or not, or to use it for some backup clients but not others.

Q: Does the backup software support tape multiplexing?

There are two different ways that backup software writes to tape: serially or multiplexing. Some software applications back up one client at a time, per tape drive. This technique is referred to as *serial backup*. Some backup software packages allow multiple clients to back up to one tape drive in parallel. This technique is referred to as *multiplexing backup*.

For small sites that have one tape drive per computer being backed up, use serial backups. For medium sites that have a relatively small number of clients to the backup server(s), your backup window will dictate whether multiplexing is advantageous. If you cannot meet the backup window you have defined, then multiplexing may speed up the backups enough that you can meet your backup window. If you have a larger site with lots of backup clients, then multiplexing is probably best for you. The number of clients writing to a tape device should be a variable with which you can, with testing, determine the best ratio for your backup server. You do not want multiplexing to be too high. If it is too high, the multiplexing will really affect the speed of the restores. It should be high enough to keep the tape drive streaming and no higher.

Q: If the backup software supports tape multiplexing, does it also support tape demultiplexing?

Once the data from the clients is multiplexed onto a tape, you might require that the data be demultiplexed and then rewritten to tape serially. You would perform backups with multiplexing to take advantage of the performance. Then after the backups are completed, you would demultiplex the backups and put them back on tapes in a serial fashion. The serial tapes are used for restores.

The advantage of this technique is that you have high throughput (via multiplexing) during backups. Then, after the backups complete, demultiplexing would be done. Once you demultiplex the tapes, you can perform restores from the serial tapes and take advantage of better restore speeds. Remember, performing restores from the multiplexed tapes does affect the restore throughput, because of the processing associated with the multiplexed tape. Therefore, restores from serial tapes are faster than restores from multiplexed tapes.

The disadvantages of this technique are as follows:

- During the demultiplexing process, the tape being demultiplexed is not available for restores.

- You utilize twice as much tape with demultiplexing.

- You are handling the data twice as much and have twice as much processing associated with backups.

You must weigh these factors to determine what is best for your site. Also, you should consider the following other points:

- To perform this technique, you must have multiple tape drives.

- Demultiplexing may or may not be able to be scheduled. If you can schedule it, you can have it occur immediately after backups complete. If it cannot be scheduled, then someone must manually start the demultiplexing process.

- If you are backing up lots of data every night, it might not be practical or cost-effective to demultiplex the data.

Q: Does the backup software support disk staging?

Disk staging is the process of backing up all the data from the clients to the disk on the backup server and then serially moving the data from the disk to tape. The process of moving the data from the disk to tape can be done while the backups are occurring or after the backups have completed.

The advantage of this technique is that the backup server can back up the client data very quickly because it is writing the data to disk. Disk staging is not limited to the slower speed of the tape drive.

The disadvantage of this technique is the additional cost and management of the hard disk space on the backup server. The backup server must have hard disk capacity to match the amount of data you are backing up. With disk staging, you have to watch the growth of your backup clients closely. As you back up more data from your backup clients, you have to add additional hard disk capacity to the backup server for the staging area.

Q: Can the product support tape duplication?

Tape duplication is an important feature. You must have multiple tape drives or a tape library connected to your backup server to use this feature. The duplicating allows you to keep one copy of the tape onsite for restores and send another copy of the tape offsite for safe keeping, in the event of a disaster. Of course, you could write a utility to copy the contents of one tape to another. However, if the backup software performs this task, it will track that the duplication has occurred. This information should be logged into the backup software's databases. When a restore is requested, the backup software knows it can use the original tapes or the duplicate tapes.

An added option is having the ability to have the duplication take place either on a scheduled basis or automatically after backups have completed. This frees you from having to remember to create the duplicate tapes. With the automatic process, you just come in and remove the duplicates from the tape drive or tape library and ship them offsite.

Hardware Platform Considerations

Q: On what hardware platforms can the backup server and backup client software run?

This question is pretty straightforward. You need to make sure whatever hardware you have for your backup server and backup clients is covered by the backup software product.

Documentation Considerations

Q: Does the product provide online help?

It is very important to have an online help facility as part of the backup software for your first line of defense when you have questions or problems. This is also important for troubleshooting from a remote location (like home) when backups are being performed (which is almost always in the middle of the night). There is a strong chance that you'll have no documentation at home and therefore will be forced to rely entirely on the online help facilities to answer any of your questions.

Q: Does the product provide online tutorials?

An online tutorial is an important way to introduce yourself to a product. By going through a tutorial, you can quickly get a feel of what is in the product and how to perform some of the basic configuration tasks. Fear of the unknown is common and makes learning a new product difficult. A good online tutorial quickly allows you to overcome the unknown and begin working within a product productively.

Q: *Does the vendor provide a full hardcopy documentation set?*

Online features are great, but we are all creatures of habit and sometimes hardcopy documentation is needed to accomplish configuration or troubleshooting. With online help features, you cannot just flip through the pages to try and find something (though there may be a search utility). The online software sometimes makes it hard to pinpoint exactly what you need to find, and hardcopy documentation lets you browse easier.

Q: *Are disaster recovery procedures well outlined and documented?*

When using backup software, the term *disaster recovery* may take on a different meaning than the one you are accustomed to. Generally, backup software refers to a complete disk failure and the steps to take to recover from this failure as disaster recovery. Disaster recovery here means much more than at most companies. Therefore, you need to see from the backup software vendor disaster recovery documentation for the steps and software required to perform a raw disk build. You need the documentation to cover what to do for a backup client as well as for a backup server.

Customer Support Considerations

Q: *What type of telephone support does the software company provide for the backup product?*

When you cannot find the answers you need from the vendor's online help and hard copy documentation, then you will need to talk to their support department. Items you should be concerned with regarding the company's telephone support include the following:

- You should first ask whether the company has a toll-free support number.

- You should know the hours of the telephone support staff. Keep in mind that backups are generally performed at night and on the weekends, so you will most likely experience most of your problems during these off hours. Also, if you are in one time zone and the vendor's support is in another, you need to make sure that you can get support during your normal hours of operation, not just during their hours of operation.

- If your company is international, then you may need technical support worldwide. Your international sites should not have to depend on technical support from the U.S. location of the vendor.

- You should find out the number of support personnel the vendor has on staff for the type of product line you are purchasing. The more staff members available for your product, the quicker a response you should receive (theoretically).

- Most people are optimistic and assume that the support will be responsive and helpful from any vendor. However, this sometimes isn't the case. Therefore, you may want to ask the vendor what the escalation procedures are if you cannot get the assistance you need to support your site. The vendor should have specific procedures and not be hesitant to share those with you.

Q: Does the software vendor have a premium support option available?

Generally, basic support will provide support for only specified hours of the day and specified days of the week. If you are willing to pay more for more support, you should be able to get support coverage 24 hours a day, 7 days a week. This type of support is commonly referred to as premium support. Depending on your site and the critical nature of your backups, you might or might not want to pay the extra money.

For some vendors, premium support includes a specific individual that supports your site. At larger sites, with custom and complex configurations, this is a big benefit. How many times have you called a vendor and had to explain to different individuals over and over how your site is configured and what systems and networks your site consists of? When you are trying to troubleshoot a problem, having to give this kind of explanation each time you call the vendor can be time-consuming and frustrating. With the same person handling your support calls, you do not have to explain the basics over and over each time. You actually build a rapport with this person, and the support becomes far more personal and less frustrating. An added benefit to premium support is that most vendors have their more senior support people as part of the premium support staff. With more seasoned support, you can generally solve your problems faster.

Q: If required, can the software company provide onsite support?

You may get into a situation where the right answer to fix a problem requires a vendor staff member at your site. This can be quite costly, but it can be comforting to know that it exists. When all other options fail, at least you still have another option.

Q: How are customer bug reports and customer-recommended engineering changes handled and responded to within the software company?

As you use a product, you are bound to uncover problems with the product or come up with ideas to improve the product. It is very import to feed that information back to the vendor, so that it can be incorporated into future releases of the product. Knowing exactly how that process is handled within the company is important. You need to know not only how to provide input to the company, but how the company will inform you of what is happening to your input. If you provide a suggestion or a bug fix, it is nice to know if it will be fixed, when it will be fixed, if there is a workaround, or if it will not be fixed. Nothing is more discouraging than to give information to a company and get no response whatsoever. You feel like you are talking to a black hole!

Q: Are product patches available via the software vendor's web site or through an FTP site?

The availability of patches via the Internet is very convenient and sometimes vital. For example, you may be having problems with your backup software product. A support staff member may tell you over the phone that the problem is fixed in a particular patch for your product. The problem may be serious enough that you cannot complete your backups, therefore causing a production failure at your site. Having patches on the vendor's network site would allow you get a patch immediately when you uncover a problem instead of having to wait for postal mail or overnight delivery to reach your site. There may be situations where even overnight is not soon enough, and having the ability to access what you need over the Internet, right away, is attractive.

Q: Does the vendor have any problem-identification or problem-resolution facility at their web site?

Once again, Internet web sites are very convenient, and one of the ways to use these is to have the option of searching the site for answers. This may provide a better way to configure the software or a more serious answer to a real problem you may be experiencing. This type of functionality provides an alternative location for you if you cannot reach the support staff (possibly because of time zone issues). Also, if problems and resolutions are available for browsing, you can go to the web site at your leisure and examine what is there. It is possible that you might find something to make the configuration of the backups at your site easier to manage or find some other bit of information you may not have found elsewhere.

Q: Are there any user groups meetings or conferences available for the backup product for you to attend?

There is nothing like talking to others in your area about technical problems or implementations related to products and vendors. It may be that you find common problems within this group that can be brought up to the vendor as group issues and concerns. Approaching the vendor as a group effort to fix problems is sometimes more effective, and you may see more responsiveness doing this than as an individual making the same effort.

User groups might or might not be sponsored or coordinated by the vendor. You might ask the vendor if they have coordinated any type of user groups or you might take it upon yourself to contact other companies in your area or region to see who is working on their backups and what they are doing to accomplish backups. If you coordinate the groups yourself, you can rotate the meetings among the different companies. A lot of technical information can be shared among individuals without revealing any company secrets.

Another type of group meeting is conferences. Some general Windows NT conferences, for instance, may have sessions (scheduled or impromptu) to discuss such things as backups. If you are attending a conference and do not see a session on backups, contact the coordinators of the conference. Let them know you are interested; perhaps a backup discussion will be scheduled. The computer vendor may also hold user conferences about their own products.

Q: Are there any mailing lists associated with the product?

There may be mailing lists that the vendor or someone else sponsors. A mailing list may provide you with information on bugs and bug fixes or general installation or configuration questions and answers. Also, you can submit questions to obtain answers from other users who may have encountered the same issues. These mailing lists are an excellent way to share information or at least read information about issues and concerns others may be experiencing.

Q: What onsite training or training courses are available from the vendor?

Some vendors provide training themselves at their own locations. Other vendors have third-party individuals or companies provide training. The vendors or third-party sources may be able to provide the training at your site. Possibly through a user's group, you may be able to get enough people together for training to make it more cost-effective to have the training at your location or another in your region. There are always the traditional ways to receive training, but you can get creative to find a different way that costs less and is more convenient.

Additional Considerations

Q: How is licensing supported by the product?

Licensing software is important for vendors to protect their interest and to be able to receive income for copies of their software being used. However, how the vendor implements the licensing restrictions is important to understand. In the area of backups, having to enter license keys on every backup client to be able to perform backups is not very scalable. As you get more and more backup clients, it becomes harder and harder to manage. The licensing restrictions should be on the backup server.

One thing to be concerned about with respect to backup server licensing is having the flexibility to move from one backup server to another without a preventative hardware dependency. For example, you may have a backup server become completely inoperable in the middle of the night. Say the power supply in the computer goes, you have no replacement power supplies, and you cannot wait until morning for a store to open because backups have to be completed that night. In this case, you might decide that you will use a completely different computer system for the backup server. One of the many issues you'll have to address is the licensing for that new backup server. The bottom line is that if you are not using the license on any other operating computer, you should be able to move it to another computer. In the example given here, you would not be breaking any license agreement, so there should not be any reason it cannot be done.

Check with the vendor on how the licensing is handled in their product. Backups almost always run at night and on weekends. These are generally when vendors' support staffs are not available. Therefore, the licensing should be flexible enough for you to make unexpected changes without breaking the licensing agreements that are in place.

Q: Does the vendor have a site license available for their product?

The larger your site, the more important site licensing is and the easier it is to handle administratively. The site license may restrict the number of backup servers, or the number of backup clients, or both, to a maximum number of hosts licensed. That way all backup servers use the same license key and there is no tracking of them to a particular backup server. Do not be surprised if with a site license, the vendor wishes to have periodic audits to make sure you are not exceeding the original number of computers agreed upon for your site.

The vendor may want a clause in your contract that states that you cannot go over a particular threshold. This might come into play in the event of your company being bought by another company or vice versa. The number of backup clients may double or triple, and of course the vendor will want more money for the substantially larger site. In the event of a situation like this, don't be surprised if the vendor wants to renegotiate the contract.

Q: Does the backup software provide archiving support?

Archiving is explained in Chapter 2, *In Addition to Backups.* If you might be implementing archiving in the future, you should know whether the products you are considering for backups also supply archive support. Remember that you can provide archiving capability other products that do not provide backup support, so that you are not boxed in if you choose a vendor for backups and decide that their archive support is not what you need for your site.

Q: Does the backup software provide Hierarchical Storage Management (HSM) support?

HSM is described in Chapter 2. If you might be implementing HSM in the future, you might be interested in knowing whether the backup products you are considering also provide HSM support. The HSM support integrated within the backup product may be able to be used to suit this requirement, or you may find another product. There are products that do not provide backup support but do have the HSM functionality. It is possible to integrate these HSM products into your backup environment.

Q: What other customers can you talk to about the product in your area of business with a similar site configuration?

Any business similar to the kind of business your company is in should have the same type of requirements and should be contacted. The other site should have a similar mix of computers and a similar size. They should have also implemented backups in a similar manner as the one that your site is considering.

You should ask the backup software vendor for recommendations of who you can talk to. If you schedule a conversation with someone, see if you can talk to them without the backup vendor's salesperson involved. You want the truth about the product you are considering, and you may get more candid answers from individuals if the vendor's salesperson is not on the telephone or in the room. Another way to find a reference is to get a name and telephone of someone on a mailing list associated with the product you are considering. In the technical arena, generally cold-calling someone from a mailing list will be well received, and you can get some great answers about a product that way.

Q: What are the vendor's test and evaluation policies?

Testing backup software is a time-consuming proposition. You will not be able to do it in a short period of time, such as a couple of weeks. You need at least a couple of months to do a thorough job. See how long you can evaluate the product and how your questions and concerns will be addressed during this evaluation period. You will definitely need a technical person at your disposal whom you can call when needed. During the evaluation period, don't let the vendor do all of the installation and configuration for your site. Whoever will be managing the backups at your site should be involved with their own hands. The vendor may gloss over some issues that need to be explained or investigated further. Some of these types of issues will surface only as you actually use the product and get your feet wet. Keep in mind that you don't buy a new car by having the car salesperson drive you around town. You have to get in the driver's seat and see how it handles.

Q: How many employees are employed by the vendor?

The number of employees employed by the vendor can mean different things. First, you should know how those employees are distributed: how many are in engineering, how many are in support, and how many are in sales. The more engineers involved with the product, the more likely it is that quick changes can be made to the product, and the more likely chances are that the vendor will stick to schedules set for new releases. Having more support staff available means that you may receive more expedient responses to your support calls. You also want a company that will stick around in the industry for a while. A large number of employees involved with the company can indicate a commitment of the company to the employees, and, ultimately, to the product itself.

Q: What year was the company founded?

How long a company has been in business can also indicate a certain amount of commitment. This information also implies a certain level of expertise.

7

Windows NT Backup Software

The Windows NT operating system is shipped with backup software called *ntbackup*. This software is commonly referred to as the *Tape Backup Utility* (TBU). The TBU can be accessed either through a GUI interface or from the command line. The GUI cannot be used for scheduled backups, but the *ntbackup* command can be used in conjunction with the *at* command and the Schedule services to accomplish scheduled backups. This backup software is a subset of the backup and restore software sold by Seagate Software and is repackaged by Microsoft to be included with Windows NT.

TBU Advantages and Disadvantages

Like most software, the TBU provided as part of Windows NT has its advantages and disadvantages, which are described in the following sections.

Advantages

The most obvious advantage is that the software is free and is available immediately after you have installed the base NT operating system. Other advantages are the following:

- The GUI provided by the TBU is easy to understand and follow.
- The TBU can perform full, incremental, or differential backups.
- The TBU can back up and restore local and remote NTFS or FAT file systems.
- The TBU can append backups to existing backup tapes and span multiple tapes.
- You can create batch files to automate the backups.
- The TBU provides log files on tape operations.

Disadvantages

Even though the TBU is free and has its advantages, there are features and capabilities missing. These features and capabilities are available in commercial products that can be purchased separately. The disadvantages include the following:

- The TBU does not have online catalogs or databases to perform restores. The catalog(s) have to read from tape for each tape that might be needed for the restore.

- The TBU will not back up open or locked files or folders, and because of this, for best results, the TBU must be used on completely quiescent systems.

- Every NT system has to be configured separately for backups.

- The TBU does not provide network backups. It allows only backups of mapped network drives.

- The TBU cannot back up special partitions or filesystems, such as those for SQL Server, Microsoft Exchange, or Lotus Notes.

- The TBU does not support tape libraries.

- The TBU supports only tape devices. It does not support optical drives, Zip drives, or Jaz drives.

- The TBU does not provide heterogeneous backups and restores.

After reading these advantages and disadvantages, you probably realize that the TBU can be used with the small backup model only. It is not scalable to support medium backup implementations and it definitely is not useful in large backup sites.

Backup and Restore User Accounts

Using the TBU, the administrator can back up and restore any directory or file on the entire system using the *ntbackup* program or the TBU. Additionally, users that are members of the Backup Operators or Administrators group can do the same.

NOTE   If a user will be performing only backups and no other administrative tasks, it is highly recommended that they be part of the Backup Operators group, not the Administrators group.

All users have access to both the command-line and GUI interface of the TBU. A user can back up directories and files that are not restricted to that user. This is important for users who wish to do ad hoc backups when data needs to be backed up. For example, let's say a user works on the weekend, but it is after the backups have completed. If they have done substantial work, they may want to perform a backup of the files that were changed, just to protect themselves, until the next full system backup is performed. Another example is if a user wishes to transfer information to another system (maybe take it home) and the file(s) will not fit on a floppy diskette. This user can put the data on tape, transfer to the other system and perform the restore. However, this does require tape drives that are compatible between the two systems.

Additions to Backup Operators or Administrators Group

To add a user to either the Backup Operators or Administrators group, log in as the administrator or as a user with administrator privileges. First go to the Windows NT Start button, under Programs, and then under Administrative Tools, click on the User Manager option. The User Manager window will appear. From this window, add the appropriate users to either the Backup Operators or Administrators group.

WARNING   The previous description is for adding users to a local machine's
              Backup Operators or Administrators group, rather than a domain. If
              you add a user to a domain's Backup Operators or Administrators
              group, be careful that you truly intend to allow that user backup
              and restore privileges for *all* machines within that particular domain.

Starting the TBU GUI

There are several different ways to start the TBU GUI:

* Start → Programs → Administrative Tools → Backup.

* Through the Windows NT Explorer or in the My Computer window, use the right mouse button and click on one of the disk drives. A pull-down window will appear; in this window, left-click on Properties. The drive Properties window will appear. Click on the Tools tab and you will see a box labeled Backups. Click on the Backup Now... button.

* If you have a MS-DOS window available, you can type in the command ntbackup and the TBU GUI will appear.

Troubleshooting Tape Devices

No matter how you start the TBU, the utility first performs an initialization. The initialization process includes a check for configured tape devices. The tape device(s) to be used for backups and restores must be installed and accessible by Windows NT before the TBU will be able to recognize them during the initialization and access them. If you start the TBU and you get the error message shown in Figure 7-1, there are a number of steps that can be taken to determine the possible problem. This section covers some of the items to check.

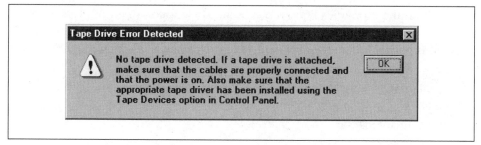

Figure 7-1. Tape drive error message

No Tape Drive Installed

It may seem obvious, but if you do not have a tape device installed in your PC and you start the TBU, you will get an error message stating that the tape device could not be detected. The fix for this problem is to install a tape drive.

Verify that Windows NT Recognizes Device and Driver

If you start the TBU and receive an error message that the tape device could not be detected, when in fact your tape drive is installed, the first step is to verify that the hardware is recognized by Windows NT.

To do this, select Start → Settings → Control Panel. The Control Panel window will appear. Select the Tape Devices icon, which will display the Tape Devices window. At this point, you have the following options:

- If the tape drive installed in your computer is displayed under the *Devices* tab with the corresponding driver listed under the *Drivers* tab, proceed to the section "Tape Device Found in the Tape Devices Window."

- If the tape drive installed in your computer is not displayed under the Devices tab, proceed to the section "No Tape Device Found in the Tape Devices Window."

Tape Device Found in the Tape Devices Window

If your tape drive is listed in the Tape Devices window, first verify that the device and driver are working properly. Double-check the following things:

- Under the Devices tab, highlight your tape device. There should be an indication on the far right side of the device name that states Driver loaded. Then click on the Properties button. A new window appears and displays all of the pertinent information about that drive. Under the General tab in the Device Status portion of the window verify that the device is working properly.

- Under the Driver tab, highlight your tape driver. There should be an indication in the far right side of the device name that says it is started. Then, in the Driver Status portion of the window, verify that the driver is installed, started, and configured.

Depending on what you find from the information acquired, take one of the following actions:

- If the status indicates the device is working properly and the driver is installed, started, and configured, then NT recognizes the hardware properly. You should be able to restart the TBU and it should begin initializing with the tape device being detected.

- If this is your first time through this verification section and the status does not indicate a properly working device and installed, started, and configured driver, verify that the hardware is connected properly by following the instructions in the section "Verify that Hardware is Connected Properly." After verifying that the hardware is connected properly, repeat the steps in the section "Verify that Windows NT Recognizes Device and Driver."

- If this is your second time through this Windows NT verification section and the Device Status indicates anything besides "working properly" and the Driver Status indicates anything besides "installed, started, and configured," then contact the store where the hardware was purchased, or contact the manufacturer of the tape drive.

No Tape Device Found in the Tape Devices Window

If your tape drive isn't listed in the Tape Devices window, click on the Detect button. The system will scan your system for devices. Based on the results from the scan, take one of the following actions:

- If the device is detected, the system will install the required drivers. Follow the steps as prompted. You will most likely need the original Windows NT CD or diskettes. After the device and drivers are installed, take one of the following steps:

   — If you can, reboot your PC. Once your computer is back up and running, follow the instructions in the section "Verify that Windows NT Recognizes Device and Driver."

   — If you cannot reboot your PC, you can start the driver manually. Note the Driver and Device name in the Tape Devices window. Start→Settings→Control Panel→Devices displays the Devices window. Find the corresponding Device name in this window and click on the Start button.

- If the device was not detected, continue to the next section, "Verify that Hardware is Connected Properly."

Verify that Hardware is Connected Properly

First, make sure that your computer has been shut down and the power cord disconnected. At this point, take one of the following actions:

- If the tape drive is an external tape drive, check to make sure the power cord and cable connection between the computer and tape drive are secure. You may want to unplug them and reconnect them, just to make sure (do this on both ends of the cable and the power cord).

- If the tape drive is an internal tape drive, remove the cover of the PC and check the internal cable and power connections to your tape drive by unplugging them and then reconnect them (do this on both ends of the ribbon cable and power connection).

Reconnect the power cord to your PC and turn on the PC. After Windows NT is up and running, repeat the instructions in the section "Verify that Windows NT Recognizes Device and Driver."

Using the TBU GUI

To help you better utilize the TBU GUI, review this section, which provides guidance on using the GUI. It is not intended to give you a detailed explanation of how to use the TBU GUI. The TBU GUI has a fully functional help feature to assist in any details you need to know that are not covered in this chapter.

Selecting and Deselecting Items

While using the TBU for backups and restores, you will be selecting and deselecting directories and files. A selected drive, directory, or file has an *X* marked in the box to the left of the item name. The box is blank if the directory or file is not selected. If the box next to a drive or directory name is grey with an *X* mark, then only parts of that drive or directory have been selected for backup.

Selecting or deselecting a drive, directory, or file can be done in one of the following ways:

- Clicking on the box next to the desired drive, folder, or file.
- Clicking on one of the two far right buttons in the Taskbar. These are the Checked or Uncheck buttons on the Taskbar.
- Using the Select menu option and selecting the Check or Uncheck options.

If a directory is selected, then every file and subdirectory within that directory automatically becomes selected. You can select an entire drive or directory, then drill down to deselect any individual files that should not be backed up. Conversely, you do not have to select the entire drive or directory: you can first drill down drives or directories and select only individual directories or files for backups.

Backup Sets

The TBU uses the concept of backup sets. If you use this product, it is important that you understand the definition of backup sets. A backup set is a group of folders and files written to tape as a single unit. These sets are folders and files from one disk drive. If you choose folders or files from different drives, different backup sets are created. For example, if you select the folder *C:\winnt* and *D:\lotus\docs*, each of these folders will be backed up as a separate backup set onto the tape.

Cataloging

A catalog is a listing of what was backed up. The catalogs created by the TBU are stored on the tape media with the backups. If the TBU is still running between the time a backup is performed and the restore, the tape catalog information will still be recognized when you use the utility. If you exit the TBU and then restart it, the tape catalog information has to be restored or reread from the media before the restore of the folder or file can start.

The alternative to this type of approach is to have the catalog or, as it is sometimes called, a database located on the hard drive of your computer. If the catalog is located on the tape media, it takes longer to perform the restore of the data. That is because the catalog has to be read from tape before the data restore can get started. If the catalog is located on your computer's hard drive, then the catalog is not read from tape; instead, it is read directly from the hard disk. This saves time on the overall restore of the required data. This option is not available with the TBU.

Backups

The TBU predominately uses the Drives and Tapes windows that are within that utility. When performing a backup, you start with the Drives window. In this window, select the desired drives, folders, or files to be backed up. Once these selections are made, there are a couple of different ways to initiate the backup:

- Clicking on the far left button in the Taskbar. This is the Backup button.

- Using the Operations menu option and selecting the Backup... option.

After initiating the backup, you will be prompted with the Backup Information dialog window, shown in Figure 7-2. This window has three sections: Tape Information, Backup Information, and Log Information.

WARNING   Performing proper backups is the key to being able to perform a successful restore. It is important to go through each option within the Backup Information window before starting any backup.

The components in the Backup Information window are pretty straightforward. Additionally, there are help entries for each option in this window. Every option should be reviewed with every backup. Don't rush when you are performing backups. Make sure that they are performed consistently and thoroughly each time. When you need data restored is not the time to be wishing you were more careful with your backups. Generally, you will be performing restores after deleting a folder or file accidently or after a hard disk crashes. So you will already be frustrated even before the restore process has started. The last thing you need is to have a poorly performed backup make a bad situation even worse.

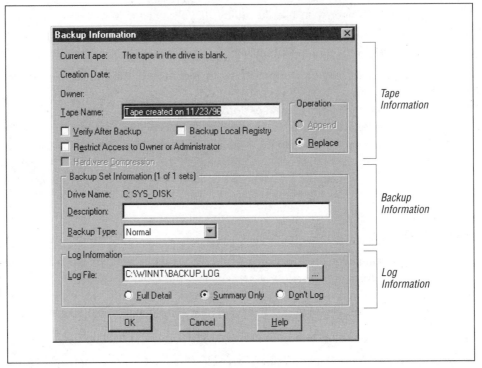

Figure 7-2. Backup Information dialog window

A few of the options in the Backup Information dialog window are worth specific comment:

Current Tape

> The name of the tape in the tape drive is displayed to the right of this label. This can be modified in Tape Name.

> If no tape is in the tape drive, it will state this. You will need to put a tape in the drive before a backup can be performed. Sometimes, if you have just placed a tape in the tape drive and the drive has not yet become ready, you will also receive the same message. Just wait a few moments; when the tape is ready, the status next to Current Tape will change to indicate this.

> If the tape in the tape drive was used for other purposes such as backups using a different software package, you will receive a message that says the tape must be erased before it can be used.

> If the tape in the tape drive is new, you will receive a message that states the tape in the drive is blank. With a blank tape, you can perform a backup.

Operation

This field is where you indicate whether you want the current tape appended to or replaced (overwritten). You will be prompted to make sure that you want to overwrite the existing tape. So if you mistakenly choose the replace operation, you will have a chance to back out and select append instead.

Verify After Backup

The success of a restore is only as good as the data on the tape. Therefore, you may wish to have the data on the tape verified after the backup is completed. This does take extra time, but it is often well worth it. This may catch a bad tape or just an error in the process of writing the backup data to tape.

Backup Local Registry

When you perform a backup, you should always consider if you would like the Registry backed up in addition to the selected folders and files. Check this option if you need a current backup of the Registry.

Backup Type

The following types of backups are possible:

Normal

This option indicates that you want to perform a full backup of the specified data. The files are marked on disk to indicate that this option was used.

Copy

This option indicates that you just want to copy the files from the disk to the tape. The files are *not* marked on disk.

Differential

This option indicates that you want to back up only the files that have changed since the last backup among the files that you specified. The difference between this option and the incremental option is that this option does *not* mark on disk that this option was used.

Incremental

This option indicates that you want to back up only the files that have changed since the last backup among the files that you specified. The files are marked on disk to indicate that this option was used.

Daily

This option indicates that you want to back up only the files that have changed that particular day. The files are *not* marked to indicate that this option was used.

After you have filled in the appropriate information in the Backup Information dialog window (shown in Figure 7-2), click on OK and the backup will start. At this point, the Backup Status window, shown in Figure 7-3, is displayed. This window is broken into two parts: Status Area and Summary. At this point in the backup process, you can watch the Summary area of this window to see the progress of the backups. The TBU shows only folders and files that are being backed up. There is no tape speed information presented.

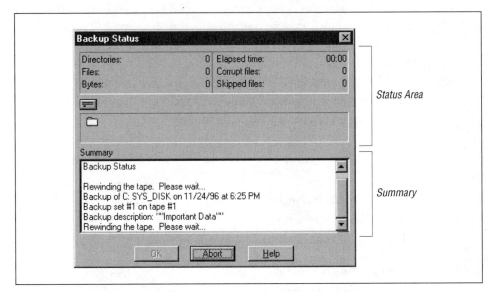

Figure 7-3. Backup Status window

If you selected the append option in the Backup Information dialog window, before the actual backup starts, the tape will move through each previous backup set on the tape being used. This process may take a while; how long depends on which type of tape device you are using and how many previous backups were on the tape you are currently using. If you selected the replace option in the Backup Information dialog window, you will be asked if you really want to replace the information on tape before the backup proceeds.

Restores

The TBU predominately uses the Drives and Tapes windows within that utility. When performing a restore, start with the Tapes window. When this window is selected, the current tape catalog from the tape currently in the tape drive is displayed. If the TBU has been restarted since the last backup, the tape catalog has to be reread from the tape. This may take a little bit of time.

After the tape catalog is displayed, you select the desired drives, folders, or files to be restored. Once these selections are made, there are a couple of different ways to initiate the restore:

- Clicking on the second button from the left in the Taskbar. This is the Restore button.

- Using the Operations menu option and selecting the Restore... option.

After initiating the restore, you will be prompted with the Restore Information dialog window, shown in Figure 7-4. This window has three sections: Tape Information, Restore Information, and Log Information.

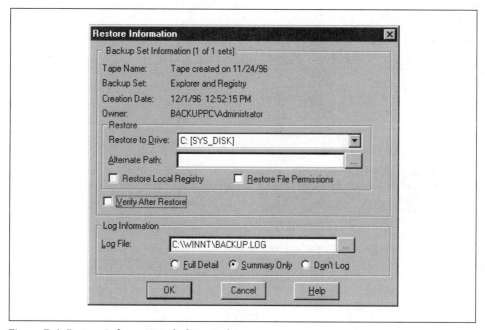

Figure 7-4. Restore Information dialog window

The components in the Restore Information dialog window are pretty straightforward. Additionally, there are help entries for each option in this window. Every option should be reviewed with every restore. A few of the options in the Restore Information dialog window are worth specific comment:

Alternate Path

This field is where you specify a different location to restore the folders or files. If you do not want to overwrite existing folders or files, you might want to restore the folder or file to a different location. For example, you might want to compare an existing file with one that was backed up to determine which copy you want to keep. By restoring the file to a different location, the comparison can then be performed.

Restore Local Registry

This is how the Registry is restored using the TBU. Unfortunately, you cannot restore only the Registry. The TBU requires some folder or file to be selected in the Tapes window, before you have the option to restore the Registry.

ntbackup Command

To schedule, backups you must use *ntbackup* from the command line. You cannot schedule backups using the TBU; you must use a combination of the command-line *ntbackup* program, the *at* command, and the Schedule service. This section describes the syntax associated with the *ntbackup* program.

NOTE   Files backed up using the *ntbackup* command can be restored using the TBU.

The *ntbackup* syntax is:

```
ntbackup operation path [/a] [/v] [/r] [/d "text"] [/b] [/hc:{on|off}]
[/t {option}] [/l "filename"] [/e] [/tape:{n}]
```

The parameters are defined as follows:

operation

This parameter should be set to **backup**.

path

This parameter is used to specify one or more paths for the folders to be backed up.

NOTE   The *ntbackup* program does not allow you to back up individual files; you must specify directories or drives. Also, it does not allow you to use wildcards.

/a

This parameter appends the specified data to the end of the last backup set on the tape. If this parameter is not used, the backup will overwrite the previous data on the tape. If more than one directory or drive is specified on the command line, the first one overwrites the data on the tape, and subsequent ones are appended.

/v

> This stands for verify. This parameter confirms that the backup data set was in fact placed on the tape.

/r

> This stands for restrict. This parameter limits access to the backup data set that is being written to tape.

/d "text"

> This stands for description. This parameter provides a very brief explanation of the backup data set being written to tape.

/b

> This stands for backing up local Registry. If this parameter is used, the local Registry will be backed up in addition to the backup data set specified.

/hc:{on | off}

> This stands for hardware compression. Depending on whether you indicate on or off, this parameter will utilize hardware compression or not.

/t {option}

> This stands for type of backup to be performed; the different types of backups are the same types described in the section "Backups." The keywords used for option are the following:

```
normal
copy
differential
incremental
daily
```

/l "filename"

> This parameter indicates that you want logging turned on with the name of the log file that should be kept on the backup. This logs full details, which include all operations information, including the names of all the files and directories backed up.

/e

> This parameter is used in conjunction with the /1 parameter, but indicates that the logs should only be the summary information, not the full details. This logging includes only the major operations and failed backups.

/tape:{n}

> If you have multiple drives attached to your system, use this parameter to specify the tape drive to back up to. The variable n is the tape drive number and can be a value between 0 and 9.

There are two additional parameters to the *ntbackup* program that require user input and therefore cannot be used in conjunction with the Windows NT scheduler. For completeness only, they are listed here.

The syntax for the additional *ntbackup* parameters is:

```
ntbackup [/nopoll] [/missingtape]
```

The parameters are defined as follows:

/nopoll

This parameter is used only with no other parameters and tells the *ntbackup* utility to erase the tape.

/missingtape

This parameter indicates that a tape is not available within a backup set of tapes. You might want to restore from one tape out of a set or you might have lost a tape that was part of a set. This parameter tells *ntbackup* that each tape should be treated as a separate unit and not part of a set of tapes.

Scheduling Backups

Scheduling backups is done by using the *at* command in combination with the Windows NT scheduler and *ntbackup*. The *at* command is used to schedule commands or programs to execute on any computer at a specific time on a particular date. So, in this context, part of the input to *at* is the *ntbackup* program.

The first thing to remember is that the Windows NT schedule service must be running to perform any scheduled backups. To verify that this service is up and operational, go to the Windows NT Start button, under Settings, and then under Control Panel, double-click on the Services icon. The Services window will appear. From this window, scroll down until you see the Schedule service. Under the Status column, it should state that this service is Started. If not, highlight the Schedule service and then click on the Start button on the right side of the window.

If you want the scheduler to start automatically when the computer is booted, then while still in the Services window, click on the Startup... button on the right side of the window. Change the Startup Type to Automatic and click OK. Note that in that same window you can indicate whether you want the scheduler service to start under the system account or a different account. This is where you can provide a specific account name that is used to manage the backups and that may be part of the Backup Operators group.

Now that the Windows NT scheduler is running, use the *at* command with the *ntbackup* command-line program. First, the syntax and how to use the *at* command will be explained. An example of how to use the *at* command with the *ntbackup* command is provided in the next section.

There are three ways the *at* command is utilized:

- To see what jobs are scheduled
- To schedule new jobs in the queue
- To delete jobs already scheduled

If you bring up an MS-DOS window on your computer and type at without any parameters, you will see a list of jobs that are currently in the queue for the computer on which you are currently running. You may see that there are no jobs scheduled in the list. If you have no jobs scheduled or you want to enter another job, use the *at* command to enter the jobs into the queue.

The syntax for the *at* command is:

```
at [\\computername] time [/interactive] [/every:date[,...] |
/next:date[,...]] "command"
```

The parameters are defined as follows:

computername

> This parameter is used only if you want to schedule a command or program on another computer. If this parameter is eliminated, the job will be scheduled on the local computer you are using.

time

> This is used to indicate what time the command or program must start. Use the 24-hour military clock notation, where 00:00 is midnight, 12:00 is noon, and 23:00 is 11:00 P.M.

/interactive

> This parameter indicates that you would like the command or program that executes to interact with the user logged into the computer where the scheduled job runs.

/every:date[,...]

> This parameter is used to specify the frequency of the job for those jobs that must run repeatedly on specified days or dates.
>
> - To specify a day, replace date with one of the days of the week, indicated with M, T, W, Th, F, S, or Su.
> - To specify a date, replace date with one of the dates of the month, indicated with numbers 1, 2, 3 through 31.

If you have multiple days or dates, use a comma to separate them. If no day or date is specified, the current day is assumed.

/next:date[,...]

This parameter is used to specify that you would like the command or program that is scheduled to execute on the next occurrence of the day or date. It will not repeat.

- To specify a day, replace **date** with one of the days of the week, indicated with **M**, **T**, **W**, **Th**, **F**, **S**, or **Su**.

- To specify a date, replace **date** with one of the dates of the month, indicated with numbers 1, 2, 3 through 31.

If you have multiple days or dates, use a comma to separate them. If no day or date is specified, the current day is assumed.

NOTE   You use either the **/every** parameter or the **/next** parameter. They cannot be used together.

"command"

This parameter indicates what you want executed. It can be an NT command, a program with an extension of *.EXE* or *.COM*, or a batch program file with a *.BAT* or *.CMD* extension. You must provide the full, absolute pathname in this parameter, including the drive letter or the server and sharename if you are using a remote computer.

It isn't mandatory to use the quotation marks, but for consistency, ease of reading the command, and so that you don't have to worry about whether you have provided the exact syntax, it is recommended that you do use quotes. The exact rules on using the quotes or not are listed under the NT help for the *at* command.

NOTE   The **command** parameter is where you indicate the name of the batch file that has the *ntbackup* command. You cannot put the *ntbackup* command directly on the command line for the *at* command. If you do, you will get errors when the system tries to execute the *at* command.

While the *at* command syntax described earlier is used to schedule jobs in the queue, the following syntax is used to remove jobs from the queue.

The *at* command syntax is:

```
at [\\computername] [[id] [/delete [/yes]]
```

The parameters are defined as follows:

computername

> This parameter is used only if you want to schedule a command or program on another computer. If this parameter is eliminated, the job will be scheduled on the local computer you are using.

id

> Every job you submit has an identification number assigned to it. You can see what identification numbers are assigned to what jobs by entering the *at* command with no parameters, which lists all jobs in the queue and their associated identification numbers.

/delete

> This parameter is used to cancel a scheduled job from the queue.

WARNING   If the `id` parameter is not provided and the `/delete` parameter is used, all scheduled jobs in the queue are canceled.

/yes

> When deleting jobs from the queue, you will be prompted from the system. This parameter is used if you what to force a yes answer to all of these queries.

Examples

This section provides a few examples to help you use the TBU program.

Example: Performing a Backup of System or User Files

This section shows you, with step-by-step instructions, how to back up a file or folder using the Windows NT TBU:

1. Start the TBU as described in the earlier section, "Starting the TBU GUI."

2. First, make sure that you have a tape in your tape drive and verify that you are using the appropriate tape. This verification is done by enlarging the Tapes window within the TBU if it isn't already enlarged. Once this window is displayed, it will show you the creation date on the tape and you can drill down to determine exactly which files and folders are on the backup tape in the tape drive. If this isn't the tape you wish to back up, replace it and find the appropriate tape before beginning the new backup.

3. Now select which files or folders you want to back up. This is done through Drives window within the utility. This window may or may not be expanded when the TBU is brought up; it may be an icon. If it is an icon, enlarge the icon, and you will see a window similar to the one in Figure 7-5.

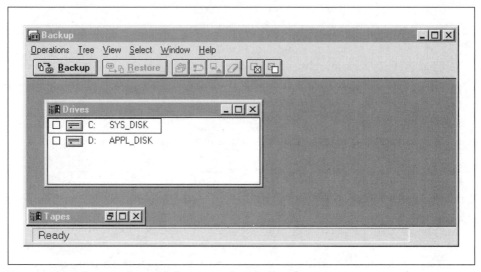

Figure 7-5. Backup window with Drives window displayed

Within the Drives window, find the files or folders that you want to back up. Click on the box to the left of what you want to back up. You will notice that once you click on the box, an *X* will be placed in the box indicating that the file or folder is to be backed up. If you see a white box with an *X* in it, it means that specific file or folder is to be backed up. If you see a grey box with an *X* in it, that means that some file or folder within that directory tree structure is marked for backup.

4. After selecting all of the files you wish to back up, the next step is to click on the Backup button in the upper-left corner of the window depicted in Figure 7-5. Once you have clicked this button, a Backup Information dialog window will appear, like the one shown in shown in Figure 7-2.

5. Now you must set the correct backup set options. The section earlier in this chapter called "Backups" discusses the most important options in the Backup Information dialog window. Every time you perform a backup you should briefly go through each option, just to make sure they are set properly for the particular backup you are about to perform.

Don't forget to configure the log options. These are on the bottom portion of the Backup Information dialog window. If you have had previous problems with a backup, go ahead and use the Full Detail option to assist you in troubleshooting. Otherwise, you may want to select just the Summary Only option. You should always keep some logs, unless you are extremely short on disk space to support the log files.

6. Once the backup options are all set appropriately, click on the OK button at the bottom of the Backup Information dialog window.

7. Finally, the backup should be running. At this point you will see a Backup Status window, like the one shown in Figure 7-3. When the status states that the backup has completed, you are finished.

Example: Performing a Full Backup of a Drive

This section shows you, with step-by-step instructions, how to back up a drive fully using the Windows NT TBU.

WARNING   It is highly recommended that you close all applications and not do any work on the computer while you are performing this full backup.

For this example, let's assume the drive to be backed up is the *C:* drive.

1. Start the TBU as described in the section "Starting the TBU GUI."

2. First, make sure that you have a tape in your tape drive and verify that you are using the appropriate tape. This verification is done by enlarging the Tapes window within the TBU (if it isn't already enlarged). Once this window is displayed, it will show you the creation date on the tape, and you can drill down to determine exactly which files and folders are on the backup tape you have in the tape drive. If this isn't the tape you wish to back up on, replace it and find the appropriate tape before beginning the new backup.

3. Now select the entire *C:* drive by clicking on the box next to the *C:* drive in the Drives window within the utility. This window may or may not be expanded when the TBU is brought up; it may be an icon. If it is an icon, enlarge the icon and you will see a window similar to the one in Figure 7-5.

   Within the Drives window, note that the box with an *X* in it next to the *C:* drive is *not* grayed in. That means that all of the files for that drive have been selected for backups.

4. After selecting all of the *C:* drive to back up, the next step is to click on the Backup button in the upper-left corner of the window depicted in Figure 7-5. Once you have clicked this button, a Backup Information dialog window will appear, like the one shown in Figure 7-2.

5. Now you must set the correct backup set options. The "Backups" section, earlier in this chapter, discusses the most important options in the Backup Information dialog window. Every time you perform a backup you should briefly go through each option, just to make sure that they are set properly for the particular backup you are about to perform.

Since this is a full backup of a drive, the following are some options you should select:

- You should Verify after Backup.

- You should Backup Local Registry.

- The Backup Type should be set to Normal.

- Depending on the tape you are using, appropriately mark Append or Replace.

- As a good rule of thumb, you should include a Description.

Don't forget to configure the log options. These are on the bottom portion of the Backup Information dialog window. If you have had previous problems with a backup, go ahead and use the Full Detail option to assist you in troubleshooting. Otherwise, you may want to just select the Summary Only option. You should always keep some logs, unless you are extremely short on disk space to support the log files.

6. Once the backup options are all set appropriately, click on the OK button at the bottom of the Backup Information dialog window.

7. Finally, the backup should be running. At this point you will see a Backup Status window, like the one shown in Figure 7-3. When the status states that the backup has completed, you are finished.

Example: Performing a Restore of System or User Files

This section shows you, step by step, how to perform a restore using the Windows NT TBU.

1. Start the TBU as described in the section "Starting the TBU GUI."

2. First, make sure that you have a tape in your tape drive and verify that you are using the appropriate tape. This verification is done by enlarging the Tapes window with in the TBU. Figure 7-6 illustrates what the TBU looks like with the Tapes window opened. If the Tapes window is in an icon, enlarge it. Now, if the appropriate tape isn't in the tape drive, replace it and find the appropriate tape before beginning this restore.

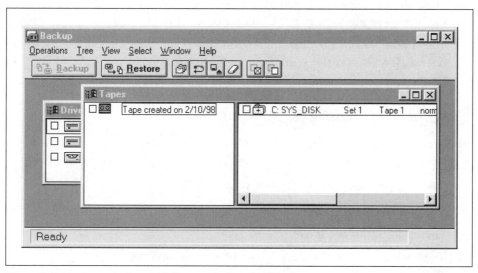

Figure 7-6. Backup window with Tapes window displayed

3. Next you must select which files or directories you want to restore; this is also done through the Tapes window. Within the Tapes window, select the files or folders that you want to restore. Click on the box to the left of what you want to restore. As with the backups, you will notice that once you click on the box, an *X* will be placed in the box indicating the file or folder is to be restored. If you see a white box with an *X* in it, that means that specific file or all the files in that folder are to be restored. If you see a grey box with an *X* in it, that means that only some files or folders within that directory tree structure are marked for restore.

4. After selecting all of the files you wish to restore, the next step is to click on the Restore button on the upper-left side of the window depicted in Figure 7-6. Once you have clicked this button, a Restore Information dialog window will appear, like the one shown in shown in Figure 7-4.

5. Now you must set the correct restore set options. The "Restores" section earlier in this chapter discusses the most important options in the Restore Information dialog window. Every time you perform a restore, you should briefly go through each option, just to make sure they are set properly for the particular restore you are about to perform.

   As with the backups, don't forget to configure the log options. These are on the bottom portion of the Restore Information dialog window. You should always keep some logs, unless you are extremely short on disk space to support the log files.

6. Once the restore options are all set appropriately, click on the OK button at the bottom of the Restore Information dialog window.

7. The restore should now be running. At this point, you will see a Restore Status window. When the status states that the restore has completed, you are finished.

Example: Scheduling a Backup

This section will show you, with step-by-step instructions, how to schedule a backup using the Windows NT *ntbackup* command and the *at* command.

For this example, let's assume the following:

* You want to backup the folder *D:\docs*.

* The backup is to occur every weekday.

* The backup is to be done at the end of the business day, 5:10 P.M.

* The backup is for your local computer.

You would then perform the following steps:

1. On your Windows NT system, bring up an MS-DOS window. To do this, select Start → Programs → Command Prompt.

2. In the MS-DOS window, if you want to, type at to see what is scheduled.

3. Now, create a batch file for the *at* command to execute. This batch file contains the *ntbackup* command with its parameters. Using *notepad*, for this example, create the file *C:\batchjobs\backup.bat*. In this file, enter the following (on a single line):

```
C:\WINNT\system32\ntbackup.exe backup D:\docs /a /v /d "Daily backup of Docs
directory" /t normal
```

Note the following points about this command:

* The full pathname, including the drive letter, is used for the *ntbackup* command.

* The backup is going to be appended to the tape.

* The backup is to be verified.

* The specified description is to be used on the backup tape.

* The backup is a normal backup (full backup).

NOTE   If you intend on running a number of different batch jobs, create a directory to hold all of these files. For example, you could call the directory *C:\batchjobs*.

---

4. Now type in the following command in the MS-DOS window to schedule the backup:

```
at 17:10 /interactive /every:M,T,W,Th,F C:\batchjobs\backup.bat
```

Note the following points about this command:

- The 24-hour military clock notation was used.

- The job runs every weekday, Monday through Friday. No weekend back-ups are run.

- The batch file is executed at the specified time.

5. After entering the previous command, you will see a message from the system stating that it was scheduled and providing the identification number associated with the job.

6. To further verify that the job was actually scheduled, you can once again enter the *at* command with no parameters.

Example: Performing a Restore from Loss of Disk

This section will show you, with step-by-step instructions, how to do a complete restore from the loss of a disk, using the TBU.

For this example, the following assumptions are made:

- The main *C:* drive is the drive that fails.

- It is a complete failure and you have installed a new hard drive.

- You are rebuilding the same computer that failed with just a new hard drive installed.

- You have your original media for the Windows NT operating system.

- You have a full backup of your *C:* drive plus any incremental backups of your *C:* drive that were performed since the last full backup.

You would then perform the following steps:

1. Install the Windows NT operating system from the system diskettes and CDs as you did originally.

2. Next you must install the tape device. You did it before (otherwise you couldn't have done backups), but as a reminder, it is done under the Control Panel and then Tape Devices. In the Tape Devices window, click on the Detect button. Your system will be scanned and your tape device will be found (if it's set up properly!). You will then have to reboot your computer to see the device.

3. Now that your system recognizes the tape device, you can start the TBU as described in the section "Starting the TBU GUI" earlier in this chapter.

WARNING   It is highly recommended that you close all applications and do no work on the computer while you are performing this full restore.

---

4. First, make sure that you have a tape in your tape drive and that you are using the appropriate tape. At this point, you should use your latest full backup tape. The incremental backups will be restored later.

   The verification of the tape is done by enlarging the Tapes window within the TBU. Figure 7-6 illustrates what the TBU looks like with the Tapes window opened. If the Tapes window is in an icon, enlarge it. Now, if the appropriate tape isn't in the tape drive, replace it and find the appropriate tape before beginning this restore.

5. The restore is done through the Tapes window. Within the Tapes window, click on the box next to the *C:* drive to indicate that you want a full restore of all the folders and files. You want the box to remain white, not grey. Remember, the white box means that all folders and files will be restored.

6. After selecting the *C:* drive to restore, the next step is to click on the Restore button on the upper-left side of the window depicted in Figure 7-6. Once you have clicked this button, a Restore Information dialog window will appear, like the one shown in Figure 7-4.

7. Now you must set the correct restore set options. The "Restores" section, earlier in this chapter, discusses the most important options in the Restore Information dialog window. Every time you perform a restore, you should briefly go through each option, just to make sure that they are set properly for the particular restore you are about to perform.

   Since this is a full restore of a drive, the following are some options you should select:

   - You should Restore Local Registry.

   - You should Restore File Permissions.

   - You should Verify After Restore.

   As with backups, don't forget to configure the log options. These are on the bottom portion of the Restore Information dialog window. You should always keep some logs, unless you are extremely short on disk space to support the log files.

8. Once the restore options are all set appropriately, click on the OK button at the bottom of the Restore Information dialog window.

9. The restore should now be running. At this point, you will see a Restore Status window. The restore will take longer than the backup. This is because the TBU has to rebuild the file system tables as it restores files. When the status states that the restore has completed, you are finished with the restore of the full backup tape.

10. Now you need to restore the incremental backup tapes. Start restoring with the earliest tape that was created on the date closest to the full backup, then restore the tape that is the next closest to the full backup date, and so on. For example, let's say you created a full backup on Sunday, an incremental backup on Tuesday, and another incremental backup on Thursday. Then on Saturday you had to replace the drive. You should start with the Sunday full tape, then restore the Tuesday incremental tape, and finally restore the Thursday incremental tape.

    For each incremental backup restore, as long as the Windows NT TBU is running, repeat steps 5 through 10. During the incremental restores, don't be alarmed if you are asked about overwriting files. Different versions of the files could possibly be on each incremental tape, so answer the question *yes*.

11. Once the complete restore is done, reboot your system.

8

In this chapter:
- *ADSM*
- *ARCserve*
- *Backup Exec*
- *Backup Express*
- *HP OpenView OmniBack II*
- *NetBackup*
- *NetWorker for NT*
- *SM-arch*
- *Feature Comparison*

Commercial Software

The Windows NT Tape Backup Utility will not scale to anything besides a very small environment. There are a lot of commercial backup and restore products available for the Windows NT platform that can scale to larger environments. This chapter covers the most popular products on the market today that have a Windows NT backup server and client product available as of the publication date of this book.* All backup products chosen have full Windows NT filesystem support of FAT, HPFS, and NTFS, including the NT Registry.

The commercial software products reviewed in this chapter are listed in Table 8-1. This chapter provides more information than you can get from the vendor literature and provides a common comparison between the products, which you cannot get from any one vendor.

Table 8-1. Commercial Software Reviewed

Product	Vendor
ADSM	IBM
ARCserve	Computer Associates
Backup Exec	Seagate Software
Backup Express	Syncsort Inc.
HP OpenView OmniBack II	Hewlett-Packard Company
NetBackup	Veritas Software
NetWorker for NT	Legato Systems, Inc.
SM-arch	Software Moguls

---

* Some products did not have Windows NT backup server software available at the publishing date, but have products in the development cycle. These products include BudTool from PDC and Alexandria from Spectra Logic. Since these products were not available, they were not reviewed in this chapter.

It is interesting to note that the NT backup products are all converging from different markets. You can actually look at them from a general perspective and group them. The ADSM product is from the mainframe marketplace. The Backup Express, HP OpenView OmniBack II, NetBackup, NetWorker, and SM-arch products were originally developed for the Unix marketplace. The ARCserve and Backup Exec products were developed for the Windows and Novell marketplace. Of course this is a generalization, and all of the products now cross into different marketplaces, but they all had to start somewhere.

All of these product choices are nice to have, but at the same time make it difficult to understand which one best fits your site. Each product is very different. The marketing and sales information for each individual product is useful, but it is also beneficial to compare and contrast the products in a concise manner. This chapter helps with comparison.

This chapter is broken into two major parts. The first part provides you with a high-level overview of how each product is designed. It covers the software design characteristics discussed in Chapter 6, *Software Features*, and how they relate to each product. The design information is not always part of the vendor's manuals or sales literature, so the information provided in this chapter should be interesting even if you have done some initial research on the backup and restore products. Also, the products are reviewed in a similar manner, providing you with comparable information to help you narrow down your search. The design of each software product doesn't change too rapidly, but the feature set of the products does. So I recommend that you visit the web sites of the vendors whose products best fit your site needs. The second part provides you with a side-by-side matrix comparison of the features for all of the vendors.

You should get a fairly good idea of which products fit your site requirements. You should narrow your search down to two or three vendors' products before you proceed into the testing phase.

ADSM

ADSTAR Distributed Storage Manager (ADSM; Version 3) is a backup, archive, and space-management* product that is supported on a wide variety of operating systems such as MVS, VM, ESA, OS/2, AS/400, Unix, and Windows NT. ADSM is an enterprise-wide storage management solution, and consists of a family of software products that integrates unattended network backup and archive with storage management and powerful disaster recovery planning functions. It is sold as a single package.

---

* ADSM's space-management capability is IBM's description of their HSM.

The ADSM product has always been an IBM product. It was initially developed on the AIX platform and ported to MVS. It has been in production since June 1993. The Windows NT version of the product has been in production since September 1996, and the server is available for both NT 3.51 and 4.0.

Backup Server

The ADSM Server component provides backup and restore services to client workstations or nodes. The server maintains the database and recovery log for ADSM resources, users, and user data.

The ADSM Server provides the storage for the backup data and consists of storage pools of randomly and sequentially accessible media. The storage pools contain files that are backed up, archived, and migrated from client nodes. The backup server also has utilities and an interface to configure the ADSM server.

ADSM is a simple server architecture. Each ADSM server has its own backup database. However, you can have tiered servers or server-to-server communications, and backup servers can be configured to share tape library resources. For example, one ADSM backup server may have a tape robot while another server may not. To handle this situation, you have the following options:

- The backup server without the robot can be configured to write directly to the tape library connected to the other backup server. The data is backed up from the backup client to its original backup server, and the backup server then moves the data to the backup server with the tape robot. This configuration is transparent to the backup client.

- The backup client can be configured to back up some data to the backup server without the tape robot and some data to the backup server with the tape robot.

- Data can be backed up to the backup server without the tape robot initially, then later migrated from the backup server without the robot to the backup server with the tape robot.

In any of these situations, the meta data about the backup is stored on the backup server without the tape library. Of course, the backups could be configured so that they can be sent directly to the server with the tape robot.

ADSM supports disk and tape devices for storing backups, archives, or space-managed files and also the migration from one media to another. The migration is true disk staging. Once the pointer to the data moves from disk to tape, ADSM notes this in the database. You set thresholds for how much data stays on the backup server's disk before it is moved from disk to tape. After the migration, a restore of the data comes directly from tape; the restore does not restore to the backup server's disk and then to the backup client's disk.

Backup Client

The ADSM Backup-Archive Client software is loaded on every workstation that must be backed up. The backup data is pushed from the backup client to the backup server. The users on the backup clients or the ADSM administrator can initiate backups or restores.

ADSM has the capability to configure a backup client to back up to different servers. However, when a user has to do a restore, they must know where to get the data and may have to logon to both servers if they are not sure where the backed-up data is located.

Configuration and Backup Information

Each ADSM backup server has one database, which is used to store all information about the data that is managed, backed up, restored, or archived by that particular ADSM Server. The database is protected by a two-phase commit process in which the server and client both have to agree that an event is successful or the transaction is backed out. The ADSM database also supports automatic triple mirroring with automatic error detection and correction. This means that you can configure ADSM to have synchronized copies of the database in three places.

The construct to manage data is made up of four parts. The parts are all related and referred to as policy objects. These four policy objects are:

Copy Group

The central, most basic policy object is the Copy Group. You have multiple but unique Copy Groups defined, which are grouped within a Management Class. When configuring the ADSM server, the Copy Group object is defined first. This group contains the backup and restore attributes or rules associated with the backup clients. This includes how many copies or versions of a file, folder, or disk to keep online, what storage pools they are stored in, and their retention dates.

ADSM handles retention of data in a unique manner. When the retention date of a file is past, the meta data about that file is removed from the ADSM database. Then ADSM tracks what percentage of data on a tape is valid. You configure what percentage of valid data is acceptable and once that percentage is reached, ADSM performs a reclamation. For example, you may set the reclamation percentage to 60%. Then any tapes with 60% of expired or invalid data will be reclaimed. The reclamation process moves the valid data to another tape volume, and the reclaimed volume is then available to be reused. This process requires two tape drives because the reclamation is a tape-to-tape copy.

The Copy Groups are defined separately for archives and backups:

Archive Copy Group

> This group is an object containing attributes that control the generation, destination, and expiration of archive files.

Backup Copy Group

> This group is an object containing attributes that control the generation, destination, and expiration of backup files.

One Archive Copy Group and one Backup Copy Group belong to one Management Class. However, you can have the same Archive or Backup Copy Groups across different Management Classes.

Management Class

> You can have multiple Management Classes; they are part of a Policy Set. A Management Class is a policy object that is a collection of rules or values for a particular group of backup clients. You have one Backup Copy Group, one Archive Copy Group, and one Space Management Copy Group per Management Class. Note that the Backup and Archive Copy Groups are defined in the Copy Group, described earlier, and the Space Management Copy Group is defined within the Management Class.
>
> As an example, you may have a different Management Class for scientific data, engineering data, accounting data, payroll data, human resources data, software development data, CEO data, managerial data, and staff member data. Each of these Management Classes define how the data is managed by the ADSM server when a file is backed up, where it is backed up to, restored, archived, or migrated from a backup client.

Policy Set

> The Policy Set is associated with a Policy Domain. You can have multiple Policy Sets, but only one can be active at one time within any Policy Domain. The Policy Set is a policy object that contains a group of Management Classes. At any one time there can be many Policy Sets within a Policy Domain but only one policy set can be active at one time.
>
> The activation of different Policy Sets is performed by a backup administrator at the appropriate time. For example, you may want a Policy Set defined for particular backups and archives at the end of the month.

Policy Domain

> The Policy Domain contains Policy Sets, Management Classes, and Copy Groups for a particular group of client backup nodes. Basically, the Policy Domain encapsulates the three objects described previously.
>
> When backup clients are registered with the ADSM backup server, they are associated with only one Policy Domain on the backup server. You can have

more than one policy domain on a backup server and both can be active at once. Each policy domain is a logical grouping of backup clients (for example, grouped by geography, type of jobs, or departments).

The database is 400 to 700 bytes per file backed up and is located in *C:\w32app\ ibm\adsm\server\db1.dsm*. The database can be backed up manually or automatically. This database contains the name, attributes, directory structure, pointer to location in storage pool, data backed up, and management class used for the backup.

Log Files

ADSM does not use the NT event logger; it uses the following five log files of its own:

Recovery Logs

These logs are located on the ADSM backup servers and are separate from the database. They keep in-flight transactions and changed database pages. A Recovery Log is a sequential log of one or more files that keep track of all client and server transactions including backup, archive, and space management. You can add more disk space dynamically to support a larger Recovery Log, as required.

Event Log

This log is part of the database and is therefore located on the ADSM backup server. It lists all of the scheduled events, whether they are scheduled in the future, if they have happened, and whether they succeed or fail. It also contains a little bit of information as to why an event might have failed and the status of the failure.

Activity Log

This log is part of the ADSM database and is therefore located on the ADSM backup server. It tracks the server activity, messages, and operator console messages. This log includes when a client and server session starts or ends, errors on devices, and mount messages for tapes.

Error Logs

These logs are located on the backup clients and the information in these logs includes communication errors, backup errors, or connection errors. The exact location of these logs on the client is configurable. These logs cannot be turned off, and administrators have to manage these files periodically to maintain a particular size.

Schedule Logs

These log files are located on the backup clients and include information about all activities, such as start time, stop time, or files sent during a scheduled event such as a backup, archive, or restore. These logs must also be managed by the administrators to make sure they do not grow too large.

The ADSM product does have a MIB and SNMP traps. The MIB is published and can be integrated into any systems monitoring software.

Special Option

The following is an additional option in support of the ADSM product:

Space-management
This option is a combination of HSM and archiving. It is heavily integrated into the AIX and Solaris ADSM products, although, for Windows NT and NetWare, third-party space-management products are available.

Company Contact Information

IBM Corporation, Storage Systems Division
5600 Cottle Road
San Jose, CA 95193
Telephone: (800) IBM-4YOU or (520) 799-6487
Fax: (404) 238-6628
http://www.ibm.com/storage/adsm

ARCserve

ARCserve (Version 6.5) delivers backup, restore, and disaster recovery for standalone Windows NT workstations, small LANs and heterogeneous enterprises. The product is designed to back up and restore data across single or multiple site enterprises and is available in three editions:

Enterprise Edition
The Enterprise Edition provides the capability to manage multiple ARCserve backup servers from a central location. It includes clients' agents for Windows NT, Windows 95, and Windows 3.1x. Additionally, there are other client agents available for systems such as OS/2, Macintosh, Unix, and NetWare. The Enterprise Edition also supports ARCserve Application Agents for databases, groupware systems, and other applications (such as Microsoft Exchange) that reside locally or remotely to the ARCserve backup server.

Single Server Edition
This product provides the same features and functions as the Enterprise Edition, but does not include support for multiple remote servers. It is intended to provide backup and restore only for local server data and a small homogeneous Windows (NT workstation, 95, and 3.1x) networked environment. The

Application Agents for databases, groupware systems, and other applications are all supported with this edition; however, they must be local to the ARCserve server.

Workstation Edition

This product provides all the features and functions of the ARCserve Single Server edition except for the client agents. There is no backup server and backup client relationship with this edition of the product. It installs on a single system running Windows NT workstation.

The ARCserve product was formerly sold under the company name of Cheyenne. Cheyenne is now a fully owned subsidiary of Computer Associates.

The ARCserve product was originally developed for NetWare. ARCserve for Windows NT was first introduced in 1995. The current version, 6.5, shipped in September 1997. The product runs with either Windows NT Server or Workstation Version 3.51 or 4.0.

Backup Server

With the Enterprise and Single Server Editions, the backup server configurations can be managed from one location by selecting the server you use from the backup client or backup server. Multiple servers can be managed from one desktop. Between backup servers there is manual failover for each backup job. There is no automation to failover.

Within the ARCserve product, the definition of a backup job is any group of backup clients with associated folders, files, or disks as configured by the user. It is a logical grouping, not a physical grouping.

There are two main components that work together within the ARCserve product to back up, copy, and restore data:

ARCserve Manager

This component enables you to control all operations of your ARCserve server from one machine. The ARCserve Manager is used to perform such tasks as submitting your backup and restore jobs, managing your database, and searching reports.

ARCserve Server

Using the information you specified in the ARCserve Manager window, the ARCserve Server is the module that performs the operations you set up. The ARCserve Server directly carries out the backup procedure controlling the job, tape, and database engines:

Job Engine

The Job Engine is responsible for processing your jobs at their designated date and time. It constantly scans the job queue. When it finds a job that is ready to run, the Job Engine sends it to the appropriate handler (backup server).

Tape Engine

The Tape Engine is responsible for communicating with and controlling your tape devices. When a tape device is needed for an ARCserve job, the Tape Engine lets your hardware know that it is needed.

Database Engine

This engine is responsible for maintaining the history of several things:

- Files, directory, drives, and machines that ARCserve has backed up or copied.

- Information about jobs that have been processed by ARCserve, such as (but not limited to) the type of job, the final result, and the start and end time.

- Tapes used by ARCserve, such as but not limited to the name of the tape, date it was first formatted, date it expires, and sessions on it (a tape session is a block of data written to tape).

By default, everything that happens within ARCserve is recorded by the Database Engine to the catalog.

Backup Client

Communications between the backup server and backup clients is accomplished with Windows NT impersonation capability. There is no ARCserve software required to be loaded on the NT backup clients. If your clients are cross-platforms, then appropriate backup client software must be loaded.

Configuration and Backup Information

The ARCserve configuration information is stored in a single catalog (database) file, which can be stored in one of two different formats: ARCserve's standard database, Raima, or as an Open Database Compliant (ODBC) database such as MS SQL Server.

As a backup job is run, the data is written to tape and a temporary catalog file is written. After the tape session finishes, the temporary catalog file is merged into ARCserve's permanent catalog.

When a backup job completes, the ARCserve catalog is automatically written to tape as a full backup, as follows:

- For the Enterprise Edition, the catalog can be local to each ARCserve server or replicated to a central location.

- For the Single Server Edition, the catalog is located on the single ARCserve backup server.

- For the Workstation Edition, the catalog is located on each individual workstation.

The ARCserve catalog contains filenames, backup dates, media pool names, job, and device information. It contains approximately 80 bytes per file backed up and is located in the *Arcserve\database* directory after installation. ARCserve provides a utility for managing the database, *dbmgr.exe,* which is located in the ARCserve home directory. As entries are made to the ARCserve database, these are recorded in the activity log.

Log Files

The ARCserve product has log files of its own and does not utilize the Windows NT event log. The ARCserve log files are located in the *Arcserve/log* directory; there are two files that are separate form the catalog mentioned previously:

Arcserve.log
>   This log file contains activity information about what occurs and when.

tape.log
>   This log file is not used by default. It is turned on for debugging and troubleshooting, if there are troubles with the hardware. It provides detailed SCSI information about what occurs between the ARCserve software and the hardware.

The logs can be pruned by setting the number of days to keep them, through configuration settings in ARCserve:

- For the Enterprise and Single Server Editions of ARCserve, both log files are local on each ARCserve server. The log files cannot be replicated to a central location.

- For the Workstation Edition, the logs are located on each individual workstation.

There is an SNMP MIB available for ARCserve for integration with other systems management or monitoring frameworks, such as CA's Unicenter TNG.

Special Options

The following are the additional options in support of the ARCserve product:

Disaster Recovery
>   This product is a disk disaster recovery solution. It saves boot disk information on a set of floppy diskettes or has ARCserve collect and update the infor-

mation automatically during backups. In the case of a disaster, the entire system, including configuration information, can be rebuilt without manual reinstallation of the operating system or backup software.

Tape Library Option

This product provides device-management functions, including bar code support, tape formatting and erasing, maintaining inventory on slots, mounting tapes, and automatic cleaning of the library's tape drives. It also supports the import/export feature on libraries offering this capability.

Image Option

This product allows high-speed backup and restore. It creates an "image" of the disk on tape, by circumventing the file system and reading data directly. With this option, you can still backup and restore file by file. This option also includes tape RAID.

RAID Option

This product increases performance and fault tolerance for devices and media. The option supports an array of similar tape drives/tape libraries that behave as a single drive/library. It concurrently stripes data across all drives when configured as level RAID 0 or RAID 5.

InocuLAN

This product integrates automatic antivirus scanning of files during a backup operation.

Backup Agent for Open Files

This product enables ARCserve to back up open data files of any application at any time safely and reliably.

Backup Agent for Lotus Notes

This product allows ARCserve to back up and restore Lotus Notes servers. It permits backups and restores to occur while Lotus Notes is open and in use.

Backup Agent for SQL

This product allows ARCserve to back up and restore Microsoft SQL servers. It permits backups and restores to occur while SQL databases are open and in use.

Backup Agent for Oracle

This product allows ARCserve to back up and restore Oracle servers. It permits backups and restores to occur while Oracle databases are open and in use.

Backup Agent for SAP R/3

This product allows ARCserve to back up and restore SAP R/3 servers whether they are based on Oracle or Microsoft SQL Server.

Backup Agent for Exchange

This product allows ARCserve to back up and restore Microsoft Exchange servers. It permits backups and restores to occur while Exchange is open and in use. The backups protect critical folders and mailboxes within the Exchange Information Store. You can back up and restore individual folders and mailboxes without affecting other users.

Data Migration Option

This product provides HSM support. Through GUIs and drag-and-drop operations, you can configure any volume on an NT network for data migration. It also provides an automated capacity management feature to eliminate out-of-disk situations.

Company Contact Information

Computer Associates International, Inc.
One CA Plaza
Islandia, NY 11788
Telephone: (800) CHEY-INC
Fax: (516) 484-3446
http://www.cai.com/cheyenne

Backup Exec

Seagate Backup Exec (Version 7.0) is a backup application for the Windows NT environment, including Microsoft SQL Server, Microsoft Exchange, and Microsoft SMS. Intelligent Disaster Recovery automates recovery of data to a user-defined point in time. Seagate Software's Agent Accelerator technology, a 32-bit multithreading design, provides the fastest backup of valuable data for the entire Windows NT enterprise. Integrated detailed reporting provides access to important information quickly and is seamless. Seagate Backup Exec is based on the Microsoft Component Object Model (COM), which makes it a scalable architecture. It supports Microsoft Tape Format and Windows NT tape and device APIs, which ensures compatibility today while providing for easy integration to future growing backup needs.

The product is sold in two editions. Note that there are no functional differences (only licensing differences) between the Single Server and Enterprise Editions of Backup Exec:

Single Server Edition

This product supports one backup server running on a Windows NT server and an unlimited number of backup clients running on anything but a Windows NT server.

Enterprise Edition

> This product supports an unlimited number of backup servers and an unlimited number of backup clients. It also bundles the backup client agents for Macintosh and a selection of Unix agents.

Seagate Backup Exec for Windows NT was introduced after Seagate provided the backup utility to Microsoft for Windows NT. Seagate writes the code for each of its backup products independently, so Backup Exec for Windows NT was not based on one of their other products, but Backup Exec for MS-DOS, Windows, NetWare, and other operating systems all work together. Backup Exec is available for both Windows NT Server Versions 3.51 and 4.0.

Seagate purchased both Storage Manager from Palindrome and Backup Exec from Arcada (Arcada was a subsidiary of Conner). Seagate's Storage Exec is the renamed Palindrome Storage Manager product and in the long term, Seagate's Storage Exec will migrate into Seagate's Backup Exec product.

Backup Server

Backup Exec is based on a single-server architecture and has two tiers, the backup server and the backup clients. Multiple backup servers can back up the same backup client, but the administration of the backup servers is performed separately and independently.

Within Backup Exec, logical groups of backup clients are defined as jobs. A job contains the files, folders, shares to back up, and the backup schedule, to mention a few items. The retention policies are applied to the media, so media pools each have their own retention policy associated with them. Within the definition of a job, you configure the job to use a particular device and a specific media pool.

The backup server for the Backup Exec product has the following services associated with it; all are located in *Program Files\Seagate Software\Backup Exec\NT*:

Server

> This is the main service. It handles communications within Backup Exec's services and handles job management and scheduling.

Agent Browser

> This service maintains a list of the backup clients found on the network. The Windows NT backup clients are found through the NT network neighborhood, and all other backup clients are contacted through the Backup Exec agent. This allows users to see a list of backup clients in the backup selection window.

Notification Server

> This service is used internally between the Backup Exec services. This service is the automated alert notification that maintains recorded logs of unattended backup message notifications.

Alert Server

> This service notifies the administrator of different things that occur during backups and restores. The alerts are configurable, so that they can be issued through Exchange email, trouble tickets, event log, paging, or printing.

Device & Media Service

> This service is responsible for managing all devices, such as tape drives, optical drives, or tape libraries, and media on the Backup Exec Server.

Job Engine

> This service handles all data movement and formatting from filesystems to tape formatting.

Naming Service

> This service maintains a list of Backup Exec servers on the network, so that the user can easily select which server to manage with the administration client software.

Backup Client

Backup Exec backup servers have two methods of communicating with Windows NT backup clients. One method is through the NT backup client agent, known as the Agent Accelerator, and the other method is through the Windows NT Remote Administration feature. When a backup or restore is performed, the backup server checks to see whether the Agent Accelerator exists on the client. If it does, it is used, and if not, the remote administration feature is used.

Configuration and Backup Information

Backup Exec contains the following databases, all located on the backup server:

Catalog Database

> There is one catalog database per tape. This catalog contains information about the files that have been backed up and contains file and folder names, size, type, modification date, and attributes. This is a proprietary database.

Device and Media Management Database

> This database contains information on device and media statistics and configuration information, such as what type of tape drives are attached to the backup server. This database is a Microsoft Access database, and you can use the Access database tools and utilities to manage it.

Job Database

This database contains the definitions of and additional historical information on the jobs configured on that backup server. This includes information on what is to be backed up, schedules, when jobs were completed, and whether they were successful. This is a proprietary database.

The databases are backed up like any other data when they are defined as part of a job.

Backup Exec allows you to read tapes created by CA ARCserve for NetWare 4.x/5.x, Seagate SyTOS Plus for OS/2, and the Windows NT backup utility.

Log Files

Backup Exec log files are all located on the backup servers; no logs are stored on the backup clients. Backup Exec also sends application events to the NT Event Log.

The default name for log files is *BEX0000*, and the name increments as new log files are created for each job. Logs contain information about backup jobs performed by the backup server. This information can be viewed by the backup server and also by a backup client using NT's Remote Administration.

All logs for all jobs are in one Backup Exec directory, and the log files are aged. You define how many log files you would like to retain, and Backup Exec will maintain only that number of files, removing the oldest log files to make room for the newer log files. You can retain 100 log files; when the 101st log file is created, Backup Exec will remove the oldest log file to maintain the 100 log file maximum.

Backup Exec offers trap alert notification and MIB support to your SNMP console for centralized network monitoring.

Special Options

Additional options available for Seagate Backup Exec include:

Storage Migration Option

The new storage migration option utilizes hierarchical storage management (HSM) functionality to automate the management of information by migrating inactive data to near-line and tertiary storage resources.

ADSM Option

Backup Exec has an ADSM option that uses IBM's ADSM system as a large data storage device and allows backups to be routed automatically to the ADSM system just as if it were a large tape library or autoloader. Multiple servers and workstations can all be protected using the ADSM option, and any number of Backup Exec systems can simultaneously connect to one ADSM system.

Intelligent Disaster Recovery Option

This feature eliminates the need to first reload the operating system and allows you to restore from your last backup set, including differential and incremental backups.

Crystal Reports Integration Option

Backup Exec offers predefined reporting capabilities and includes five canned reports within the base product.

ExecView Option

This option enables you to monitor all backup operations across your enterprise from a single console for both Windows NT and NetWare installations. Seagate ExecView enables you to obtain real-time statistics related to all scheduled, active, and completed backup jobs from any Windows NT system or Windows 95 client. It is also possible to monitor backup operations at remote sites.

Open File Manager Option

This option provides uninterrupted data protection for network environments that must remain accessible 24 hours a day and 7 days a week. Open File Manager provides protection for active email, database, and other data files even while information is being entered or changed by users. This is for data security, integrity, and reliability.

Media Mirror Option

This option provides fault tolerance and offsite media duplication for Windows NT by providing RAID level 1 support for tape devices.

Resource Manager Option

This option is a web-based application that provides consolidated views and trends of storage resource layout, configuration, capacity, utilization, and health information. It enables administrators to track disk defects, partition configuration, largest files, largest directories, file creation, file modification, and access trends across an entire NT domain.

Autoloader Module

This option provides the interface between Backup Exec and a number of autoloaders, giving users the ability to perform high-capacity unattended backup operation.

Agent for Microsoft SQL Server

This option provides client and server functionality for integration of SQL database backup into existing network backup routines. Online database support allows critical databases to be protected without taking them offline.

Agent for NetWare

> This option provides multithreading Agent Accelerator technology for data protection of complete NetWare 3.1x and 4.x servers.

Agent for Microsoft Exchange Server

> This option provides client and server functionality for integration of Exchange Server backups into existing network backup routines. Online support allows critical Exchange Servers to be protected without taking them offline.

Company Contact Information

> Seagate Software, Network and Storage Management Group
> 400 International Parkway
> Heathrow, FL 32746
> Telephone: (800) 327-2232 or (407) 531-7500
> Fax: (407) 531-7730
> *http://www.seagatesoftware.com*

Backup Express

Backup Express (Release 2) provides distributed backup with centralized control for a wide variety of heterogeneous, networked environments and is administered through a GUI. Large file systems, partitions, or files can be split over multiple backup devices, and the use of multiple tape drives on the restore is supported as well.

The product was originally coded on Unix (specifically, Sun Solaris). It was then recompiled for other Unix platforms and Windows NT and changed to support the structure of those operating systems.

The Backup Express product line has been in production since February 1996 and is available for Versions 3.51 and 4.0 of Windows NT Server.

Backup Server

Backup Express is designed for a single master server and multiple device servers:

Master server

> Allows you to configure the backup clients and maintain the backup catalog (database). The master server can also function as a device server. You can have multiple master backup servers, but there is no interaction between master servers.

Device server

> A device server is a backup node (client) that has a device, such as a tape drive or tape library, directly attached to it. The optimal configuration is to have the data from a node backed up by a device attached to that specific node, having no network involved.

A Backup Express *job* is a logically grouped unit of work and can be defined as an entire enterprise (all nodes) or grouped by every node in a department. The grouping of jobs is used to manage such parameters as retention policies, schedules, media pools, or copies of tapes. For example, a job could be the entire accounting department or all of the *C:* drives of the computers used by executives, each with its own parameters applied.

Multiple backup jobs can happen at one time on a backup node. One job could be writing to that node's own devices and another job could be writing to a device across the network. The device destination is configurable by job.

The following Backup Express services run continually on the master server:

CMAGENT

> This service is the main Backup Express service. It is the communication agent responsible for TCP/IP connections between the backup server, the device servers, and the backup nodes.

SSSCHED

> This service is responsible for all scheduling of the backup jobs.

There are also the following Backup Express dynamic programs that execute on the master server as needed:

DMTAPE

> This program is referred to as the disk data movers and tape movers program. It is used to move data from backup client disks to the backup devices, such as tape devices.

JOBMON (Job Monitoring GUI)

> This program monitors all active jobs on the master server. It allows the administrator to watch the progress of a job running and includes percent completed, number of bytes of data moved, how much data is left, and the approximate time the job will complete based on current throughput.

JOBHND

> The job handler is initiated by the scheduler to track the status of the jobs.

The device servers run *CMAGENT* and *DMTAPE*. They do not run *SSCHED*, *JOBMON*, or *JOBHND*.

Backup Client

The backup clients are referred to as the backup nodes. A node can become a device server by adding devices during the initial installation, or it can be reconfigured as a device server at a later time. The configuration of the backup nodes is performed on the master server. The following service runs continually on each backup node:

CMAGENT

This service is required and is the communication agent responsible for TCP/IP connections to the backup server.

The following program runs on each backup node as needed:

DMTAPE

The data movers and tape movers program is required on the clients to move the data from the disk to the appropriate device server.

Configuration and Backup Information

Backup Express has a single database, stored on the backup server, which is called the *catalog*. It is made up of multiple files that are located in *Backup\db\ *.db* in a proprietary format. There are catalog files associated with every backup node, and there is one global catalog file.

Repairs to a possibly corrupted catalog are built into the product. There is a commit process that guarantees that information is put into the database. The catalog itself is backed up through a user-defined job that is scheduled for a static time or when required. It is treated like any other defined job.

There is a catalog condense feature that removes information from the catalog about files on tapes that have expired. This is based on the retention time that is associated with each backup job. Once all of the files on a tape have expired, the status of a tape changes to empty during the condense so that it can be reused. The catalog condense operation is scheduled like any other job.

All information for the backup catalog is written to the catalog, on the master server, at the end of a job. The size of the catalog is approximately 0.5% to 1% of the backed-up data, using 80–100 bytes per file that is backed up. This accounts for 70 bytes for attributes plus the length of each file in the pathname.

Log Files

Backup Express does not use the event logger; it uses its own log files. The product has several different types of logs that are located on the master server, device servers, and backup nodes.

The master server has a group of log files associated with the management of the server itself. This includes such logs as the Communication Manager Log, Data Manager Log, Jukebox Handler Log, Message Logger Log, Main Scheduler Log, Script Processing Log, and SNMP Log. There are up to 10 of each of these log files. The master server also has a group of log files associated with the execution of the jobs. This includes such logs as the Main Job Logs, Event Handler Logs, Script Processing Log, Job Handler Logs, Node Browser Log, Restored Files Log, Scheduler Logs, Command Line Interface Logs, and Job Handler Sort Logs. There is one of these log files per job or per group of jobs. Finally, under certain circumstances the Cataloguing Temp File Log may be created.

The device server also has log files. Remember a device server can be the master server or it can also be a backup node that has been configured as a device server. The log file on the device server associated with the backup jobs is the Tape Mount Manager Log, and there is one of these logs per job. There is also a log file associated with moving data, the Data Mover Log. There is one to two of these logs per disk backed up and per tape used. Finally, under certain circumstances the Tape Browser Log file may be created.

The backup nodes also have log files. The logs associated with the backup jobs are the Event Handler Log, File Browser Log, and Node Browser Log. There is one of each of these files per job. The backup node also has the Data Mover Logs associated with moving the data from the node to the device server. There are one to two of these logs per backup.

There is a correlation between the logs on the master server, device server, and the backup nodes. You have to look through the job log on master server to see what type of errors occur and then look at the device server or node specific logs. The node specific logs may be located on the master server or client nodes.

Backup Express does support SNMP traps for important status notification.

Special Options

Syncsort does not provide HSM or archiving. However, you can define jobs using unlimited or lengthy tape retensioning that satisfy the archiving requirement.

The following other options are available for Backup Express:

Microsoft Exchange Interface
  Using this interface, any Exchange file system can be viewed, backed up, or restored from the GUI through a new icon.

OFM Interface
  This interface utilizes the Open File Manager product from St. Bernard with Backup Express for online backups of SQL Server, Lotus Notes, or Windows NT.

SQL Backtrack Interface

This interface integrates the SQL Backtrack product from BMC with Backup Express for online backups of databases that can be performed for Oracle, Sybase, and Informix.

SAP R/3 Interface

This interface is certified by SAP for backing up SAP R/3 on the Sun Solaris, HP-UX, IBM AIX, Windows NT, Sinux, and DEC OSF platforms.

Company Contact Information

Syncsort Incorporated, Marketing Department
50 Tice Boulevard
Woodcliff Lake, NJ 07675
Telephone: (201) 930-8200
Fax: (201) 930-8290
http://www.syncsort.com

HP OpenView OmniBack II

HP OpenView OmniBack II (Version 3.0) for Windows NT provides data protection, high accessibility, lights-out operation, and efficient device and media management. It can save valuable time on installation and daily operation.

OmniBack II has an architecture for all sizes and mixes of environments in which backups can be managed from one central point. From one cell manager, all data in homogeneous Windows NT or mixed Windows NT, NetWare, and Unix environments can be backed up locally or over the network.

The architecture allows distribution of all backup functionality to required destinations. OmniBack II integrates into your existing information technology infrastructure and allows protection of Microsoft BackOffice data and usage of existing Microsoft BackOffice–based management processes. Online backup for Microsoft SQL Server, Microsoft SMS, and SAP R/3 business data provides high application availability.

HP offers a modular product structure for OmniBack II. They have an entry price for the product that includes the base functionality. Enhancements are added by purchasing modules, each of which provides advanced functionality.

OmniBack was formerly a product of Apollo, a workstation company acquired by HP in 1989. The name changed in 1994 from OmniBack to OmniBack II because of a major redesign. The NT server product has been in production since 1996 and runs on NT 3.51 and NT 4.0 on both the Server and Workstation platforms.

Backup Server

OmniBack II's server architecture is split into two components. These components can run on different systems for better scalability and flexibility:

Cell Manager

This is the system from which the OmniBack II backup environment is managed. The Cell Manager services client systems that are all configured in the OmniBack II cell. Each cell can only have one Cell Manager system. If needed, you can move configuration data between cells by importing and exporting data from the database.

Configuration files and the OmniBack II log database are installed on the Cell Manager, which remotely initiates and controls backup and restore sessions to transfer data between Device Servers and Disk Agents. If the Cell Manager is not accessible or is not running, these activities are not possible. For high availability environments, the cell manager can run on Microsoft Cluster Servers for NT or HP MC/ServiceGuard for HP-UX versions of the product.

The Cell Manager runs session manager processes for different types of sessions, such as GUI administration sessions, backup sessions, or restore sessions.

Device Server

This is the OmniBack II software component that controls reading from and writing to a media drive: for example, a tape drive. During a backup session, the Device Server gets data from the Disk Agent and writes it to media. During a restore, the Device Server reads data from media and sends it to the Disk Agent, which writes the data to disk. There is no requirement for the backup devices to be connected to the Cell Manager. OmniBack II has the capability to have backup devices on any system in the cell.

Backup Client

The Disk Agent is OmniBack II's software that allows the Cell Manager to access data on the client system's disks. It runs on all systems that are backed up. Operation of the Disk Agent is controlled by the session managers on the Cell Manager. There are different Disk Agents for different operating system platforms.

The Disk Agent and Device Server directly communicate between each other. Only status and catalog information is sent to the Cell Manager, which is the controller of all backup and restore sessions and keeps lots of data in the OmniBack II database about used and available devices and media, backup catalog information (which file was backed up when and where it is stored on which media), user access rights, and scheduled backup sessions, to mention a few things.

Configuration and Backup Information

The Cell Manager holds the OmniBack II database, which contains all the information about backup and restore sessions as well as reporting, scheduling, and licensing.

There is only one database per OmniBack II cell. The database itself consists of multiple files. You can find the database files in the *OmniBack\Config\db* directory. There are utilities to maintain the integrity of the database. Omniback II maintains the integrity of the database by preventing you from backing up a corrupted database.

The folder or file information recorded in the database depends on the properties you can get from the filesystem about that file or folder. For all filesystems the name, directory, size, attribute, creation data, last backup date, and type of last backup are recorded. If the information is available from the filesystem, the user, group, and access rights are also recorded.

The database is used to store additional summary information about all backup or restore sessions. This includes the media used in the session, the devices used for this media, the condition and usage of media, the list of files and directories backed up or restored, the location of the data on the media, the messages resulting from a backup or restore session, and the protection for data on the media.

When a chunk of data is written to tape during a session, the catalog data relating to the chunk of data is sent to the Cell Manager, specifically, to the the session manager process, and is then written to the database. The session manager process only writes the catalog data to the database after the chunk of data has been successfully saved on tape. If a session fails in the middle, the database contains the catalog information only about the successfully backed-up objects.

The growth and size of the OmniBack II database are determined by the number of logged messages, the amount of details on backed-up files and directories stored in the database, and the number of backup and restore sessions. There is a complicated formula to compute the OmniBack II database size depending on the number of files, number of directories and subdirectories, number of full backups, number of incremental backups, and rate of modified files by incremental backups. It mainly depends on the number of files and number of directories and subdirectories in which you want to store detailed information. With the 1% estimate, you are on the safe side—in most cases it will be less.

The following is recommended for backing up the OmniBack II database:

- Create a separate backup specification for the database to simplify scheduling and restoring.

- Make the database back up on a separate media; if possible, on a separate device, such as a standalone drive, to greatly simplify restores.

- Create and use a separate media pool (a set of media of the same type used and tracked as a group) for backing up your database.

- Schedule a database backup every night.

You cannot run an interactive backup of the database directly. The database is in use whenever you are using the user interface or when a backup or restore session is in progress. If you start the interactive backup of the database, you must exit all user interfaces and stop all other running sessions for the backup to start. If you schedule a backup of the database, OmniBack II will wait until the other sessions are finished to perform this backup. OmniBack II needs exclusive access for database backups and restores.

In order to use OmniBack II for NT, users must be configured as HP OmniBack II users on the cell manager. An admin user can perform any function within the cell, an operator can start and stop backups and restores and monitor the sessions, and an end user can restore only data that they own. This ensures that unauthorized users cannot use OmniBack II.

Log Files

OmniBack II uses the Windows NT event log in addition to its own logs. The logs are not separate for OmniBack II; they are an integral part of the database and located on the Cell Manager. They are referred to as the Session Log. This log contain information such as started processes and backed-up systems, filenames, and directories. If there is an error during a backup session, the administrator should use the Session Log file to check on the details of the error.

The OmniBack II product does have support for SNMP traps. There is no SNMP MIB available.

Special Options

The following OmniBack II extensions all provide optional advanced functionality:

Online Extension for Windows NT
  This extension is required for each OmniBack II Cell Manager supporting the following online database and applications backup on Windows NT systems: Microsoft SQL Server, Microsoft Exchange, Oracle, and SAP R/3.

Cluster Extension
  This extension is required once for each OmniBack II Cell where OmniBack II is an integral part of the high availability cluster: HP's MC/ServiceGuard or Microsoft's Cluster Server.

Manager-of-Managers Extension

This extension is required for each OmniBack II Cell, which is part of the OmniBack II Manager-of-Managers.

61–250 Slot Library Extension

This extension is required once for each OmniBack II Cell managing libraries with 61 to 250 media slots. Multiple OmniBack II Cells sharing the same library require only one license.

Unlimited Slot Library Extension

This extension is required once for each OmniBack II Cell managing libraries with no slot limitation. Multiple OmniBack II Cells sharing the same library, require only one license.

Company Contact Information

Hewlett-Packard Company
3000 Hanover Street
Palo Alto, CA 94304
Telephone: (415) 857-1501
Fax: (415) 857-5518
http://www.hp.com/go/openview

NetBackup

Veritas NetBackup (Version 3.0) is a mainframe class backup and recovery product for distributed data resources. The NetBackup product provides backup, archiving, and recovery services for Unix, NT, and PC client systems in client and server networks. It can be scaled to serve virtually any size operation ranging from a standalone system to an entire enterprise.

NetBackup is packaged as two separate pieces of server and client software. With robotic extensions and database extensions sold separately. Prices for each component are published by platform type.

Originally, the product was owned by Control Data Corporation. In 1992, the product became an OpenVision product and was called Axxion NetBackup. In 1997, OpenVision and Veritas Software merged and the product became Veritas NetBackup.

The NT server NetBackup product has been in production since April 1997. It is available for both NT Server Versions 3.51 and 4.0. The NetBackup product was originally developed and designed for the Sun platform (specifically, SunOS). It was designed for the enterprise marketplace.

Backup Server

NetBackup has two different types of backup servers, which are listed next. It is possible to have the master server and the slave server two different systems or in the same system. Both types of servers are capable of backing up data to attached tape, optical, or disk devices. The NetBackup backup server types are:

Master server

> The master server is capable of interfacing with the configuration, file, and volume databases. It provides the main administrative controller for all the backups in a backup domain. The master server is responsible for setup and control of all backups and restores for all servers and clients in the domain.

Slave server

> The slave server is capable of interfacing with the media database and the device database. It receives control and directions from the master server to perform backups and restores of clients to the attached storage devices that are connected to the slave server. There can be many slave servers under one master server.

Backup Client

The clients in the network are any computers that back up data to a backup master or slave server. They read data from the client disk and send the backup data or image to a tape storage device on the Master or Slave Server. At the same time, they send the file information data to the master server for storage in the File Database.

Client-initiated functionality is not typical in large enterprise environments. The client software is usually run by the administrator on the master, and push restores are performed for the client from the master server.

Configuration and Backup Information

There are three groups of different databases associated with the NetBackup product. They are the configuration, file, error, and media management databases. The media management database is a combination of three databases: volume database, media database, and device database. The media management database set is used by the media manager, which manages secondary storage for both Net-Backup and HSM. All NetBackup databases are a collection of either flat ASCII files or binary files. The NetBackup databases are:

Configuration database

> This database contains the information required to perform backups and is used by the configuration manager. It is stored on the master server and con-

tains all of the configuration information for all of the storage units (collection of standalone drives or a tape library) and the information to tell NetBackup where to go to for backups, restores, and archives. It provides NetBackup with the mapping between the virtual names of the storage units and the real names of the storage units (which are in the device databases described later in this section). This database has no tape (media) information.*

This database is relatively small and static, with one line of information (100 to 150 characters) for each storage unit. It contains no specific information of the storage unit. For example, all it knows is that it is robot 1 and has 2 drives and which backup slave server is used to access that robot.

File database

This database stores the file attribute information and is located on the master server and used by the file manager. The information stored in this database includes permissions on the file, owner of the file, group to which the file belongs, file size, modification and creation date of the file, and full directory name of the file.

The file databases are stored by backup client name. For each backup client, there are multiple file databases. They are set up with one folder defined for each backup client and a file database per day within this folder. They are located in *netbackup/db/images/{clientname}/{encoded date and time}* on the backup master server.

These databases can get large. Their size is mostly dependent on the file name length and the number of filenames (full filename with folder names included) in the database. Average entry length, based on average filename length, is approximately 100 to 150 characters. The database indexing adds an additional 2 characters per average entry.

Job database

The job monitor uses the job databases to watch the jobs for backups. These databases are stored under *db/jobs/{job id}*. The job databases are very small and are removed when no longer needed.

Error database

This database contains information about NetBackup operations. This database resides on the master server and has two parts. The first part is the error portion. It contains information recorded during backup operations and used in the NetBackup reports. The second part is the failure history. It contains the daily history of backup errors.

---

* The configuration database can also be used by the Veritas HSM product to allow both NetBackup and HSM to utilize the same tape devices—but different pools of tapes—in a tape library configuration.

Volume database

The volume database contains information about the media and where they are in the drives and robots; they are used by the volume manager. This includes all of the slot numbers of all the pieces of media, all of the pool information and which tapes are in which pool, expiration dates of each piece of media (not the expiration of image data on the tape), and the mount information. The mount information is used to determine how many times the media was mounted, and, after a certain number of hours of mount time, shuts down the media for backups. This is because with a specific number of mounts, tapes can wear out.

The volume database resides normally only on the master server; there can be one or more. Having one database gives central control of tapes. You can have as many multiple databases as the total number of slave servers, but that is not recommended.

The volume database can grow large, depending on the number of pieces of media you have at your site. It contains information for each piece of media, and is approximately 100 to 150 characters per piece of media.

Media database

There is a media database on each master and slave server; they are used by the media manager. Each server maintains its own media database for the storage units configured on that backup server. The database contains information on the images stored on that server's storage units.

The volume database is a superset of the media databases. The volume database has every tape ID on every server. There is a media database for each server; it contains the IDs of the tapes on that particular server. Since this is really a redundant database, there are plans to remove this database in future releases of the NetBackup product.

The media database is very small. It contains only the media identification numbers associated with the media managed by that server.

Device databases

There is one device database for each master or slave server; it is used by the device manager. The volume manager utilities are used to define storage devices (for example, tape drives) to the volume manager and database, so NetBackup can use them for storage units. NetBackup does not query device managers and databases; it queries the volume manager and database with the virtual names of the devices, and the virtual names of the devices are then mapped to the real operating system names through the device databases.

The device databases are small and contain only the operating system device drivers that are associated with the virtual names of devices in the configuration database.

The databases listed here can be backed up automatically by the scheduler or manually. The manual backup can be through the GUI or command line. The database backup is always a full backup and must be performed when the backups and restores are quiescent.

The product needs to have backup and restore authority within the user's rights. The user who starts up the services must be in the same user group as the individuals performing backups and restores, unless you are restoring data that you own. NetBackup follows standard NT security implementation.

Log Files

NetBackup does not use the NT event logger. There are NetBackup log files located on both the backup clients and the backup server. The NetBackup log files are:

Progress logs

These logs are the client logs and are a result of end user–initiated operations, such as archives, backups, or restores. Progress logs provide information on operations as they are underway and indicate whether the operation succeeds or fails. The location of the logs defaults to where NetBackup was installed on the client side, or the user can specify where these logs are stored. You can have NetBackup create a separate progress log file for each type of user-directed activity. These logs are removed automatically after a configurable number of days.

Job monitoring logs

The server performs all logging for all other tasks that are not user-initiated. They are located on the master backup server in *netbackup/logs/{function}*.

Critical information is also posted in the event viewer. For example, process start and stop and drive failure information is included in the event view in addition to the NetBackup logs.

The NetBackup product uses SNMP traps to forward alarm conditions to Network Managers such as CA Unicenter, HP Operations Center, or Tivoli. The product currently has no MIB.

Special Options

Veritas also has the following additional options:

Robot Extension, Tier 1 through Tier 4

This option comes in four different levels referred to as *tiers*. Small robots would be supported with the Tier 1 Extension and large robots would be supported with the Tier 4 Extension. There are two tiers in the middle for medium robots.

Client Agents

This option provides backup client support for a wide array of systems. These include Macintosh, OS/2, Windows 95, and a wide variety of Unix operating systems.

Sybase Extension

This option allows NetBackup to integrate with and back up Sybase databases.

Oracle Extension

This option allows NetBackup to integrate with and back up Oracle databases.

Informix Extension

This option allows NetBackup to integrate with and back up Informix databases.

SAP R/3 Extension

This option allows NetBackup to integrate with and back up SAP R/3.

Datatools Extension

This option allows NetBackup to integrate the SQL Backtrack product, which was developed by BMC.

Company Contact Information

Veritas Software
1600 Plymouth Street
Mountain View, CA 94043
Telephone: (800) 258-UNIX(8649)
Fax: (415) 335-8050
http://www.veritas.com

NetWorker for NT

Legato NetWorker (Version 5.1) for Windows NT is a storage management solu\
tion for the protection of file and print, database, and application servers, and their networked clients regardless of operating system. NetWorker provides backup, recovery, archive, and automated disaster recovery for networks of all sizes. The product is sold in the following packages:

Workgroup Edition

This edition is for small networks and is suited for remote branch offices, mixed Windows NT and NetWare LANs, and new deployments of Windows NT LANs. It provides support for up to four client connections and two storage devices, allows attachment of a single one-to-eight–slot autochanger software module, and includes client software for Microsoft Windows NT, Windows 95, and Windows 3.1x.

Network Edition

This edition is for multiplatform, enterprise-wide installations. It is preconfigured to support 10 client connections and is bundled with NetWorker client software for Windows NT, Windows 95, and Windows 3.1x.

Power Edition

This edition provides protection for the very largest, mission-critical NT servers. The Power Edition features local architectures to utilize large symmetric multiprocessor servers.

Backup Server

The NetWorker product has two different types of servers:

Primary backup server or central server

This server is dedicated to the role of resource manager. This includes the following tasks:

- Administration of backup schedules and policies.

- Scheduling for routing parallel client data streams to storage nodes or directly connected devices. The server can perform simultaneous backups and restores or parallel backups and restores.

- Operating concurrent devices, including dynamic load-balancing among available storage nodes or directly connected devices.

- Maintaining separate online indices for client file directories and media.

- SmartMedia management to handle and automate such tasks as media labeling, media rotation, and media tracking in a way that is device-independent.

The backups are grouped on the central server as savegroups. A savegroup consists of a group of savesets. A saveset is the combination of a backup client and drive(s), folder(s), or file(s) to back up. For example, one saveset could be a backup client and drive *C:*, and another saveset could be a different backup client and the folder *C:/Program Files* and drive *D:*. Both of these savesets can be grouped into the same savegroup.

Secondary backup server or storage node

This server is dedicated to the role of device management. Once the storage node receives instructions as to which saveset to back up or restore and which device to use, it actually performs the task. When the backup or restore is initiated, the storage node communicates directly with the backup client itself. After the backup or restore is completed, the backup database information is passed from the storage node to the master server.

Backup Client

In the NetWorker storage management model, the client has several active roles:

Smart client

> The client automatically responds to backup requests it receives through an NT network service. It then generates the appropriate data stream and pushes the data to the backup server. Details of the client, such as how to read files in its operating system environment, are dealt with only in the client. This includes client-side data compression, encryption, and password protection.

Administrative mode

> This role provides the interface for monitoring and controlling the primary or secondary servers from any client.

User mode

> This role provides the interface for user-initiated backup and recovery operations from any client.

Immediate restore

> This feature bypasses the TCP/IP stack overhead associated with local restore operations. The software knows that it is a local restore and eliminates the network stack for that restore.

Configuration and Backup Information

The NetWorker product has two databases to maintain the configuration and backup information. They are both in a proprietary format, and NetWorker utilities are available to mange the database and repair any corruption. The databases are automatically backed up in full when a savegroup is finished being backed up. You can also perform a full backup for the databases at any time as required. The NetWorker databases are:

File index

> This database stores the information about the files backed up by NetWorker. There is one file index for each backup client. Each entry in the file index typically includes the following information for a backed up file: filename, number of blocks, access permission, number of links, owner, group, size, last modified time, and backup time. How long the information is stored in the file index is configurable by setting the browse policy. Once the browse policy is set for each backup client's file index database, the software automatically removes the file index entries older than the browse policy plus one cycle.

Media index

> This database stores information about the NetWorker media and the backup savesets. The media index does not recognize individual files, but instead recognizes the savesets to which the file belongs. There is one media index data-

base for each primary backup server at your site. How long the information is stored in the media index is configurable by setting the retention policy. Media index entries older than the retention policy plus one cycle are marked as recyclable in the media index, making the backup volume (tape) available for relabeling and overwriting with new data, if that is desired. You can choose not to relabel and reuse tapes. The tape can be stored and at a later time manually rescanned to regain the information.

The total size of both databases together grows at a rate of approximately 220 bytes per file backed up.

Log Files

NetWorker does logging on the backup server; it utilizes the NT event log. The NT event log contains all savegroup, error, and operations messages, which are reported by severity level. The NetWorker-specific log files are all located on the backup primary server:

Savegroup log
> This log is one of two places in which the savegroup completion messages get written to (it is also written to the NT event log). The savegroup completion message is generated at the end of each savegroup, and indicates the success or failure of each saveset run during the backup.

Messages log
> This log is where the NetWorker server writes RM protocol messages to. These are the same messages that appear in the administrator's GUI message window. The RM protocol messages are informational messages used to inform the user of important operations that the NetWorker server is performing.

Daemon log
> This log is where all of the NT service process messages are redirected. This information is application trace information used to diagnose NetWorker problems. By default, only a limited amount of information is put in the file; to get more details, the NetWorker services can be started with the debug argument set.

NetWorker does have an SNMP add-on module that can send traps to HP Open-View, SunNet Manager, and other third-party frameworks. The product does not have a MIB available at this time.

Special Options

Legato has the following modules to provide additional support:

GEMS

GEMS has a web-based GUI that provides a consistent, policy-based approach to managing enterprise-wide distributed storage management. GEMS provides a single control zone to perform administration, distribute Legato software, manage licensing, and track all tape media on all of your GEMS-managed nodes (backup servers) and data zones.

NetWorker Archive

This add-on is an advanced data management application that delivers file-level archiving and file-grooming services for network clients.

Autochanger Software Modules

This feature enables hands-free, automated data protection using a wide variety of autochangers. The modules are licensed according to the number of slots supported by the tape library.

NetWorker Business Suite

This group of products provides online protection for popular databases and applications. There are modules available for Microsoft SQL Server, Microsoft Exchange, Lotus Notes, Informix, SAP R/3, Sybase, and Oracle.

Open File Manager

This add-on module provides protection for open files on NT servers. Even if changes are made during backup, NetWorker backups will contain a complete and accurate copy of the file. Open File Manager works with all leading email, database, word processor, and spreadsheet packages, including Lotus Notes, Microsoft Exchange, Sybase, Btrieve, and Novell GroupWise.

SNMP Module

This module provides an enterprise system management strategy by providing seamless integration of NetWorker with system monitoring frameworks.

Disaster Recovery Module

This module provides bare metal restore of NT systems from diskettes and provides block-level image backups and restores for enhanced performance.

Company Contact Information

Legato Systems, Inc.
3210 Porter Drive
Palo Alto, CA 94304
Telephone: (650) 812-6000
Fax: (650) 812-6032
http://www.legato.com or *http://www.legato.com/nt*

SM-arch

SM-arch (Version 4.2) is backup and retrieval software for heterogeneous enterprise networks. It offers a remote distributed environment for consistent, disaster-proof backup and retrieval of critical data. SM-arch offers your enterprise-wide network the ability to perform distributed backup with single-point control. It runs on both Unix and Windows NT servers and supports many more client platforms, including MS-DOS, Windows NT, Novell, and Macintosh, among others.

There are three packages available:

Personal Backup Edition
> This edition provides automatic scheduling and volume management for individual Windows NT workstations. It supports one locally attached tape drive.

Workstation Backup Edition
> This edition provides unlimited data backup for your Windows servers and Windows-based workstations in a workgroup network. You have the option of adding a second tape drive and backing up shared data on remote computers.

Enterprise Backup Edition
> This edition is for distributed client and server backups in a heterogeneous network. It includes features of the Workgroup Backup Edition, plus remote intelligent client support, distributed device support to connect to drives at remote clients as well as the backup server. You can also add the Archive Module, the Jukebox Module, or the Database Backup Module to this edition.

SM-arch has been in production on the Unix platform for six years and originated on the Unix operating system. It has been in production on the NT platform since the end of 1996 and runs on Windows NT Server Versions 3.51 and 4.0.

Backup Server

The backup server software is the same in the previously described three editions. The difference in editions is the licensing. Cataloging and backup scheduling is implemented and administered from one central server. The system administrator requires just one server console to monitor and control backup activities. You can have more than one backup server to multiple clients, but SM-arch does not have the capability to failover from one server to another.

The SM-arch backup server directs the backups through two services:

Scheduler
> This service runs the backups, manages media expiration, and maintains the online catalog.

SMClient

This service performs data collection and tape drive operations when needed.

SM-arch network backup is never server-centric. The intelligent clients gather data independently from the server and communicate directly with backup devices. This allows the host backup server to perform its role as backup manager efficiently, irrespective of network size.

Backup Client

On the SM-arch NT backup clients, there is one service, SMClient. This service performs data collection and tape drive operations when needed. It gives the backup clients a built-in technology that prepares the files ahead of time for backup and then puts the data where the server has instructed the client to put it, either on the server's storage device or a storage device connected to another backup client. The Scheduler service on the backup server puts the SMClient service on the backup client in touch with the SMClient service on the backup server.

Configuration and Backup Information

The configuration and backup information is stored centrally on the backup server, and the SM-arch backup catalog is compact. Multiple files make up the catalog, which can be considered a single logical entity. Data structure and relationships among the catalog files are proprietary to the SM-arch architecture. Software Moguls has utilities to repair the catalog in the event that it becomes corrupted.

The data on the backup clients is added to and grouped by classes. The original order entry sequence within that class is how the priority is set for the backup clients. The highest priority backup classes should be scheduled earliest in the backup window.

SM-arch automatically defines a backup class for the catalog, which is backed up as a full backup. Once this class is scheduled by the administrator the backup of its catalog runs automatically as a full backup after the backups are done.

The catalog records the size of the backed-up file, the time it was modified, who can access the file, the name of the file, and where it is stored on tape. Its size is about 44 bytes per file with a one-time overhead of 38 bytes.

All end users can recover their own files to their own machines. Administrators can recover any file to any location. The user's logon identity is used to restrict operations for users that are not in the Administrator group.

Log Files

SM-arch integrates with the NT event log, but does have its own log files. Logs are generated for each backup or restore event and are named with a one-up naming convention. Backup logs are located on the server in a set location and can automatically be emailed to the administrator and/or other parties. Diagnostic logging on remote clients can be enabled for troubleshooting purposes.

SM-arch provides no integration with SNMP.

Special Options

Software Moguls also has the following options available:

Archive Module
> This module automatically transfers large and infrequently used files from hard disk drives to low-cost archival media. Retrievals are driven by intuitive "tracer" files that let you know exactly when and where a file was archived.

Database Backup Module
> This module allows you to include backup and retrieval of third-party relational database management systems into your regularly scheduled SM-arch backups with the Database Backup Module. With this module, SM-arch supports backup of live databases and object-level recovery. This module provides native backup and recovery of the Microsoft Exchange and SQL Server databases.

Jukebox Module
> This module supports all the leading brands of autoloaders and works independent of network topology. Interfacing your jukeboxes and SM-arch with the Jukebox Module provides full automation through premounting capabilities and after-hours "lights-out" operations. This module supports multiple drive libraries, which can be connected to different computers, reducing SCSI and network bottlenecks. Splitting the drives eliminates this problem.

Company Contact Information

> Software Moguls
> 6400 Flying Cloud Drive
> Eden Prairie, MN 55344
> Telephone: (612) 944-0770
> Fax: (612) 944-1660
> *http://www.moguls.com*

Feature Comparison

The vendor survey outlined in Chapter 6 provided a checklist of questions and the rationale for each question to help you determine which backup and restore features are needed to suit your site's needs. This section takes each of the features and each of the commercial software vendors listed previously to give you a side-by-side matrix comparison of features versus vendors. Across the top of each matrix is the name of the commercial software and the Windows NT Server version that was reviewed.

The features were not evaluated, just documented as existing or not existing. It is up to you to perform the evaluation of the features and functionality to see if they fit your needs. The matrices should help you narrow down which vendors fit your site's needs; remember, you should choose no more than three vendors to evaluate.

As you narrow down your vendor choice, remember to check the vendor's web site for further (and possibly more up-to-date) information. This book may be slightly out of date with the current product shipped by the vendors, and there may be new features you should consider.

Due to the large size of the following table matrices, the abbreviations listed in Table 8-2* were used in this chapter to help save space.

Backup Server Considerations

An important aspect to backups is the Windows NT backup server. The backup server is the heart and soul of the network backups if you have a medium or large site. At small sites, every one of your hosts is a backup server itself. You have many considerations to weigh with respect to the backup server. Table 8-3 lists features associated with backup server considerations. Note that the features described below are for the Windows NT backup server software. This is important, because some vendors have different or additional features on their different backup server operating system versions.

Backup Client Considerations

If you are implementing backups at a medium or large site (where you use the network) there are naturally backup clients. Table 8-4 provides you with a list of all backup clients supported by the different vendors when using a Windows NT backup server. Even though this book is focused on Windows NT systems, I realize that most sites do not have an NT-exclusive environment, because most sites

---

* The rest of the tables in this chapter have been placed together at the end of the chapter.

have legacy systems. Remember, it is technically possible to have a backup server of one type of operating system back up clients of a different operating system. Therefore, it may be desirable at your site to have the backup server back up a mixed–backup client environment.

Note that Table 8-4 does not include many specific operating system version numbers for the types of different backup clients. You should contact the vendor to verify that you are using an operating system version that they specifically support. Generally, if your site is on the latest version, the backup software vendors will suit your needs.

Site Considerations

It is important to fit the backup solution into the infrastructure that already exists at your company. The better the fit, the easier the integration of the software will be. Table 8-5 lists other software you may have at your site and how the different backup vendors support this software with an Windows NT backup server.

Administrative and Configuration Considerations

As a site grows, the administration and configuration overhead of the backup server and clients becomes more time-consuming. Understanding how the administration and configuration is handled by the backup software will help you choose the best product for your site. Any of the features in Table 8-6 that make your life easier are worth considering. The features listed in Table 8-6 are available with a Windows NT backup server.

Monitoring, Reporting, and Logging Considerations

Monitoring, reporting, and logging are all important for your Windows NT backup server. You cannot have just one or two of them—you must have all three to manage your backup environment efficiently. Monitoring is important for operational and administrative staff members to watch the backups and restores in real time. Reporting is important for administrators and management to understand what did and did not get backed up and to be able to watch for trends. Then, when there are problems, the log files are vital to be able to troubleshoot the exact problem before it can be fixed. Table 8-7 lists these features and their availability by vendor.

Data Considerations

The features listed in Table 8-8 relate to the data being backed up by a Windows NT backup server. How data on the backup client is handled before it is backed up, while it is being backed up, and after it is backed up are all important considerations.

Security Considerations

After the backups start to run, the backup server has all vital data for your site. This means that it should be the best secured system you own. It is not appropriate for everyone to have access to all data on the backup server. There may be proprietary or sensitive information on the Windows NT backup server to which certain individuals should not have access. Table 8-9 outlines some security features that you should consider when making a choice of backup software vendor.

Tape Considerations

Tape considerations are also important. What hardware you are planning on using can help you determine what software you are going to use on your Windows NT backup server. Table 8-10 lists these features by vendor support.

Hardware Platform Considerations for Backup Server

Table 8-11 outlines which hardware platforms are supported by each vendor for the Windows NT backup server system.

Hardware Platform Considerations for Backup Clients

The site survey described in Chapter 4, *Requirements Definition*, includes a question to define what backup client hardware platforms (for any backup client operating system) are supported when using a Windows NT backup server. Based on which hardware platforms you have at your site and using Table 8-12, you may be able to narrow down which applications best suit the hardware mix at your site.

Documentation Considerations

Documentation is very important. It is where you and your end users should go first, before contacting the vendor. There are all forms of documentation; Table 8-13 provides an overview of the type of documentation provided by the different vendors.

Customer Support Considerations

The customer support considerations are worth considering when purchasing backup software. You have to deal with the vendor frequently, and therefore should be aware of some basics, which are covered in Table 8-14.

Additional Considerations

Other features that did not fit neatly into the categories above, landed in this section. These are features in an environment implementing a Windows NT backup server. The items in Table 8-15 are by no means less important than any of the other features in the other tables.

Table 8-2. Abbreviations Used in Vendor/Feature Matrices

Abbreviation	Full Word
admin	administrative
amt	amount
auth	authentication
avail	available
ave	average
bckp	backup
config	configuration
clnt	client
cmpr	compression
distrib	distribution
docs	documentation
db	database
eng	engineering
exp	expressions
ident	identification
info	information
lang	language
lib	library
min	minimum
mgt	management
mods	modifications
mstr	master
os	operating system
prob	problems
reg	regular
req	required
rst	restore
srvr	server
sppt	support
sw	software
wrkst	workstation

Table 8-3. Backup Server Feature Matrix

Bckp Srvr Features	ADSM Version 3	ARCserve Version 6.5	Backup Exec Version 7.0	Backup Express Release 1	HP OpenView OmniBack II Version 3.0	NetBackup Version 3.0	NetWorker for NT Version 5.1	SM-arch Version 4.2
Bckp Srvr Windows NT Versions	NT Srvr/Wrkst V3.51 or V4.0	NT Srvr V3.51 or V4.0	NT Srvr/Wrkst V3.51 or V4.0	NT Srvr V3.51 or V4.0	NT Srvr/Wrkst V3.51 or V4.0	NT Srvr V3.51 or V4.0	NT Srvr V3.51 or V4.0	NT Srvr/Wrkst V3.51 or V4.0
Other Bckp Srv OS Sppt	VSE/ESA OS/400 OS/2 VM MVS AIX Solaris HP-UX	NetWare	NetWare MS-DOS Windows OS/2 Windows 95	HP-UX IBM AIX Solaris SunOS DEC Unix SCO Unix OpenServer V NCR SRV4 DG/UX Sinix SGI IRIX	HP-UX	Auspex OSF1 HP-UX IBM AIX SGI IRIX Solaris SunOS NetApp NDNP	Solaris SunOS IBM AIX HP-UX NetWare Digital Unix SGI IRIX	Solaris IBM AIX HP-UX SGI Irix
Multithreaded Srv SW	yes	yes	yes	yes	no	yes	yes	yes
Failover Sppt	no	no, use CA's Identica product for failover	no	no	yes	yes	yes, using storage nodes	yes, optional standby srvr
Min Bckp Srvr: RAM Disk Space Processor Speed	32 MB 90 MB 486DX or Pentium	16 MB 30 MB X86 or Pentium	24 MB 35 MB x86, Pentium, or Alpha	32 MB 33 MB x86 or Pentium	64 MB 270MB Pentium	32 MB 12 MB Pentium or Alpha	64 MB 30 MB Pentium or Alpha	64 MB 80 MB x86, Pentium, or Alpha
Installation Media for Bckp Srvr	CD-ROM	CD-ROM	CD-ROM	CD-ROM	CD-ROM	CD-ROM or floppy diskettes	CD-ROM	CD-ROM

Table 8-4. Backup Client Feature Matrix

Bckp Clnt Features	ADSM Version 3	ARCserve Version 6.5	Backup Exec Version 7.0	Backup Express Release 1	HP OpenView OmniBack II Version 3.0	NetBackup Version 3.0	NetWorker for NT Version 5.1	SM-arch Version 4.2
Windows NT	yes	yes	yes	yes	yes	yes	yes	yes
Novell, NetWare 4.x	yes	yes	yes	yes	yes	yes	yes	yes
Novell, NetWare 3.1x	yes	yes	yes	yes	yes	yes	yes	yes
SUN, Solaris	yes	yes	yes	yes	yes	yes	yes	yes
SUN, SunOS	no	yes	yes	yes	yes	yes	yes	yes
HP, HP-UX	yes	yes	yes	yes	yes	yes	yes	yes
SGI, IRIX	yes	yes	no	yes	yes	yes	no	yes
DEC, Ultrix	yes	no	no	yes	yes	yes	no	no
IBM, AIX	yes	yes	no	yes	yes	yes	no	yes
SCO, Unix	yes	yes	yes	yes	yes	yes	no	yes
Windows 95	yes	yes	yes	yes	yes	yes	yes	yes
Windows 3.x	yes	yes	yes	yes	yes	yes	yes	yes
MS-DOS	yes	no	yes	no	no	yes	yes	yes
Banyan, VINES	no	no	no	no	no	no	no	no
Macintosh	yes	yes	yes	no	no	yes	yes	yes
IBM, OS/2	yes	yes	yes	no	no	no	yes	no

Table 8-4. Backup Client Feature Matrix (continued)

Bckp Clnt Features	ADSM Version 3	ARCserve Version 6.5	Backup Exec Version 7.0	Backup Express Release 1	HP OpenView OmniBack II Version 3.0	NetBackup Version 3.0	NetWorker for NT Version 5.1	SM-arch Version 4.2
Other	MVS O/E, NEC EWS-UX, AT&T Unix, SNI Sinix,	none	Interactive, UnixWare	SNI Sinix, Openserver V	SNI Sinix	Auspex, Cray, OSF1, CD-4000 EPIX, V88R3, V88R4, NCR SRV4, Pyramid DCOS, Sequent Dynix/PTX	MPE/ix	Linux
Installation Media for Bckp Client SW	CD-ROM	CD-ROM	CD-ROM	CD-ROM	CD-ROM or network distribution	CD-ROM or floppy diskettes	CD-ROM	CD-ROM or network install

Table 8-5. Site Feature Matrix

Site Features	ADSM Version 3	ARCserve Version 6.5	Backup Exec Version 7.0	Backup Express Release 1	HP OpenView OmniBack II Version 3.0	NetBackup Version 3.0	NetWorker for NT Version 5.1	SM-arch Version 4.2
MS SMS Integration	no	yes	yes	no	yes	no	yes	no
Other SW Distrib Mechanism	yes, using Tivoli Courier	yes	no	no	yes	yes	yes	no, next release
Bckp Prtion. Sppt:								
Lotus Notes	yes	no	no	no	yes	no	yes	no
MS SQL Server	yes	yes	yes	no	yes	yes	yes	yes
MS Exchange	yes	yes	yes	yes	yes	yes	yes	yes

Table 8-5. Site Feature Matrix (continued)

Site Features	ADSM Version 3	ARCserve Version 6.5	Backup Exec Version 7.0	Backup Express Release 1	HP OpenView OmniBack II Version 3.0	NetBackup Version 3.0	NetWorker for NT Version 5.1	SM-arch Version 4.2
Network Installation Sppt	yes	yes	yes	no, planned for future	yes	no, Unix only	yes	yes
Sppt for read-only filesystem for Clnt Binaries	yes	yes	yes	no	yes	yes	yes	yes

Table 8-6. Administrative and Configuration Feature Matrix

Admin & Config Features	ADSM Version 3	ARCserve Version 6.5	Backup Exec Version 7.0	Backup Express Release 1	HP OpenView OmniBack II Version 3.0	NetBackup Version 3.0	NetWorker for NT Version 5.1	SM-arch Version 4.2
Information Stored in Bckp DB for Individual Files	name, attributes, directory structure, pointer to location in storage pool, data backed up, management class used	tape ID, tape name, serial number, media pool name, format date, expiration date, file path, session number, file size, number of files	name, size, type, modified date, attributes	node, data, size, number of links	name, folder, size, attribute, creation date, last backup. If available: user, group, access rights	permissions on file, owner of file, group file is in, file size, modification date, creation date, and full directory name	filename, number of blocks, access permission, number of links, owner, group, size, last modified time, backup time.	record size, time of modification, access, name, and location on tape
Amt of Disk Space Req, Ave Bckp Clnt	450–600 bytes/file or 3% to 5% of backed up data	80 bytes/record	[not available]	1/2% or 1% of backup data	less than 1% of backup data	1.5% of backup data	220 bytes per file	44 bytes per file
Bckp Restart	yes	yes, configurable at job setup	yes	yes	yes	no	yes, by saveset	yes

Table 8-6. Administrative and Configuration Feature Matrix (continued)

Admin & Config Features	ADSM Version 3	ARCserve Version 6.5	Backup Exec Version 7.0	Backup Express Release 1	HP OpenView OmniBack II Version 3.0	NetBackup Version 3.0	NetWorker for NT Version 5.1	SM-arch Version 4.2
Bckp Retry	yes	yes, configurable at job setup	yes, manually	yes	yes	no	yes, configurable	yes
Initiation of Bckps	clnt or srvr	srvr only	srvr only	clnt or srvr	clnt or srvr	clnt or srvr	clnt or srvr	clnt or srvr
End-User Restores	yes	yes	no	yes	yes	yes	yes	yes
Remote Restores	yes	yes	yes	yes	yes	yes	yes	yes
Cross Restores	yes	yes	yes	yes	yes	yes	yes	yes
Allows wildcard or Reg Exp, Bckps	yes	yes, through filter options	yes	yes	yes	yes	yes	yes
Allows wildcard or Reg Exp, Rstrs	yes	yes, through filter options	yes	yes	yes	yes	yes	yes
GUI and command-line interfaces	yes	yes	yes	yes	yes	yes	yes	yes
Printable Bckp Srvr Config Info	yes	yes	yes	yes	yes	yes	yes	yes
Sppt Host Grouping Host Ordering	yes	no	no	yes	yes	yes	yes	yes
Host Priorities Sppted	yes	yes	no	no	yes	no, only class priorities	yes	yes
Multilevel Bckps Sppted	yes	yes	yes	yes	yes	yes	yes	yes
Calendar-Based Bckps Sppted	yes	yes	yes	yes	yes	no	yes	yes
Sppt Bulk Entry for Config	yes	yes, through SMS	no	yes	yes	yes	yes	yes

Table 8-6. Administrative and Configuration Feature Matrix (continued)

Admin & Config Features	ADSM Version 3	ARCserve Version 6.5	Backup Exec Version 7.0	Backup Express Release 1	HP OpenView OmniBack II Version 3.0	NetBackup Version 3.0	NetWorker for NT Version 5.1	SM-arch Version 4.2
Sppt Srvr Bckp Exceptions	yes	yes	yes	yes	yes	no	yes	yes
Sppt Clnt Bckp Exceptions	yes	yes	yes	yes	no	yes	yes	no, planned enhancement

Table 8-7. Monitoring, Reporting, and Logging Feature Matrix

Monitoring, Reporting, & Logging Features	ADSM Version 3	ARCserve Version 6.5	Backup Exec Version 7.0	Backup Express Release 1	HP OpenView OmniBack II Version 3.0	NetBackup Version 3.0	NetWorker for NT Version 5.1	SM-arch Version 4.2
Arbitrary Command Notification Sppt	no	yes, through Alert	yes	no, email and paging in future	yes	yes	yes	yes
Bckp Srvr Monitoring	by scheduled events	by backup srvr	by file/folder	by job	by cell or by job	by job	by backup client	by class
Tape Device Monitoring	yes	yes	yes	yes	yes	yes	yes	yes
Central Monitoring	Event monitoring with Tivoli	yes	With Seagate ExecView	yes	yes	yes	yes with NetWorker Server or GEMS	yes
Remote Monitoring	yes	yes	yes, through NT's Remote Administration	yes	yes	yes	yes	yes, through email
SNMP Monitoring	yes	yes	yes	yes	yes, traps only	yes, traps only	yes, traps only	no

Table 8-7. Monitoring, Reporting, and Logging Feature Matrix (continued)

Monitoring, Reporting, & Logging Features	ADSM Version 3	ARCserve Version 6.5	Backup Exec Version 7.0	Backup Express Release 1	HP OpenView OmniBack II Version 3.0	NetBackup Version 3.0	NetWorker for NT Version 5.1	SM-arch Version 4.2
Log File Sppt	yes	yes	yes	yes	yes	yes	yes	yes
Location of Log File	srvr and clnt	srvr	srvr	srvr and clnt	srvr	srvr and clnt (clnt only if needed)	srvr	srvr and optionally on clnt
Reporting Mechanism	ODBC SQL interfaces	GUI, command line	5 canned reports, customer reports through Crystal Reports	GUI, command line	GUI, command line, HTML output, web-based	GUI, command line	GUI, command line, GEMS	GUI, command line

Table 8-8. Data Feature Matrix

Data Features	ADSM Version 3	ARCserve Version 6.5	Backup Exec Version 7.0	Backup Express Release 1	HP OpenView OmniBack II Version 3.0	NetBackup Version 3.0	NetWorker for NT Version 5.1	SM-arch Version 4.2
Bckp Clnt or Bckp Srvr Data Cmpr	clnt cmpr	clnt cmpr	clnt or srvr cmpr	clnt or srvr cmpr	clnt or srvr cmpr	clnt cmpr	clnt or srvr cmpr	clnt cmpr
Multi-Lang Sppt	yes	yes	yes	no	yes	yes	yes	yes
Open File Sppt	yes	yes	yes	yes, with Open File Manager[a]	yes	yes, with Open File Manager[a]	yes, with Open File Manager[a]	yes, with Open File Manager[a]

Table 8-8. Data Feature Matrix (continued)

Data Features	ADSM Version 3	ARCserve Version 6.5	Backup Exec Version 7.0	Backup Express Release 1	HP OpenView OmniBack II Version 3.0	NetBackup Version 3.0	NetWorker for NT Version 5.1	SM-arch Version 4.2
Hot DB Bckp Sppt	yes, with ADSM agents	yes, with Database Agent	yes, with SQL Back-track[b] and Open File Manager[a]	yes, with Open File Manager[a]	yes	yes	yes, with Database Suites	yes, with SQL Back-track and natively planned
Pre- and Post-processing	yes	yes	yes	yes	yes	yes	yes	yes

[a] The Open File Manager product is available from St. Bernard.
[b] The Backtrack product is available from BMC (formally a Datatools product).

Table 8-9. Security Feature Matrix

Security Features	ADSM Version 3	ARCserve Version 6.5	Backup Exec Version 7.0	Backup Express Release 1	HP OpenView OmniBack II Version 3.0	NetBackup Version 3.0	NetWorker for NT Version 5.1	SM-arch Version 4.2
Permissions Granted for Restores	standard NT security, plus ADSM login and pass-word	standard NT security	standard NT security	standard NT security	standard NT security	standard NT security	standard NT security	standard NT security
Security for Bckps	standard NT security, plus ADSM login and pass-word	standard NT security	standard NT security	standard NT security	standard NT security	standard NT security	standard NT security	standard NT security

Table 8-9. Security Feature Matrix (continued)

Security Features	ADSM Version 3	ARCserve Version 6.5	Backup Exec Version 7.0	Backup Express Release 1	HP OpenView OmniBack II Version 3.0	NetBackup Version 3.0	NetWorker for NT Version 5.1	SM-arch Version 4.2
Auth for Admin and Config Functions	standard NT security, plus ADSM login and password	standard NT security	password protection for tapes and database	standard NT security	standard NT security	standard NT security	standard NT security	standard NT security
Encryption Sppt	no	yes	no	yes	yes	yes	yes	yes

Table 8-10. Tape Feature Matrix

Tape Features	ADSM Version 3	ARCserve Version 6.5	Backup Exec Version 7.0	Backup Express Release 1	HP OpenView OmniBack II Version 3.0	NetBackup Version 3.0	NetWorker for NT Version 5.1	SM-arch Version 4.2
Tape Drive Sppt:								
QIC	yes	yes	yes	yes	no	no	yes	yes
4mm (DAT)	yes	yes	yes	yes	yes	yes	yes	yes
8mm	yes	yes	yes	yes	yes	yes	yes	yes
DLT	yes	yes	yes	yes	yes	yes	yes	yes
AIT	yes	yes	no	yes	no, future release	yes	yes	yes
Other Tape Drives Sppted	IBM 35xx	none	none	none	none	IBM 1/2" Cartridge, Sony DTMF		none
Tape Format	proprietary	proprietary	Microsoft Tape Format	proprietary, system-independent data format	proprietary	GNU-tar for serial backups, proprietary for multiplexed backups	Open Tape Format	compatible with Unix tar

Table 8-10. Tape Feature Matrix (continued)

Tape Features	ADSM Version 3	ARCserve Version 6.5	Backup Exec Version 7.0	Backup Express Release 1	HP OpenView OmniBack II Version 3.0	NetBackup Version 3.0	NetWorker for NT Version 5.1	SM-arch Version 4.2
Tape Lib Sppt								
Entry/Exit Door	yes	yes	yes	yes	yes	yes	yes	yes
Cleaning Tape Sppt	yes	yes	yes	yes	yes	yes	yes	yes
Bar Code Sppt	yes	yes	yes	yes	yes	yes	yes	yes
Tape Library Media Grouping Sppt	yes	yes	yes	yes	yes	yes	yes	yes
Tape Drive or Tape Slot Locking Sppt	yes, tape drive and no, tape slot	yes, both	yes, both	no, tape drive and yes, tape slot	yes, both	yes	yes	yes
Tape Library Replenish Sppt	no	yes	yes	yes	yes	yes	yes	yes
Maximum Tape Drives Sppted	unlimited	32	hardware limited	unlimited	5 (configurable) drives/session × 50 sessions/cell	unlimited	unlimited	256
Tape Drive Controllers Sppt	SCSI	SCSI	SCSI	SCSI	SCSI	SCSI	SCSI	SCSI
Tape RAID Sppt	no	yes	yes	no	no	no	no	no
Tape Retention Sppt	no	yes	yes	yes	yes	yes	yes	no
Tape Verification Sppt	yes	yes	yes	yes	yes	yes	yes	yes
Bckp Clnt Multiplexing onto Tape	yes	no	no	yes	yes	yes	yes	no
Demultiplexing Sppt	not needed	no	no	yes	no, next release	yes	yes	no

Table 8-10. Tape Feature Matrix (continued)

Tape Features	ADSM Version 3	ARCserve Version 6.5	Backup Exec Version 7.0	Backup Express Release 1	HP OpenView OmniBack II Version 3.0	NetBackup Version 3.0	NetWorker for NT Version 5.1	SM-arch Version 4.2
Disk Staging Sppt	yes	no	no	no	no	no, Unix only	yes	no
Tape Duplicating Sppt	yes	yes	yes	yes	no, next release	yes	yes	yes

Table 8-11. Backup Server Hardware Platforms Matrix

Bckp Srvr Hardware Platforms	ADSM Version 3	ARCserve Version 6.5	Backup Exec Version 7.0	Backup Express Release 1	HP OpenView OmniBack II Version 3.0	NetBackup Version 3.0	NetWorker for NT Version 5.1	SM-arch Version 4.2
Intel	yes	yes	yes	yes	yes	yes	yes	yes
Alpha	no	yes	yes	yes	no	yes	yes	yes
MIPS[a]	no	yes	no	no	no	no	no	no
Power/PC[a]	no	yes	no	no	no	no	no	no
Other	none	none	none	none	none	none	none	none

[a] Microsoft no longer supports the MIPS or PowerPC hardware platforms. They are included for backup compatibility of existing equipment at your site.

Table 8-12. Backup Client Hardware Platforms Matrix

Bckp Client Hardware Platforms	ADSM Version 3	ARCserve Version 6.5	Backup Exec Version 7.0	Backup Express Release 1	HP OpenView OmniBack II Version 3.0	NetBackup Version 3.0	NetWorker for NT Version 5.1	SM-arch version 4.2
Intel	yes	yes	yes	yes	yes	yes	yes	yes
Alpha	yes	yes	yes	yes	yes	yes	yes	yes
MIPS[a]	no	yes	no	no	no	no	no	no

Table 8-12. Backup Client Hardware Platforms Matrix (continued)

Bckp Client Hardware Platforms	ADSM Version 3	ARCserve Version 6.5	Backup Exec Version 7.0	Backup Express Release 1	HP OpenView OmniBack II Version 3.0	NetBackup Version 3.0	NetWorker for NT Version 5.1	SM-arch version 4.2
Power/PC[a]	no	yes	no	no	no	no	no	no
Other	none	none	none	none	none	none	none	none

[a] Microsoft no longer supports the MIPS or PowerPC hardware platforms. They are included for backup compatibility of existing equipment at your site.

Table 8-13. Documentation Feature Matrix

Doc Features	ADSM Version 3	ARCserve Version 6.5	Backup Exec Version 7.0	Backup Express Release 1	HP OpenView OmniBack II Version 3.0	NetBackup Version 3.0	NetWorker for NT Version 5.1	SM-arch version 4.2
Online Help	yes	yes	yes	yes	yes	yes	yes	yes
Online Tutorials	yes	no	yes	no	no	no	yes	yes
Hard Copy Doc Set	yes	yes	yes	no, on CD-ROM	no, on CD-ROM	yes	yes	yes
Disaster Recovery Docs	yes	yes	yes	yes	yes	yes	yes	yes

Table 8-14. Customer Support Feature Matrix

Customer Sppt Features	ADSM Version 3	ARCserve Version 6.5	Backup Exec Version 7.0	Backup Express Release 1	HP OpenView OmniBack II Version 3.0	NetBackup Version 3.0	NetWorker for NT Version 5.1	SM-arch Version 4.2
Type of Phone Sppt	8:00 A.M.–5:00 P.M. weekdays, 7×24 optional	8:00 A.M.–10:00 P.M. EST weekdays, 10:00 A.M.–6:00 P.M. EST Sat, 10:00 A.M.–3:00 P.M. EST Sun, 7×24 optional	8:30 A.M.–8:00 P.M. EST weekdays, 7×24 optional	8:00 A.M.–8:00 P.M. EST weekdays, 7×24 optional	7×24 with contract	8:00 A.M.–8:00 P.M. weekdays, 7×24 optional	8:00 A.M.–8:00 P.M. PST weekdays, 7×24 optional	7:00 A.M.–7:00 P.M. CST weekdays, 7×24 optional
Premium Sppt Avail	yes	yes	yes	yes	yes, business continuity support contracts	yes	yes	yes
Onsite Sppt	yes	yes	yes	yes	yes	yes	yes	yes
Bug Reports, Eng Changes	IBM Support Structure	through technical support	std escalation between tech sppt, QA and R&D member of TSANet[a]	browser-based early warning system used by support	HP's Customer Response Center Organization	processed through support desk, then prioritized by development	identified through technical support, then sent to engineering	detailed log of all bugs and enhancements
Patches Avail through the Web or FTP site	yes	yes	yes	no	yes	yes	yes	yes
Prob Ident / Resolution Facility through the Web	no	no	yes	not for customers	no	no, currently under development	yes	support database of technical notes and FAQs
User Groups	yes	yes	yes	no	no	yes	yes	no

Table 8-14. Customer Support Feature Matrix (continued)

Customer Sppt Features	ADSM Version 3	ARCserve Version 6.5	Backup Exec Version 7.0	Backup Express Release 1	HP OpenView OmniBack II Version 3.0	NetBackup Version 3.0	NetWorker for NT Version 5.1	SM-arch Version 4.2
Mailing Lists Avail	yes	yes	yes	yes, newsletters	no	no	yes	yes
Training Avail	yes, at vendor site	yes, third-party	yes, Seagate Software Academy	yes, onsite available	yes, at vendor site	yes, onsite, at vendor site, or third party	yes, onsite or at vendor site	yes

a TSANet is a technical support alliance comprised of over 80 leading hardware and software vendors, which allows members to quickly find answers to multi-vendor support issues.

Table 8-15. Additional Feature Matrix

Additional Features	ADSM Version 3	ARCserve Version 6.5	Backup Exec Version 7.0	Backup Express Release 1	HP OpenView OmniBack II Version 3.0	NetBackup Version 3.0	NetWorker for NT Version 5.1	SM-arch Version 4.2
Licensing Sppt	number of backup srvrs and backup clnts and type of features	number of backup srvrs	number of backup srvrs	number of backup srvrs and backup clnts	number of backup clnts and number of drives	number of backup srvrs and backup clnts	number of backup srvrs and backup clnts	number of backup srvrs
Sppt Site Licensing	no	yes	yes	no	yes, has to be negotiated	yes	yes	yes
Archiving Sppt	yes	yes	yes	no	yes	yes	yes	yes
HSM Sppt	yes	yes	yes	no	yes	no	yes	no
Customer References	testimonials on web site	yes	yes	yes	yes	yes	yes	yes
Test and Evaluation Policy	60-day trial	60-day trial	60-day trial	30-day trial	60-day trial	60-day trial		30-day guarantee

Table 8-15. Additional Feature Matrix (continued)

Additional Features	ADSM Version 3	ARCserve Version 6.5	Backup Exec Version 7.0	Backup Express Release 1	HP OpenView OmniBack II Version 3.0	NetBackup Version 3.0	NetWorker for NT Version 5.1	SM-arch Version 4.2
Number of Employees	200,000 corporate-wide, 5,000 in Storage Systems Division	over 10,000	1400	proprietary	approx 120,000	over 700	over 400	45
Year Founded	1914	1971	1993	1968	1939	1989	1988	1986

9

Hardware

When implementing a backup solution, you have to be familiar with the hardware as well as the software; you need to be a jack of all trades. This chapter covers hardware considerations that affect backups, including tape drive hardware, tape library hardware, and backup server hardware. Since tapes are the most popular backup media, this chapter focuses on tape technology.

With local backups, the server hardware typically is not a concern, because there is only the data of one computer to back up. Therefore, one tape drive is normally sufficient, and the computer you are backing up is acting as the backup server for itself. Usually there are no tape libraries. If you have a smaller site, you may want to focus on the tape drive hardware section in this chapter. There are different tape sizes and tape drive speeds to accommodate varying amounts of vital data.

For networked backups, you should focus on all sections in this chapter. The performance of the backup server, the tape drive hardware, and the tape library are all important considerations. The backup throughput allows you to meet the backup window; the restore speed allows you to recover lost data quickly. For ease of tape management, medium and large sites should seriously consider an implementation using tape library technology.

Tape Drive Hardware

There are five basic types of tape drive technology commonly used in the NT marketplace today. The following sections describe each type, followed by a matrix that compares the technologies side by side.

Quarter Inch Cartridge (QIC)

The development standards for the QIC technology were established and are maintained by the QIC Drive Standards Committee, Inc. There are minicartridge drive and tape standards and data cartridge drive and tape standards. The QIC minicartridge tapes* are 3.5 inches, and the QIC data cartridge tapes are 5.25 inches. The data cartridge tapes support a higher density, and therefore an increased capacity in contrast to the minicartridges. The QIC drives are an inexpensive design and are widely used. The QIC technology uses MP tape media. When the tape is placed in drive, it requires an automatic retensioning of tape before reliable read/write operations can occur and then records data in a linear serpentine manner.

An advantage to the QIC technology is that the drives and media are inexpensive. However, it is slow and has a low tape capacity. Since the QIC technology is low end, low speed, and low capacity, it is best suited for individual workstations or home use.

4mm

The 4mm technology is also referred to as Digital Audio Tape (DAT); the terms are used interchangeably. The 4mm drives and tapes adhere to one of three Digital Data Storage (DDS) standards. Each standard is an evolutionary stepping stone:

DDS-1

In 1989, this standard was the first generation of DDS and supports a maximum tape capacity of 1.3 GB. In 1991, this standard was improved to support a capacity of 2 GB. This latter standard is sometimes referred to as DDS-DC (Data Compression).

DDS-2

The DDS-2 standard was formalized in 1993 and supports a maximum tape capacity of 4 GB. This standard is twice as fast as the DDS-1 standard.

DDS-3

The DDS-3 standard was formalized in 1996 and supports a maximum tape capacity of 12 GB. This standard is four times as fast as the DDS-1 standard.

The DDS standards are backward-compatible for both read and write. For planning purposes, it is important to find out which DDS standard a manufacturer adheres to before making your purchase. All 4mm drives use the helical scan technique for recording and the MP tape media.

---

* Travan is a QIC minicartridge solution.

The DAT technology is cost-effective and well established. However, it is slow, has low tape capacities, and has a 20% duty cycle. Since the 4mm technology is low end, low speed, and low capacity, it is best suited for individual workstations or small workgroups.

8mm

Together, Sony and Exabyte design, manufacture, and market all 8mm tape drives, with the exception of the Mammoth drive. Exabyte solely designed, manufactures, and markets the Mammoth drives.

The Mammoth drive uses the AME tape media technology, and other 8mm tape drives use the MP tape media technology. The Mammoth drive is designed to read the MP tapes, but the heads must be cleaned before the AME tapes can be used again. The 8mm drives are designed to use the helical scan technology (like the 4mm technology).

The advantage of the 8mm technology is that it is well established. It has been around since 1985 and is stable and well supported. This has also made 8mm technology very cost-effective. The major disadvantage is its 10% duty cycle. The 8mm technology is in the midrange performance and capacity category and is generally best suited for small or medium networked backup sites. Sometimes it can be used in large sites with multiple backup servers if the backups can be accomplished within the duty cycle rating.

Digital Linear Tape

The Digital Linear Tape technology was originally developed by Digital Equipment Corporation, but was subsequently acquired by Quantum Corporation. Some companies repackage Quantum drives, but they all have the same origin.

There are multiple Digital Linear Tape models with the same physical drive and tape size, but with increased data transfer rates and tape capacities. The Digital Linear Tape drives are backward-compatible for both reading and writing because they uses MP tape media technology. The Digital Linear Tape drives are designed to use the leader-type tape technology. A leader tab on the tapes is mechanically grabbed by the tape drive and the tape is threaded through a path that puts the tape in contact with the stationary read/write heads (it is not wrapped around a rotating head). The Digital Linear Tape drive models before the DLT 7000 write to tape using normal linear serpentine tracks. The DLT 7000 writes to tape using the SPR linear serpentine tracks.

The advantages to this technology are the 100% duty cycle, high reliability, and high tape capacity. The major disadvantage is that the drives and media are more

expensive than the other technologies. The Digital Linear Tape technology is high
end, high speed, and high capacity, and is best suited for medium or large networked backup sites.

Advanced Intelligent Tape (AIT)

The AIT technology is the latest in tape drive technology. It is solely designed and
manufactured by Sony, and it is the first drive of a planned line of products.

The AIT incorporates a new recording format. This design decision was based on
increasing capacity, reliability, and performance requirements from the computer
industry. This makes the AIT format incompatible with any other 8mm data cartridges, even though it uses the same AME media and the helical scan recording
method. The tape drive supports Memory In Cassette (MIC), which is a 16-kilobit
flash memory chip built into the tape cartridge that stores the tape's data structure, history, and other tunable information. The physical media does not have to
be read to acquire this information. By using the MIC, the data access time is
reduced, the data handling is improved, and there is therefore less wear on the
AIT tape drive and tapes.

The advantage to this technology is that it incorporates the latest in technology.
The disadvantage is that Sony is currently the only company supporting the tape
format for the AIT tapes and the only source for media. The AIT technology is
high end and is best suited for medium or large network backup sites that are
interested in a product that embodies the latest technology.

Tape and Tape Drive Comparisons

Table 9-1* provides a quick side-by-side comparison of the tape drive information.
The other tables in this chapter list the tape and tape drive models available today
and compare them in the areas of recording, reliability, maintenance, and pricing.
The vendors selling the drives are listed in Appendix C, *Hardware Vendors*.

For clarification, the following items should be noted about the matrices in this
section:

- Only tape drive technology that can backup 1 GB of data or more (uncompressed) is covered. Drives that support smaller capacities are not discussed.

- The QIC drives are manufactured by many different vendors, so specific tape
  drive models are not listed. The QIC technology is listed by the most popular
  recording format. Sometimes the naming convention for the QIC recording format gets confused with the QIC tape cartridge types. Table 9-2 lists both the

---

* All tables in this chapter have been placed together at the end of the chapter.

recording formats and the cartridge types for the QIC technology and should help eliminate confusion.

- The 4mm drives are listed by format type, rather than model type. As with QIC technology, there are many different vendors of 4mm drives.

- Discontinued products are not listed. For example, the Exabyte 8200, 8200SX, 8500, and 8500c and the DLT 600 and DLT 2000 are not listed in the tables.

Recording Capability

Table 9-2 compares the following recording capabilities of the different tape technologies:

Tape capacity

This is the capacity of the tape drive, with and without compression. Generally, the compression is 2:1, but it depends on the type of data being compressed. For example, if the backup application compresses the data first, it will not reach a 2:1 ratio when utilizing the hardware compression. Also, binary data is not likely to reach a 2:1 ratio. On the other hand, spreadsheet data or text data will most likely reach the 2:1 ratio.

Data transfer rate, sustained

This is the maximum rate at which the tape drive will run continually. The drives may spike at higher rates, but that information is not listed. The transfer rate will go up in direct proportion to the compression achieved.

The ability to achieve these rates is dependent on a number of other things. For local backups, the tape backup software and the system performing the backups will determine if the data transfer rate can be achieved. For networked backups, the tape backup software, the backup server hardware configuration, the network speed, and the configuration of the backup clients will determine what data transfer rates can be obtained.

Reliability and Maintenance Factors

Table 9-3 compares the reliability and maintenance factors of the different tape technologies. The following factors are covered in the matrix:

Mean time between failures (MTBF)

Currently the mean time between drive failures is the only reliability metric available. The most important information is the duty cycle associated with the MTBF. For larger sites, where backups will run many hours or sometimes days, you must have a 100% duty cycle associated with the tape drive technology.

At one site, I saw tape drives with a 10% duty cycle basically wear out. When the backup servers and drives were installed, the best technology available was used at that time. As the drives aged, the site had to have one or more drives, out of 20, serviced every week because of the high usage (backups were run every night for 12 or more hours and every weekend for 36 or more hours). It became an operational headache and critical to upgrade the hardware.

Cleaning frequency and additional cleaning notes

Every drive technology has special requirements. As a site increases in size and number of tape drives in use increases, the maintenance of the drives may become a time-consuming factor.

Pricing

Table 9-4 compares the pricing of the different tape technologies. The following information is provided:

Tape drive price

The prices are for comparing one tape and tape drive technology to another and to get an idea of the cost. They are an approximation based on an over-the-counter single-quantity purchase. There will be variations; many corporations may get quantity discounts.

Media price

Similar to the tape drive prices, the price listed is for over-the-counter single-quantity purchases. Most companies can get better prices. You will note that the media is listed by cartridge type. Any cartridge under 1 GB was not included.

Cleaning tape price

Keep in mind, when purchasing cleaning tapes, that they come with a varying number of passes. This is the number of times the cleaning tape can be reused before it has to be thrown away. That may cause price differences; the more passes, the more expensive the cleaning tape. As with the tape media and drives, you'll be able to find quantity discounts.

Tape Library Hardware

This section provides a list of features commonly found in tape libraries and formulas you can use to calculate the size of the tape library required for your site. Tape libraries are sold by many different vendors. The vendors design the library chassis, the robotic arm, and the cartridge slots. The libraries are designed to support one of the types of tape drives and its corresponding media from the list in the section above. An initial list of vendors is available in Appendix C. Note that you may find more in your local area.

Tape Library Features

Tape libraries have some features that you may not be aware of: these are listed here, with an explanation of each. Keep in mind that not every feature is available in every tape library. Go through the feature list and determine what is important for your site. Then, while you gather information on libraries, you can use those features required for your site to determine which library meets your needs. The features listed here, in no particular order:

Tape drive support

All of the tape drives listed are supported by tape libraries. Once you decide on a tape technology, you can then search for that technology in your tape library.

Maximum number of tape drives supported

For future growth, you should know the maximum number of drives the tape libraries can support. You may chose one library over another because of the ability to expand. Another important piece of information to ask the library vendors is whether an increase in the number of tape drives will decrease the number of tapes in the library. Some tape library designs will sacrifice tapes to install additional tape drives.

Tape drive replacement

Mechanical parts in anything are the most likely components to fail. Therefore, the tape drives in the tape library are the most likely component to fail (followed by the robotic arm). Ask the library vendor to describe the exact steps that are taken to replace a tape drive. Some jukeboxes have far more repair steps than others. The simpler the replacement process, the less chance of error, and the less time wasted. Also ask the vendor how the robotic arm calibrates the location of the new drive. The calibration will be either manual or automatic, depending on the manufacturer. Some vendors will say that their libraries are so reliable that you shouldn't worry about the replacement time or steps. The reality is that everything can break, and you should know the replacement steps for planning purposes.

Hot-swappable tape drive support

This type of support has be designed into the tape library. You have to be able to replace the tape drive while the rest of the tape library is functioning.

Tape drive interface

The tape drives in the libraries have SCSI interfaces. You need to know how the tape drives are configured in the jukebox. The tape drives may each be on their own SCSI interface, or they may be daisy-chained together in some preconfigured fashion. It may be possible to specify how they are configured. To design your backup server environment accurately and order the proper number of cables and SCSI controller boards, these details are needed.

Robotic arm interface

You should ask the vendor what type of robotic arm interface is in the tape library. If the robotic arm has a SCSI interface, you'll need to know if the robotic arm is on its own interface or is daisy-chained with the tape drives. This may be configurable to suit your needs. Remember, if the robotic arm is on the same interface as one or more of the tape drives, you cannot replace those tape drives without affecting the robotic arm and vice versa.

Library inventory time

When a library is opened and then closed, most jukeboxes must perform an inventory of the contents. The intelligence associated with the library assumes that something probably has changed and it therefore verifies the contents. The manufacturer, the size of the library, and what the inventory process entails determine the length of this process.

The library may need to read each tape header to perform the inventory. You should know how many tape drives will be used for this process.

Another approach is for the library to read each tape's bar code label. If there is a tape in a tape slot, the bar code is read and recorded. If there is no tape in the tape slot, the process of verifying the empty slot(s) is library-dependent. This is predominately because of how the robotic arm in the library detects an empty slot. Some robotics can automatically sense that there is no tape drive in the slot and other robotics have to physically check every slot to verify that it is empty. The manual, physical check takes more time to perform.

Ask the vendor about the amount of time the inventory process takes when the library is full of tapes and the time it takes when the library is empty (or almost empty).

Entry/exit door support

Many of the jukeboxes have entry/exit doors that allow you to add or remove tapes from the library without the main library door open. By using the entry/exit door, the robotic arm does not have to reinventory the tape library completely. The larger the tape library, the more important it is that you have this feature. The entry/exit door may handle one or many tapes at a time. There are entry/exit doors that can handle as many as 10 tapes, which saves your operators time when replenishing the library.

Tape cartridge load/unload time

This is the average amount of time it takes for the tape library to load or unload a tape cartridge into or out of a tape drive. You may also want to ask about the best and worst times for loading and unloading tapes.

Bar code label support

If you want to use bar-coded labels on your tapes, you must find out if the robotic arm in the tape library is designed to read the bar code format on the labels. The task of managing tapes can become large, especially at larger sites. To make this job easier, you should consider using bar-coded labels on your tapes instead of hand-written labels. Bar code labels have the tape number in both human-readable format and bar-coded machine-readable format.

Library capacity

You should know the total uncompressed and compressed amount of data the tape library can hold. Also, you should find out how many tapes fill the library. When you purchase the library, you will have to buy the tapes separately. So the initial cost of the library is not only the library cost, but the tape cost. As you get into the faster tape technology and the larger tape libraries, the cost of fully populating a library is substantial.

Expansion of tape library

When investigating tape libraries, you should ask whether the tape library is expandable, and if so, how this is accomplished. Some tape libraries can be daisy-chained together to expand, while others have special tape-only expansion cabinets. You may find that the amount of data you would like to store online in the library is growing, and that more tape cartridges in the library would be desirable, not more tape drives. Get a photograph to see how the expansion units are added to the tape library, so that, if possible, you can position the tape library in a location where you can add on without moving the original library cabinet.

Physical dimensions of tape library

For planning purposes, you will need to know the library's overall dimensions. This is obvious, but don't forget it! Also, if the library has an expansion unit, get those dimensions, too.

Rack mount support

Depending on the size of your site and the configuration of your data center, you may prefer to get a rack-mountable tape library. They are often available as an option. Note that these types of units are on the small side, due to the physical limitation of the rack.

Circuit boards

Finding out how many circuit boards are part of the tape library is an interesting bit of information. There will always be a circuit board on each tape drive, and usually one on the robotic arm. However, there will be others scattered throughout the library. After the tape drives and the robotic arm, the next part that can fail is the circuit board. They don't fail often, but where they are located and how many there are will determine how long the replacement process will take. Finding out this information may not necessarily make or break the decision about vendor, but it is good information to know.

Firmware upgrades

Firmware upgrades do happen often; you should know the steps involved with performing an upgrade. There are two different firmware upgrades in a tape library: tape drive firmware upgrades and tape library firmware upgrades.

Tape drive upgrades are generally done by creating a special tape or receiving one from the vendor and placing the tape in the tape drive. The basic process is the same for all tape technology that has this capability.

The tape library firmware is different depending on the library manufacturer. This upgrade might or might not require a site visit from the vendor. Generally, the process requires a PC hooked up to a serial port on the library or a new floppy diskette that you use when you reboot the library. In any case, you should find out how this process is accomplished.

Reliability of tape library

There are separate reliability statistics associated with the tape library. The individual tape drives and tape cartridges within the library have their reliability statistics, but that is not the same as the library or robotic arm's reliability.

SNMP support

Any hardware or software can have built-in support for the Simple Network Management Protocol (SNMP). If your site has SNMP management software, or you are planning on implementing it in the future, you should ask the library vendor if they can integrate it into your environment. SNMP allows the hardware or software to send traps or be queried (this requires an SNMP MIB) by a management computer. The management computer would have an application running that is configured to take the appropriate steps based on the information received from the tape library.

Diagnostic support

In addition to the SNMP, or sometimes instead of the SNMP, the tape library will have some sort of diagnostics. This support is commonly accessed through the front panel of the tape library. The diagnostics can sometimes be accessed through a serial port connection to the jukebox via a PC. Information on tape drive problems or robotic arm problems is commonly available. You should specifically ask the tape library vendor what troubleshooting information can be obtained and if all the steps involved with using the diagnostics are thoroughly documented.

Year initially introduced

It is important to know how long the tape library has been manufactured and sold. With any product, the longer it has been available to the industry, the more time the vendor has had to work out any kinks. However, the older it is, the more likely it is close to being obsolete. Once you have narrowed your search to two or three different tape library vendors, go ahead and sign a non-disclosure agreement with them to find out what their plans are for newer technology in the near future (the next six months) and the long-term future (the next 18 months). Ask the vendor how they intend to migrate customers to the new technology. You should consider a clause in your contract with the vendor that states this upgrade path will be taken when the technology is available. You will pay for this upgrade, but then you are guaranteed state-of-the-art tape library technology when available.

Customer support availability

As with the backup software, it is important to be able to receive help with your tape library at any time of the day or night and on weekends. Backups run during these times, and you need to be able to reach technical support for the tape library during these times. You should also ask the vendor how they handle onsite support during these hours. See if the vendor has local field engineers or contracts with other companies that have local support. You also need to know the availability of parts in the vicinity of your site. If you are in a large metropolitan area, there should be local parts available. If not, you should know where the closest location is that does have parts for the tape library you are considering. Most of the time, for an added cost, the vendor will allow you to have parts at your site for a field engineer to use in the case of an emergency. Check into this information well before the crisis actually occurs.

Number of installed sites

The popularity of a tape library will reflect how heavily it is used. The more the product is used, the more issues and concerns will be uncovered.

References

See who the vendor can recommend as a reference for the hardware you are considering. The other site should be a site of comparable size as your own. If possible, the other site should also be using the same backup software that you are planning on using. The more closely aligned the reference is to your site, the better the reference. Call or visit the reference site without the software or hardware vendors, so that you get the complete picture without the reference site feeling pressured by the vendors.

Calculating Tape Library Capacity

Calculating the tape library capacity is the process of determining how many gigabytes or terabytes you need in your tape library to fit your site's requirements. There are three decisions you must make before you can calculate the library requirements:

- How many weeks' worth of data do you intend to have available in the tape library online at all times?

- What backup schedule you will be implementing at your site?

- What is the total amount of data to be backed up at your site for your workstations and servers (see Chapter 4, *Requirements Definition*)?

Once you have the answers for these questions, the equation to determine the total library capacity is as follows:

$$library\_capacity = num\_weeks\_online \times total\_week\_backups$$

The variable *num_weeks_online* is the total number of weeks for which you wish to have data accessible within the tape library. Most restores are going to be fairly recent, for instance, in the past few weeks. As time goes by, the requests for older restores go down. You must also check with your legal and compliance departments to see if there are any legal reasons why the backup tapes should not be kept in the tape library for long periods of time.* Based on experience, I would recommend a minimum of four weeks, if there are no contrary legal or compliance reasons and if you can afford a tape library large enough.

The variable *total_week_backups* is the sum of data that you anticipate you will back up in a one-week period. This will be very different for each site and is dependent on how much data you back up and on which backup schedule you choose to implement. Following are a few examples based on schedule types to help you calculate the *total_week_backups* variable. If your site doesn't match a schedule listed, you need to extrapolate from the examples to calculate how much data you will be backing up in a one-week period.

Full daily

For this schedule, you will perform full backups every day of the week. Calculate the variable *total_week_backups* as follows:

$$total\_week\_backups = 7 \times total\_full\_backups$$

where the new variable is defined as the following:

$$total\_full\_backups = total\_workstation\_data + total\_server\_data$$

---

* There may be legal or compliance reasons that the tapes have to be offsite in an alternative location in a short period of time. This may be to protect the data in the event of a disaster or because of regulatory requirements.

The variables *total_workstation_data* and *total_server_data* are calculated as described in Chapter 4.

Full three times weekly

For this schedule, you will perform full backups three times a week. This may be enough at smaller sites or at sites where data is not changing drastically on a daily basis. Calculate the variable *total_week_backups* as follows:

```
total_week_backups = 3 × total_full_backups
```

where the new variable is defined as the following:

```
total_full_backups = total_workstation_data + total_server_data
```

The variables *total_workstation_data* and *total_server_data* are calculated as described in Chapter 4.

Full weekly/differential daily

For this schedule, once a week, a full backup is done (maybe on weekends, maybe on weekdays) and between full backups (the other six days a week), a differential backup is performed. Calculate the variable *total_week_backups* as follows:

```
total_week_backups = total_full_backups + total_diff_backups
```

where the new variables are defined as follows:

```
total_full_backups = total_workstation_data + total_server_data
total_diff_backups = total_full_backups × .15
```

The variables *total_workstation_data* and *total_server_data* are calculated as described in Chapter 4.

Assume that the backup schedule will be one differential backup and one day of full backups. With this type of schedule, every differential backs up the data that was changed since the previous full backup.

Assume that the amount of data backed up with differential backups is approximately 15% of the full backups (this may vary at some sites, but it is a starting point).

Full weekly/incremental daily

For this schedule, once a week, a full backup is done (maybe on weekends, maybe on weekdays), and between full backups (the other six days a week), an incremental backup is performed. Calculate the variable *total_week_backups* as follows:

```
total_week_backups = total_full_backups + total_incr_backups
```

where the new variables are defined as the following:

```
total_full_backups = total_workstation_data + total_server_data
total_incr_backups = 6 × (tot_full_backups × .10)
```

The variables *total_workstatation_data* and *total_server_data* are calculated as described in Chapter 4.

Assume that the backup schedule will be six days of incremental backups and one day of full backups. With this type of schedule, every incremental backs up the data that was changed since the previous incremental *or* full backup.

Assume that the amount of data backed up with incremental backups is approximately 10% of the full backups (this may vary at some sites, but it is a starting point). You many note that this value is close to the percentage used for differential backups. That is because the data that changes from day to day is generally the same data. People will work on the same document, spreadsheet, or program today as they did yesterday. Once a file has changed since the last backup, it is backed up with the eincremental.

Finding the Right Tape Library

Most vendors will provide a total capacity rating for their tape libraries. You can compare your calculated value against this value, but it is important to know whether the vendor is basing the capacity on compressed or uncompressed data on the tapes.

For planning purposes, you should *not* plan based on the compressed capacity of the library capacity. By using the uncompressed capacity, you have a built-in fudge factor to account for the following:

- How your data compresses depends on the type of data you are backing up. Some data compresses more than other data. For example, binary files may compress at a 1.5 to 1 ratio, image data (like from the Microsoft Paint program) may compress at a 4.5 to 1 ratio, and already compressed data or encrypted data may not compress at all.

- There must be a number of blank tapes in your tape library at all times. These add a little bit of overhead to the total number of tapes that you must have at any one time.

- Many backup software packages allow you to configure different tape groups or pools within the library. You may choose to have a tape pool separate for all email data that expires weekly versus the rest of the backup data that expires after one or two years.*

Therefore, to be conservative and to allow yourself plenty of room to configure the library as you please, you should use the uncompressed library capacity value. Remember that you will never have less data. Using the uncompressed

---

* Your legal department may feel that the email data is more susceptible to a subpoena than other data. Therefore, they may choose to remove the data quickly so that it is unavailable for a court to subpoena. The penalty charge for not having the data is much smaller than the cost of defending the company in a court battle with the data.

total capacity value for planning means only that you have plenty of room for growth.

If you feel uncomfortable using the uncompressed capacity value, then compromise and use a compression ratio of 1.5:1, not 2:1. For example, if you are considering using DLT 4000 tapes (20 GB uncompressed tape capacity) in a library that holds 50 tapes:

- Total uncompressed library capacity is 1 TB

- Total compressed library capacity as stated by vendor (2:1) is 2 TB

- Total compressed library capacity (1.5:1) is 1.5 TB

So if you have calculated your total library requirement in the previous section to be between 1 TB and 1.5 TB, the library in the example would fit your needs.

Calculating Library Capacity Example

Say that your company, Genorff Engineering Inc. (GEI), has determined that they are going to purchase a tape library and need to know what size library is required. GEI has made three decisions:

- They have decided to have a total of five weeks of data online for the users' and administrator's restores.

- They have decided to implement a backup schedule with differential backups Monday through Friday and a full backup on Saturday. Since no one works on the weekends at GEI, it was assumed that no backups on Sunday would be necessary.

- Their total server and workstation data to back up is 80 GB.

With this information, you calculate their library requirements as follows:

```
library_capacity = num_weeks_online × total_week_backups
  num_weeks_online = 5
total_week_backups = total_full_backups + total_diff_backups = 140 GB
total_full_backups = 80 GB
total_diff_backups = 5 × (80 GB × .15) = 5 × 12 GB = 60 GB
  library_capacity = 5 × 140 GB = 700 GB
```

Based on the calculation, GEI should look into purchasing any tape library that can store at least 700 GB of uncompressed data.

Library Capacity Quick Reference Matrix

For your server sizing, a quick reference matrices is provided in Table 9-5. Down the right side of the matrix, choose the value that most closely matches the total amount of vital data that has to be backed up at your site in a one-week period.

This is the sum of *total_diff_backups* and *total_full_backups* variables. Then, select from the top of the table the number of weeks for which you would like to have the data available in the tape library for restores, and you can quickly see the total number of GB or TB your library must be able to hold to meet your requirements. The table below covers only 12 weeks of data in the tape library, but it can be a longer time frame, depending on your site dependencies.

Remember, this is the data that is in just the tape library. As you need to rotate new tapes into the tape library, the tapes that are taken out can be stored in tape racks near your tape library or possibly moved to a warehouse offsite. The life span of the tapes removed from the tape library should be managed as a separate issue. Just because tapes are removed from the library doesn't mean they cannot be used for restores. They can be put back into the library as necessary. Since the majority of the restores are for data that was most recently backed up (within the past two to three weeks), the tapes in the library should cover those restore requests.

Design Tips

There are some details you should not overlook as you prepare to purchase the hardware for your backup implementation. The tips in this section start with the backup server and extend to the tape drives and tape library. If you are implementing networked backups, you should definitely read this section. If you are implementing local backups with a very large system, you should also read this section.

Backup Server Design Tips

The backup server hardware is a very important consideration. The larger your site, the more concerned you should be with your backup server's performance. With lots of clients to back up or lots of data on your backup clients, you will become increasingly concerned with limited time to perform backups. Backups are generally performed when the computers are not being used, and this window of time does not change. You may get more and more computers or more and more data to back up, but your backup window will probably remain constant. Your backup server plays an important role in performance and throughput.

The backup server(s) could become the most powerful system(s) at your site. These systems are handling all of the critical data for your firm. Generally, critical data is spread across many systems within your company, but with networked backups, you are backing up all of that critical data to a few backup servers. Therefore, do not skimp on the backup server hardware. If you are on a limited budget, make sure that the system you initially install can grow with your needs.

That way, as the money becomes available, you can upgrade. For example, if you think you should purchase a two-CPU server, consider purchasing a chassis that can handle up to four CPUs and initially populate it with two CPUs.

The backup server(s) will be used in a manner different from that of most other computers. All components (the network, memory, tape devices, disks, and CPU) are heavily used for a sustained amount of time. There are really no other systems that use all these components for hours—and sometimes days—on end. There are other types of systems that use some of the components heavily, but not all components. For example, a web server or file server uses the network, disk, and memory heavily. A data entry system uses the disk and memory heavily. A calculation engine or development server uses the memory and CPU heavily. However, a networked backup server is unique because of the stress applied to all aspects of the hardware and the length of time for which this stress is applied. I used to test new releases of operating systems on the test backup server, because if the backups worked, chances were that the operating system was stable enough to release to the rest of our company. The backup server's hardware and software exercise a large part of your overall computer system, and the use is constant.

Table 9-6 provides information on how the backup server uses each of the system's components and provides some recommendations for your backup server design. As you can tell from the information in Table 9-6, network backups are quite extensive. Any of the backup server components can become the bottleneck and negatively affect the performance of your backups. You may be wondering why the backup client components were not mentioned. Yes, it is true that the backup client can become the bottleneck and affect the overall backup server performance. As a matter of fact, each of the components listed previously (except the tape drive component) could become a bottleneck on the backup clients. You could optimize the backup server, then go to every backup client and optimize the backup clients so that the entire environment is just perfect. However, as your site grows into hundreds or thousands of backup clients, it becomes ineffective and too costly to optimize every backup client.

So, if optimizing every backup client is not a scalable approach to gaining the optimum performance in your backup implementation, how do you gain the best performance? Once you've optimized the hardware, the implementation and configuration of the software on your backup server must be tuned. You can purchase software that allows you to have multiple backup clients write to a tape device at the same time. If multiple backup clients are writing to one tape device, then the backup server can keep data streaming to tape. When the backup server senses one client is not sending data, it turns to another client. Another answer may be to back up from backup clients that are located on different network segments at the same time, as opposed to backing up the clients on one network segment and then moving to another segment. This type of tuning of the backup server's configuration will allow your backup server to be most effective, without having to go to every backup client for tuning. Basically, you leave the backup clients the way they are and configure the backup server to keep moving the data from the network to the tape drives. During this configuration, your best bet is to use monitoring software to find the bottlenecks on the backup server and try to alleviate those bottlenecks.

SCSI Tape Drive Design Tips

Considering in advance how you will connect the SCSI tape drives to your backup server during the hardware planning process will save you pain, time, and effort later during the maintenance phase of your backup project. Once you choose a tape configuration option, remember to verify that the computer you are choosing can support the number of SCSI controller boards you have decided to use. You may need to make adjustments to the system you are using for your backup server.

When configuring SCSI devices, there are two basic SCSI bus rules you must follow:

- There must be a device with a terminator at the end of each bus.
- Each device on the SCSI bus must be set to a different and unique identification number.

The number of SCSI devices supported on a SCSI bus is dependent on the type of SCSI used (see Appendix B, *SCSI Fundamentals*). To fully utilize the SCSI bus, you may choose to put multiple SCSI tape devices on a single SCSI bus. However, before making that decision, you should consider the advantages and disadvantages.

When configuring the tape drives, you have multiple options. It is important to consider your site's requirements before deciding on a configuration for your SCSI tape drives. If your backups require a large backup window, you have lots of restore requirements, or you cannot take the time to have your backup server's tape drives inaccessible, then I recommend that you put each tape drive on a separate SCSI controller. Spend the extra money to allow for more flexible maintenance options. For some sites, paying for the additional SCSI controller boards and SCSI terminators is more acceptable than having tape drives inaccessible at unpredictable times.

For example, let's say you are going to use three SCSI tape devices on your backup server. You can connect these three tape drives in three different ways (assume the same tape drives are used for all three options), as shown in Figure 9-1.

Option 1

The first option, shown in Figure 9-1, is to connect all three drives to one SCSI bus.

Advantage

This option is the least expensive of the three. The amount of hardware required is minimal. You would buy one SCSI controller card for your computer, three tape drives, three SCSI cables, and one terminator.

Disadvantages

One disadvantage is realized when a tape drive has to be replaced or serviced. Since the tape drives are on a SCSI bus that must be terminated to function properly, when one tape drive is removed, all tape drives become inaccessible. Therefore, you cannot replace a tape drive when a different tape drive is required for backups or a restore. Another disadvantage is that the SCSI bus could become the bottleneck on your backup server.

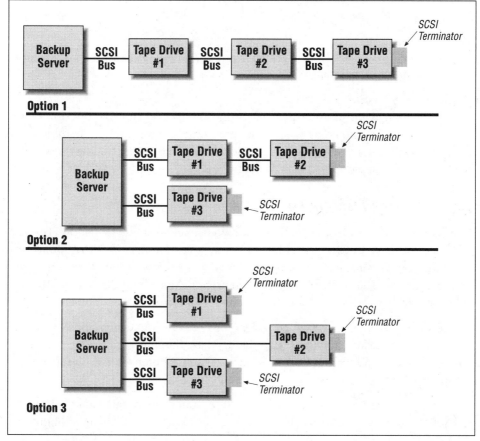

Figure 9-1. SCSI tape drive configurations for backups

Option 2

The second option, shown in Figure 9-1, is to connect two drives to one SCSI bus and the third drive to a second SCSI bus. Basically, it is a hybrid of the other two options.

Advantages

> This option is less expensive than the third option. You would buy two SCSI controller cards for your computer, three tape drives, three SCSI cables, and two terminators. Another advantage is that if tape drive #3 is replaced, no other tape drive is affected.

Disadvantages

> This option is more expensive than the first option. Also, if tape drive #1 or #2 has to be replaced, the other drive becomes inaccessible.

Option 3

The third option, shown in Figure 9-1, is to connect all three drives to different SCSI buses.

Advantage

> Any drive can be replaced without rendering the other drives inaccessible. This is the most flexible option for maintenance.

Disadvantages

> This option is the most expensive of the three. You have to buy three SCSI controller cards for your computer, three tape drives, three SCSI cables, and three terminators. You also have to make sure your backup server has enough slots to support the SCSI controllers.

Tape Library Design Tips

You may decide to use a tape library for your backup implementation. The section "Tape Library Hardware" earlier in this chapter provides a list of library features for you to consider. However, in addition to the features, there are design tips to consider. This section covers different items that should be taken into consideration and provides tips for configuring tape libraries.

The previous section covered considerations when connecting individual tape drives to your backup server. A tape library has different configuration issues to consider, which are covered in this section. These differences are due to the following reasons:

- The library has a robotic arm. There are connections and cabling from the robotic arm inside the tape library to the outside chassis of the tape library.

- You do not connect the backup server directly to the back of the tape drives, but instead, you make the connection to the back of the library. Then there are connections and cabling from the outside chassis of the tape library to the back of the tape drives.

Tape library tip #1

The robotic arm within the tape library is generally a SCSI device. All of the commands, such as to load or eject a tape, are sent from the computer system to the robotic arm over the SCSI bus. Especially for larger sites, you should design your backup server and tape library with the robotic arm on a separate SCSI controller from the tape drives for the following reasons:

Performance

The robotic arm should be on a separate SCSI controller so that it can operate independently of the tape drives. You do not want the robotic arm commands to compete with the data being sent to a tape drive. If the arm and the drives are on the SCSI bus, one or the other would get a higher priority, and that is not desirable.

Flexibility

If the robotic arm is on its own SCSI controller, you have the option of changing or fixing the robotic arm without affecting the tape drives.

Tape library tip #2

When purchasing your tape library, ask the vendors how the internal SCSI cables are configured inside their jukebox. This question is important for the following two reasons:

- The library has a SCSI robotic arm. This is an additional SCSI device to consider besides the tape drives.

- The library's internal cabling cannot be seen from the outside of the library. You see only the external SCSI bus connection.

Every tape library vendor has a different approach when connecting the internal cables to the tape drives and the robotic arm. Before purchasing a tape library, you should know how the internal cabling is configured for the tape drives and the robotic arm. You should also find out whether the internal cabling can be changed to suit your configuration requirements.

For example, say you are purchasing a tape library with three tape drives. There are many different ways to connect the three SCSI tape drives and the SCSI robotic arm. Four of these options are illustrated in Figure 9-2. The rule of thumb should be that if the vendor supports the configuration and your backup server

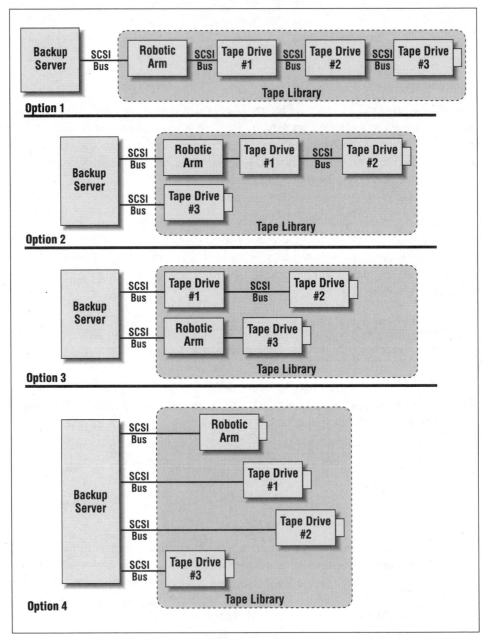

Figure 9-2. Tape library SCSI tape drive and robotic arm configurations for backups

can support the SCSI controllers, implement Option 4. You will have the flexibility of having each SCSI device on its own SCSI bus.

While shopping for a tape library vendor, you should ask them how their internal SCSI cabling is configured. The answer to that question will be one of the following configurations:

- Their internal cabling matches that illustrated in Option 4. In this case, you can consider the vendor as a possible candidate for your site.

- Their internal cabling cannot be changed and is configured like one of the other options (not Option 4). In this case, you can eliminate that vendor from consideration for your site.

- Their internal cabling can be changed to suit your site's needs. In this case, draw the vendor a diagram of exactly what you need. Have the vendor's salesperson commit to that configuration in writing. That way, if you do choose that vendor, when you receive the jukebox from the manufacturer you have some written proof of your agreement in case a mistake is made.

The internal SCSI cabling in the library between the tape drives may or may not be flexible enough to fit the SCSI configuration you want to implement. How a tape library is designed dictates what options you have with respect to the SCSI tape drive and robotic arm configuration. Therefore, when choosing a tape library (also see the earlier section "Tape Library Hardware"), you must know how you intend to connect the drives and the robotic arm in the library. Then you can ask the tape library vendor the right questions and make the appropriate library choice.

Tape library tip #3

When using a parallel SCSI bus in your backup implementation it is important to remember that the maximum of 3 or 25 meters imposed when using either the single-ended or differential parallel SCSI alternative does not refer just to external SCSI cabling. This is a total of 3 or 25 meters of cabling both inside the chassis that houses the SCSI device and outside the SCSI chassis. This is a factor especially with tape libraries.

Ask the library vendor how much SCSI cable is internal to the jukebox. They may have substantial cabling inside the library for the tape devices itself. That internal cabling counts as part of the 3 or 25 meters and should not be ignored. When you exceed the maximum SCSI length, the devices do not just stop working. Excess SCSI bus lengths can result in some difficult and time consuming troubleshooting of problems that may not be obvious. The following are a few examples:

Excessive read or write errors
> You may suspect a bad head in a tape drive. After cleaning the drive head or completely replacing the drive the errors continue.

Slow tape devices

You may suspect performance problems. After investing lots of time and effort in troubleshooting and tuning your system, the tape drive is still slow.

SCSI errors

You may see SCSI time-out errors occurring on a regular basis. After troubleshooting, thinking it may be a tape device not ready or a drive that has gone bad, you still have the error messages.

So, for your backup project, don't go overboard with SCSI cable lengths (especially single-ended SCSI). Be conservative and use only the length you really need.

Tape library tip #4

When considering different tape library vendors, ask them specific questions about how different types of maintenance are performed. The different answers will amaze you and sometimes make your choice between like vendors easier. At a minimum, you should ask the following questions:

- How do you replace a tape drive, and how long is the average replacement time? Have the vendor take you through the exact steps required to replace a tape drive within the library. Have them provide a detailed explanation as though you are the maintenance person performing the task.

- How do you replace the robotic arm, and how long is the average replacement time? The robotic arm will not have to be replaced often, but it is nice to know the steps involved with this type of maintenance. Have the vendor take you through the exact steps required to replace the robotic arm within the library. Have them provide a detailed explanation as though you are the maintenance person performing the task.

- How is the firmware updated for the tape library, and how long does this task take? Does the vendor have to visit the site to perform firmware updates or can you do it yourself? If the vendor has to perform the updates, make sure that they can perform this maintenance task at an appropriate time to suit your site's needs.

- From the time you turn the tape library on, what is the minimum and maximum amount of time required before the tape library is ready and can be used and what is done during that time? The library has to perform some sort of inventory (and possibly other functions), and this will provide you with that information. If the tape library has to be turned off to perform some maintenance, you must take into consideration the time to perform that maintenance plus the time it takes for the library to become ready when calculating your total outage window.

The information you obtain from these questions will allow you to make a better vendor choice. Also, it will give you time estimates for maintenance functions that will need to be performed. You can use those time estimates to provide your users with more accurate time outage windows when you are performing any of these functions.

Table 9-1. Tape Drive Matrix Comparison

Tape Drive Type	Quarter Inch Cartridge (QIC)	4mm	8mm	Digital Linear Tape	Advanced Intelligent Tape (AIT)
Description	There are minicartridge tape drive and tape standards and data cartridge drive and tape standards. The QIC minicartridge tapes are 3.5 inches and the QIC data cartridge tapes are 5.25 inches. The data cartridge tapes support a higher density and an increased capacity in contrast to the minicartridges.	The 4mm technology is also referred to as DAT, and the terms are used interchangeably. The DDS-1 standard has the slowest tape drive throughput and the lowest capacity tapes; the DDS-3 standard has the fastest tape drive throughput for DAT tapes and the highest tape capacity.	The Mammoth drive uses the AME tape media technology, and the other 8mm tape drives use the MP tape media technology. The Mammoth drive is designed to read the MP tapes, but the heads must be cleaned before the AME tapes can be used again.	There are multiple Digital Linear Tape models each with the same physical drive and tape size, but increased data transfer rates and tape capacities. The Digital Linear Tape drives are backward-compatible for both reading and writing.	The AIT incorporates a new recording format. This makes the AIT format incompatible with any other 8mm data cartridges, even though it uses the same AME media and the helical scan recording method.
Distinctive Feature	The QIC technology uses MP tape media and when the tape is placed in the drive, it requires an automatic retensioning of tape before reliable read/write operations can occur and then records data in a linear serpentine manner.	All 4mm drives use the helical scan technique for recording and the MP tape media.	The 8mm drives are designed to use the helical scan technology (like the 4mm technology).	The Digital Linear Tape drives are designed to use the leader-type tape technology. A leader tab on the tapes is mechanically grabbed by the tape drive and the tape is threaded through a path that puts the tape in contact with the stationary read/write heads. The Digital Linear Tape drive models before the DLT-7000 write to tape using normal linear serpentine tracks. The DLT-7000 writes to tape using the SPR linear serpentine tracks.	The tape drive supports Memory In Cassette (MIC), a 16-kilobit flash memory chip built into the tape cartridge and it stores the tape's data structure, history, and other tunable information. The physical media does not have to be read to acquire this information. By using the MIC, the data access time is reduced, the data handling is improved, and, therefore, there is less wear on the AIT tape drive and tapes.
Advantage	Inexpensive	Cost-effective, well-established technology	Cost-effective, well-established technology	100% duty cycle, high reliability, high capacity	High reliability, high capacity

Table 9-1. Tape Drive Matrix Comparison (continued)

Tape Drive Type	Quarter Inch Cartridge (QIC)	4mm	8mm	Digital Linear Tape	Advanced Intelligent Tape (AIT)
Disadvantage	Slow, low tape capacity	Slow, low tape capacity, 20% duty cycle (4.8 hours/day)	10% duty cycle (2.4 hours/day)	Expensive	One source for drives/media
Interface	IDE or SCSI	SCSI	SCSI	SCSI	SCSI
Recommended Use	The QIC technology is low end, low speed, and low capacity. It is best suited for individual workstations.	The 4mm technology is low end, low speed, and low capacity. It is best suited for individual workstations or very small workgroups.	The 8mm technology is in the midrange performance and capacity category. It is generally best suited for small or medium networked backup sites. Sometimes suited for large sites with multiple backup server.	The DLT technology is high end, high speed, and high capacity. It is best suited for medium or large networked backup sites.	The AIT technology is high end, high speed, and high capacity. It is best suited for medium or large network backup sites that are interested in a future based product.

Table 9-2. Recording Capability

Tape Drive	Tape Capacity		Data Transfer Rate, Sustained	
	Without Compression	With Compression[a]	Without Compression	With Compression[a]
QIC-3010 Mini Cartridge	340 MB to 2.2 GB	680 MB to 4.4 GB	79 KB/s	158 MB/s
QIC-3020 Mini Cartridge	680 MB to 1.7 GB	1.4 GB to 3.4 GB	158 KB/s	317 KB/s
QIC-3040 Mini Cartridge	840 MB to 3.2 GB	1.7 GB to 6.4 GB	150 KB/s	300 KB/s
QIC-3095 Mini Cartridge	2 GB to 5 GB	4 GB to 10 GB	250 KB/s to 750 KB/s	500 KB/s to 1.5 MB/s
QIC-3210 Mini Cartridge	2.3 GB to 5.7 GB	4.6 GB to 11.4 GB	100 KB/s	200 KB/s
QIC-1000 Data Cartridge	1.2 GB	2.4 GB	150 KB/s	300 KB/s
QIC-2GB Data Cartridge	2.5 GB	5 GB	300 KB/s	600 KB/s
QIC-4GB Data Cartridge	4 GB	8 GB	185 KB/s	370 KB/s

Table 9-2. Recording Capability (continued)

Tape Drive	Tape Capacity Without Compression	With Compression[a]	Data Transfer Rate, Sustained Without Compression	With Compression[a]
QIC-5010 Data Cartridge	13 GB	26 GB	750 KB/s	1.5 MB/s
4mm, DDS-1	1.3 GB	no compression	183 to 400 KB/s	no compression
4mm, DDS-DC	2 GB	4 GB	183 to 400 KB/s	366 to 800 KB/s
4mm, DDS-2	4 GB	8 GB	366 to 800 KB/s	732 to 1024 KB/s
4mm, DDS-3	12 GB	24 GB	800 KB/s to 1.6 MB/s	1.6 to 3.2 MB/s
8mm, Exabyte 8205XL	3.5 GB	7 GB	256 KB/s	500 KB/s
8mm, Exabyte 8700	7 GB	14 GB	500 KB/s	1 MB/s
8mm, Exabyte 8700LT	5 GB	10 GB	500 KB/s	1 MB/s
8mm, Exabyte 8900 Mammoth	20 GB	40 GB	3 MB/s	6 MB/s
DLT 2000XT	15 GB	30 GB	1.25 MB/s	2.5 MB/s
DLT 4000	20 GB	40 GB	1.5 MB/s	3 MB/s
DLT 7000	35 GB	70 GB	5 MB/s	10 MB/s
AIT	25 GB	50 GB	3 MB/s	6 MB/s

[a] Assuming a 2:1 compression ratio (compression will vary depending on the data at your site).

Table 9-3. Reliability and Maintenance Factors

Tape Drive	Mean Time Between Failures[a]	Cleaning Frequency	Additional Cleaning Notes
QIC	80,000 to 250,000 hours at a 10% duty cycle[b]	Vendor-specific.	Vendor-specific.
4mm, DDS-1 4mm, DDS- DC	60,000 to 200,000 hours at a 20% duty cycle[b]	For 4mm, clean tape drive every 8 to 10 hours of data transfer or after each initial pass with a new tape cartridge.	If the 4mm tape drive's green LED is slowly flashing green, you should clean the tape drive.[c] If cleaning does not eliminate the flashing LED you may have a bad tape or one at the end of its life.
4mm, DDS-2 4mm, DDS-3	180,000 to 200,000 hours at a 20% duty cycle[b]		

Table 9-3. Reliability and Maintenance Factors (continued)

Tape Drive	Mean Time Between Failures[a]	Cleaning Frequency	Additional Cleaning Notes
8mm, Exabyte 8205XL 8mm, Exabyte 8700 8mm, Exabyte 8700LT	160,000 hours at a 10% duty cycle	For 8mm, clean the tape head and tape path every 30 hours of data transfer OR once a month.	Clean the 8mm tape drive if you receive excessive read or write errors. In extremely high use situations, clean the tape drive daily.[c]
8mm, Exabyte 8900 Mammoth	250,000 hours at a 10% duty cycle		
DLT 2000XT DLT 4000	80,000 hours	For DLT, no periodic cleaning or maintenance is required.	The DLT tape drive should be cleaned only if the tape drive's cleaning tape light is on or if you receive excessive read or write errors. Overcleaning DLT tape drives will reduce head life.
DLT 7000	200,000 hours		
AIT	200,000 hours at a 10% duty cycle	For AIT, no periodic cleaning or maintenance is required.	The AIT tape drive monitors output to check for possible problems and will request the built-in Active Head Cleaner when appropriate.

a The MTBF is not a literal number of hours; rather, these figures are provided for comparison between products only (i.e., 200,000 hours is equal to twice 100,000 hours, but is not a literal measurement).
b This value is manufacturer-dependent.
c Do not use data or cleaning tape cartridges designed for audio DAT or 8mm machines; you must use data quality DAT and 8mm tapes.

Table 9-4. Pricing[a]

Tape Drive Model	New Tape Drive Price per Drive[b]	Media[c] Cartridge Type	Uncompressed Capacity	Price	Cleaning Tapes # of Passes	Price
QIC-3010 Mini Cartridge	$125 to $150	QIC-165	2.2 GB	$31	10	$35
QIC-3020 Mini Cartridge	$150 to $250	QIC-165	1.7 GB	$33		
QIC-3040 Mini Cartridge	$250 to $350	QIC-148	1 GB	$23		
QIC-3095 Mini Cartridge	$250 to $350	QIC-164	4 GB	$24		
QIC-3210 Mini Cartridge	$250 to $350	QIC-163	2.3 GB	$28		

Table 9-4. Pricing[a] (continued)

Tape Drive Model	New Tape Drive Price per Drive[b]	Media[c] Cartridge Type	Uncompressed Capacity	Price	Cleaning Tapes # of Passes	Price
QIC-1000 Data Cartridge	$700	QIC-136	1.2 GB	$25	10	$45
QIC-2GB Data Cartridge	$830	QIC-136	2.5 GB	$30		
QIC-4GB Data Cartridge	$850	QIC-136	4 GB	$33		
QIC-5010 Data Cartridge	$2250	QIC-139	13 GB	$45		
4mm, DDS-1	$500 to $630	60 meters	1.3 GB	$6	40	$13
4mm, DDS- DC	$530 to $760	90 meters	2 GB	$9	50	$15
4mm, DDS-2	$645 to $930	120 meters	4 GB	$16		
4mm, DDS-3	$1000 to $1280	125 meters	12 GB	$38		
8mm, Exabyte 8205XL	$1200	54 meters	1.2 GB	$7	12	$14
8mm, Exabyte 8700	$1,200 to $1,500	112 meters	2.5 GB	$13	18	$18
8mm, Exabyte 8700LT	$1,500 to $2,000	160 meters	7 GB	$17	20	$20
8mm, Exabyte 8900 Mammoth	$3,500 to $4,000	160 meters	20 GB	$90	12, 18	$19, $24
DLT 2000XT	$2,400	DLT IIIXT	10 GB	$41	20	$48
DLT 4000	$3,400 to $4000	DLT IV	20 GB	$47		
DLT 7000	$8,000	DLT IV	35 GB	$100		
AIT	$5,000	AIT	25 GB	$90		

[a] All prices in this table are dependent upon vendor, manufacturer, and quantity.
[b] These prices will vary greatly. For example, differential SCSI is more expensive than single-ended SCSI and external drives are more expensive than internal drives.
[c] You should *not* use video or audio tapes for backups.

Table 9-5. Library Capacity Sizing Matrix

Total Amount of Data Backed up Per Week	Number of Weeks Data Stays in Library											
	1 Week	2 Weeks	3 Weeks	4 Weeks	5 Weeks	6 Weeks	7 Weeks	8 Weeks	9 Weeks	10 Weeks	11 Weeks	12 Weeks
5 GB	5 GB	10 GB	15 GB	20 GB	25 GB	30 GB	35 GB	40 GB	45 GB	50 GB	55 GB	60 GB
10 GB	10 GB	20 GB	30 GB	40 GB	50 GB	60 GB	70 GB	80 GB	90 GB	100 GB	110 GB	130 GB
15 GB	15 GB	30 GB	45 GB	60 GB	75 GB	90 GB	105 GB	120 GB	135 GB	150 GB	165 GB	180 GB
20 GB	20 GB	40 GB	60 GB	80 GB	100 GB	120 GB	140 GB	160 GB	180 GB	200 GB	220 GB	240 GB
25 GB	25 GB	50 GB	75 GB	100 GB	125 GB	150 GB	175 GB	200 GB	225 GB	250 GB	275 GB	300 GB
30 GB	30 GB	60 GB	90 GB	120 GB	150 GB	180 GB	210 GB	240 GB	270 GB	300 GB	330 GB	360 GB
35 GB	35 GB	70 GB	105 GB	140 GB	175 GB	210 GB	245 GB	280 GB	315 GB	350 GB	385 GB	420 GB
40 GB	40 GB	80 GB	120 GB	160 GB	200 GB	240 GB	280 GB	320 GB	360 GB	400 GB	440 GB	480 GB
45 GB	45 GB	90 GB	135 GB	180 GB	225 GB	270 GB	315 GB	360 GB	405 GB	450 GB	495 GB	540 GB
50 GB	50 GB	100 GB	150 GB	200 GB	250 GB	300 GB	350 GB	400 GB	450 GB	500 GB	550 GB	600 GB
55 GB	55 GB	110 GB	165 GB	220 GB	275 GB	330 GB	385 GB	440 GB	495 GB	550 GB	605 GB	660 GB
60 GB	60 GB	120 GB	180 GB	240 GB	300 GB	360 GB	420 GB	480 GB	540 GB	600 GB	660 GB	720 GB
65 GB	65 GB	130 GB	195 GB	260 GB	325 GB	390 GB	455 GB	520 GB	585 GB	650 GB	715 GB	780 GB
70 GB	70 GB	140 GB	210 GB	280 GB	350 GB	420 GB	490 GB	560 GB	630 GB	700 GB	770 GB	840 GB
75 GB	75 GB	150 GB	225 GB	300 GB	375 GB	450 GB	525 GB	600 GB	675 GB	750 GB	825 GB	900 GB
80 GB	80 GB	160 GB	240 GB	320 GB	400 GB	480 GB	560 GB	640 GB	720 GB	800 GB	880 GB	960 GB
85 GB	85 GB	170 GB	255 GB	340 GB	425 GB	510 GB	595 GB	680 GB	765 GB	850 GB	935 GB	1.02 TB
90 GB	90 GB	180 GB	270 GB	360 GB	450 GB	540 GB	630 GB	720 GB	810 GB	900 GB	990 GB	1.08 TB
95 GB	95 GB	190 GB	285 GB	380 GB	475 GB	570 GB	665 GB	760 GB	855 GB	950 GB	1.05 TB	1.14 TB
100 GB	100 GB	200 GB	300 GB	400 GB	500 GB	600 GB	700 GB	800 GB	900 GB	1 TB	1.1 TB	1.2 TB
110 GB	110 GB	220 GB	330 GB	440 GB	550 GB	660 GB	770 GB	880 GB	990 GB	1.1 TB	1.21 TB	1.32 TB
120 GB	120 GB	240 GB	360 GB	480 GB	600 GB	720 GB	840 GB	960 GB	1.08 TB	1.2 TB	1.32 TB	1.44 TB

Table 9-5. Library Capacity Sizing Matrix (continued)

Total Amount of Data Backed up Per Week	Number of Weeks Data Stays in Library											
	1 Week	2 Weeks	3 Weeks	4 Weeks	5 Weeks	6 Weeks	7 Weeks	8 Weeks	9 Weeks	10 Weeks	11 Weeks	12 Weeks
130 GB	130 GB	260 GB	390 GB	520 GB	650 GB	780 GB	910 GB	1.04 TB	1.17 TB	1.3 TB	1.43 TB	1.56 TB
140 GB	140 GB	280 GB	420 GB	560 GB	700 GB	840 GB	980 GB	1.12 TB	1.26 TB	1.4 TB	1.54 TB	1.68 TB
150 GB	150 GB	300 GB	450 GB	600 GB	750 GB	900 GB	1.05 TB	1.2 TB	1.35 TB	1.5 TB	1.65 TB	1.8 TB
160 GB	160 GB	320 GB	480 GB	640 GB	800 GB	960 GB	1.1 TB	1.28 TB	1.44 TB	1.6 TB	1.76 TB	1.92 TB

Table 9-6. Backup Server Design Tips

System Component	Description	Design Tip
Network	The backup data will be coming from across the network, so the network board will be heavily used. Remember, the data packets will be coming in not only from the backup clients but from the backup server sending acknowledgments back to the clients to verify receipt of the data. When you are backing up only a few clients with one tape drive on the backup server, this may not constitute much network traffic. However, if your site is trying to back up hundreds of clients and you have multiple tape drives on the backup server, this traffic becomes substantial and prolonged.	You should use a PCI network board to take advantage of the faster mother board bus technology. Also, if you have a large site, make sure your backup server is on a 100 MB/s network segment or higher. With all the data coming over 10 MB/s from the backup clients, it is easy to see that so many clients driving 10 MB/s would overpower a backup server that was also on a 10 MB/s segment. The larger your site, the more this is amplified.
Memory	The memory in your backup server must be scalable. If your organization grows, your backup requirements will grow, and this growth may require more system memory to meet the backup window. Also, the memory requirements of the backup software may be higher than expected, causing the memory in the backup server to become a bottleneck.	For scalability, you should purchase dense memory SIMMS and leave room for more SIMMS within your server in case you need to use them. The denser SIMMS are more expensive, but are worth the flexibility of adding more memory at a later time if needed. Also, buy a server with a large memory capability.

Table 9-6. Backup Server Design Tips (continued)

System Component	Description	Design Tip
Tape Device	The majority of the data coming in from the network has to be written to tape. Even if you stage the backup data to disk initially and then later migrate it to tape, you are still using the tape devices heavily. Therefore, the interface(s) and connection(s) to the tape drive(s) will be heavily used. You can connect a tape drive to the Integrated Drive Electronics (IDE) controller[a] or a Small Computer System Interface (SCSI) controller.[b]	SCSI tape devices can obtain higher throughputs than the IDE tape drives; therefore the SCSI tape drives are more popular for backups. Purchase a PCI SCSI board. As with the network board, you want to take advantage of the increased performance you gain with the PCI mother board bus. At large sites, as a minimum, you should use the class of SCSI tape drives that operates at a minimum rated speed of 1.5 MB/s (see details in the following tape drive section). The slower drives are not adequate for the larger sites.
Disk	Every backup package must track what is being backed up and to what location. This information is tracked in some sort of a database(s). The database is the heart and soul of the backup server. As the data is written to tape from specific backup clients, that information must be written to the database on the hard disk, so that it can be restored at a later time. Without this information, you cannot restore the data from tape.	You should seriously consider storing your backup database(s) on RAID to provide fault tolerance. Also, any hard disks connected to your computer should be on a separate SCSI bus than the tape drives. The backup software continually makes database updates and queries as the backups or restores are occurring. It is important that this disk activity does not compete with the tape drive's writes and reads. They should be separated as a basic design strategy.
CPU	The CPU has to process a lot of information, causing backups to be CPU-intensive. The TCP/IP stack data has to be processed, the data from the backup clients has to be converted to the appropriate format for the tape device, and the information required for the backup database(s) has to be generated and written to disk. Therefore, the more CPU processing power you have available, the faster you can perform your backups.	Especially with large sites, make sure that your backup server has the capability to grow beyond a single CPU. The CPU is the real workhorse in the backup system.

[a] Sometimes the IDE controller is referred to as the floppy controller.
[b] Note that Windows NT does not support parallel tape devices and Extended IDE (EIDE) supports only hard disks and CD-ROM drives.

225

10

In this chapter:
- *Lab Testing*
- *Functionality Testing*
- *Catastrophic Data Loss Testing*
- *Tape Library Testing*
- *Performance Testing*

Testing

By the time you reach the stages discussed in this chapter, you have picked software and hardware that are possible candidates to fit your site's environment. You are probably pretty excited about the testing and are ready to have the backups running in production. Your manager is probably anxious too, and has been putting a little pressure on you. Whatever you do, push back a little bit on this pressure, and *do not skip the evaluation testing*, regardless of which backup model you are implementing.

Testing will take time, but you will learn more about your configuration than you will from reading this book or the literature provided by the vendors. You will better understand what is involved with installation and configuration and what has to be done in the event of an emergency situation (such as the loss of a hard drive). The steps involved with recovering data after a catastrophic loss are not always well defined, and the testing process allows you to perform, refine, and document these important steps. Inevitably, when you have a complete system failure, the users, your boss, and others will be hounding you on how the restore is proceeding and how long it will take. Having these answers ahead of time can make a stressful situation a little bit easier to handle.

During your testing phase, be as scientific and deliberate as possible. You need to be careful not to fall for a product just because the salesperson is nice and takes you to lunch. This may sound cynical, but always remember that you and your coworkers are ultimately the ones responsible for what is installed and for day-to-day operations. If you have problems with backups, invariably in the middle of the night or on weekends, the salesperson will most likely not be there for you. Distance yourself from your emotions, be objective as possible, and stick to the facts.

This chapter covers the testing that should be done in your environment. It includes some direction on how to perform the testing as well as some assumptions you should *not* make from the results of your testing.

Lab Testing

Your site may have a test lab. The vendors you are dealing with may also have test labs. There are advantages to using test labs, but you should be well aware of the disadvantages surrounding the use of test labs as well:

Advantage

Evaluating software and hardware products in test labs is very convenient. Generally, the systems in the lab are yours to do whatever you want with, and you can perform whatever testing you need to at any time.

Disadvantage

There are always going to be some differences between the test lab and your real production environment. These differences, no matter how small, can affect the test results. The more components (system or network) involved with the backups, the more likely differences are. Performing backups over the network inherently makes you depend on more components.

I recommend that you *not* use a test lab if you are implementing networked back-ups. You should use your production environment for the testing. The whole goal of testing is to evaluate and gain experience on the behavior of the software and hardware you are considering purchasing to determine the best products for your site. The results gained from a test lab may not be completely realistic due to the software or hardware differences between the lab and the production environment. Also, labs are usually much smaller than the real environment. Even though using your production environment for testing may mean that the testing (especially performance testing) has to be performed during off hours, you will collect realistic data and gain confidence that your backup implementation will behave as you predict once you are using it daily.

You are going to base your decision on the test results, and the more realistic the results, the more confidence you will have in your final decision. Your professional reputation and success are partially linked to successfully implementing technical solutions, and testing in a production environment for network backup will help you achieve this goal.

If you are not using the network to perform your backups, then the testing can be done in a lab environment. The only caution is that you should use the exact same hardware and software configuration in the lab environment as you will use in production. Make sure the same amount of memory is in the lab computer as well as the exact same boards in the exact same location are in the lab computer. You also should make sure the same type of tape device is used for testing as that used in production. The system(s) used for testing should also have the same operating system level and service pack level. Additionally, any other software packages that you anticipate being loaded in the production environment should be loaded on the test system. This may seem a bit extreme, but you want to uncover problems during the testing. You do not want surprises when you implement the solution in your production environment.

Functionality Testing

The first part of the testing is functionality testing. At this point, you should have the number of software vendors down to no more than three possibilities. Testing is a rigorous, time-consuming business, and it is unlikely that you will have the time or resources to test more than three products. The functionality testing should be done for any size site. Any exceptions to this are noted in the following steps.

You should get a notebook—even one for each product. You should keep notes on each of the steps outlined here and include the pros and cons of your experiences as you test. No one can remember all details, and the engineering notebook will help you review your test results at the end of the functionality testing. The following sections provide steps to accomplish the functionality testing.

The first step is to go through the following suggested testing sections and create a list of the features you would like to verify and validate. The features are from Chapter 8, *Commercial Software*, and you will note that not every feature is included. This is because a particular feature may have been for narrowing down which vendor should be evaluated at your site, but not applicable for specifically testing. Also, some of the features will naturally be tested without having to make a specific effort to test them.

The following sections also provide suggestions on how to test a particular feature. Choose which features you will test. You may want to test every feature, but there may be time constraints that require you to choose only the most important features for your site. Also remember that not all of the features listed are in every product.

Write down exactly what will be tested and keep a checklist for yourself. This is especially important if you are working with different groups within your company. The checklist allows everyone to know exactly what will be evaluated, so there will be no misunderstandings.

Some features in the following list must be tested. Others are tested in other sections in this chapter; these were listed for completeness and to avoid confusion, but do not need to be tested during the functionality testing. Table 10-1 lists features in each of these categories. The remaining features should be tested if they exist at your site.

Table 10-1. Mandatory and Optional Testing Needs for Functionality Features

Must Be Tested	Tested Elsewhere
Remote monitoring	Backup of special partitions
Hot database backup support	Tape library features
	Tape library media grouping support
	Tape drive or tape slot locking support
	Tape library replenish support
	Tape verification support
	Backup client multiplexing onto tape
	Tape duplicating support
	Disaster recovery documentation

Backup Server Features

Multithreaded server software

Multithreading is difficult to verify. You can have multithreading without multiple CPUs installed in your system. However, if you do have multiple CPUs, the best you can do is to use monitoring tools to check to make sure you are using the multiple CPUs in a consistent manner. Basically, you want to make sure each CPU is used at about the same utilization as the other CPUs.

Failover support

The vendor's implementation of failover will dictate how it should be tested. If you can failover from one backup server (master or slave) to another, you should simulate the failure on the primary backup server to make sure the backups will continue with the secondary backup system.

Site Features

Microsoft SMS integration

If you are using SMS at your site, you should first integrate the backup client software into your SMS server. Then verify that the backup client software can be installed on the identified backup clients you are using for this functionality testing.

Other software distribution mechanism

If you have a distribution package in house, add the backup client software to that package and make sure that it can install the software on the backup clients you have identified for your functionality testing.

Backup of special partitions

The process of backing up and restoring special partitions (for example, SQL Server partitions) is handled as a separate step in this section. It is important enough that it needed to be explicitly listed as a test step.

Network Installation Support

If you are planning on installing the backup client software over the network, make sure that you perform this same type of installation on the backup clients you are using for the functionality testing.

Support for read-only file systems for Client Binaries

If you intend to have your backup client software located on a read-only centrally managed file system, make sure that the backup clients in the functionality testing use the backup client binaries in the same manner.

Administrative and Configuration Features

Information stored in backup database for individual files

After running backups, verify that the information in the backup database contains the information you expect it to have. This can be done by querying the database on the backup server directly and verifying the information you get back from the query. Also, perform a restore and verify that you can find the information about the backed-up file or folder with the restore utility.

Amount of disk space required for average backup client in backup server database

Perform backups, one file or one folder at a time. After the backup, verify the size of the database on the backup server to test its growth as items are backed up. This may take many iterations of backups and checks of the backup server database to verify the size increments of the database.

Backup restart

If the backup software has the ability to restart backups in the middle of a backup and then continue where you stopped, this must be verified. Perform a backup with a few backup clients. After the first backup client has completed and you have started on the second backup client, restart the backups. Once it restarts, you should watch to make sure the first backup client is not backed up, but the backup server starts the backup with the second backup client.

Initiation of backups

With the previous testing, you will naturally test the initiation of backups from the backup server. If the backup software supports backups to be initiated on the backup clients, test this feature.

End-user restores

Perform a restore on the backup client. This restore should be performed by an ordinary user who does not belong to any special backup group within NT. See if this user can restore other user's folders or files or just folders and files that they own.

Remote restores

Test the ability to perform a restore from the backup server, placing the restored data onto a backup client.

Cross restores

Test the ability to perform a restore from one backup client system (not the backup server) to another backup client system.

Allows wildcard backup

Configure a backup on the backup server to perform a backup using whatever the wildcard feature is in the backup software. Also, perform a backup initiated by the backup client using the backup software's wildcard feature.

Allows wildcard restores

Perform a restore using the backup software's wildcard feature.

GUI and command-line interfaces

Everything you can accomplish through the backup server's GUI, you should be able to perform through a command line or program's scripting language. As a minimum, you should test the following from a command line or script: adding a backup client, changing a backup client's configuration information, getting the status of a current backup, and removing a backup client from the configuration of the backup server.

Printable backup server configuration information

If you have the option of printing the backup server configuration information, you should try it out. Look through the printout, so you know exactly what information you have access to using this feature.

Support host grouping and host ordering

If the backup software supports host grouping, create a small group of hosts. Perform a backup to verify all hosts get backed up. Also note how the hosts are ordered and if they are ordered as described by the backup vendor.

Host priorities supported

Place a high priority on one or more clients and run a backup. Make sure that host or hosts with the priority are put in front of all other clients backed up. Put a very low priority on a host and rerun the backup. Verify that the low priority host is backed up last.

Multilevel backups supported

If the backup software supports full, incremental, and differential backups, run backups with each of the levels. Perform a restore from a backup client just backed up to verify that the data backed up is the level you expected. You may also want to query the backup database on the backup server to verify the backup level.

Calendar-based backups supported

This test may take a few days. Use the calendar utility available with the backup software and schedule different types of backups over the next few days (even add a skipped day in your configuration). Each day, verify that the type of backup you expected did happen.

Support bulk entry for configuration

> This would be tested in conjunction to the command line interface testing mentioned previously. The idea is that you want to use a script tool to enter backup configuration information, so that it can be done automatically in bulk versus through the GUI, one client at a time.

Supports server backup exceptions

> If the backup software supports backup exclusions on the backup server, put one in place, perform a backup, and then perform a restore to confirm that what you excluded is not backed up. For example, backup the entire *C:\folder*, but exclude the *pagefile.sys* file. During the restore, it should not be present or available for a restore. If the backup software supports both kinds of backup exclusions, perform a test with one of each and verify the results.

Support client backup exceptions

> If the backup software supports backup exclusions on the backup client, put in one, perform a backup of a couple of systems, and then verify that the exclusion happened on the backup client you specified, but is not on the backup client you didn't have an exclusion on. If the backup software supports both kinds of backup exclusions, perform a test with one of each and verify the results.

Monitoring, Reporting, and Logging Features

Arbitrary command notification support

> With this feature, the backup software notifies you or other administrators when particular events occur. These events might include when backups complete, a tape is required, or a backup client fails or completes. The most flexible notification system would allow you to put in any command for the notification: you could send an email, or, if you have an automated paging system, send a page. Each notification available should be tested with the different events triggering an email message to advise you of what is happening. If you have time, you should try other command-line options besides sending out email messages. For example, you may want to test the ability to trigger an automated paging system (if you have one at your site) through the backup software's notification system. If you are constrained by time, then at a minimum, test those notifications that you think are pertinent to your site.

Backup server monitoring

> This feature will naturally be tested as you are performing other functional tests. You need to note what you can watch and what information you can obtain through the monitoring tool. You may also want to note what you don't see through the monitoring so that you can investigate whether there are other ways to obtain that information.

Tape device monitoring

This feature will be obvious as you test other functions listed in this table. You should note how the information is displayed to you. Is it in KB/s of individual drives or one aggregate value for all drives? It is possible that this information is not available with some products. If not, is there some other way (possibly in log files) you can obtain this information?

Central monitoring

You should test central monitoring if you can run multiple backup servers during the functional testing and the backup vendor's product supports central monitoring of all backup servers. To test this feature, start backups on all backup servers and use the central monitoring tool to see what information is available for you to monitor. It should be easy to go from backup server to backup server to acquire the information about the backups.

Remote monitoring

Since backups run at night, it is likely that you will be performing administration tasks from home. If you have remote access, this should be evaluated for each product you are considering. Actually perform this testing from home to get the most realistic results as possible. You definitely should be comfortable with administrating the backups as well as the restores via remote access.

SNMP monitoring

Testing this feature requires an SNMP manager to be configured to receive the SNMP traps or perform SNMP polls to the backup server. You may choose not to evaluate this feature, because it could be time-consuming and out of your area of expertise. If you do test this feature, make sure that you can receive traps on the SNMP manager, tune the trap parameters on the backup server, and poll the backup server from the SNMP manager—at a minimum.

Log file support

After performing some backups and restores, you need to watch the log files and see what type of information is available for you to perform troubleshooting. Success information as well as failure information should be included in the logs. If the backup software product provides log watch software or your site has third-party log watch software, configure the software to register on a particular error message. Then simulate that type of error event to make sure that the log watch software notifies you as configured.

Location of log file

Verify that the logs are only in the locations indicated in the vendor's documentation and that there are not additional logs spewed out across the backup server or backup client. Browse through these logs so you can begin to understand what information is located in them.

Reporting mechanism

As you perform backups and restores, there should be reports generated. Look at these reports to see whether you can obtain information required for your site. Note whether there is any information you need that is not available in the report. Also, if you can generate ad hoc reports, do so to see what they look like and how flexibly this can be performed.

Data Features

Backup client or backup server data compression

If the backup software supports backup client compression, it should be tested to make sure no data is lost. To do this, turn on the client compression, perform a backup, perform a restore of the data to an alternate location, and then compare the original data to the restored data. Many times the compression by the backup server is done by the device driver for the tape device. To test this, perform backups with no client compression. Keep performing backups until the backup tape you are using is full. At this point, compare the total amount of data you were able to place on the tape with how much data the tape is rated to hold. For example, if the tape is rated at a capacity of 20 GB without compression and 35 GB with compression, then you should have been able to obtain a tape capacity between these two values. The amount of compression you can obtain depends on the type of data you backed up. If it is all image files (which are highly compressed already) then the value will be close to the 20 GB figure. If the backups are all binaries, then the value will be closer to the 35 GB figure.

Multilingual support

This may be difficult to test unless you have files or folders stored in a different language. If so, back up these files or folders. Restore them to an alternative location and make sure that the names on the files and folders remain the same as the original file or folder names.

Open file support

To test this feature, open a word processor on a backup client and edit a file. Try to back up this file. If it fails, then the open file support is not working properly. You should note if there is an error message and how easy or difficult it is to understand the error message as well as noting if the software retries the backup. Alternatively, it may succeed. If it is successful, recover the file just backed up and verify that it is intact.

Hot database backup support

If you have a database that must be able to be backed up while it is being used, you should test this feature. After backing up a hot database, it should be restored to an alternative location and compared with the original database.

Pre- and postprocessing

This feature is the ability to customize backups to have something occur before the backups and/or after the backups complete. A common test for this is if you have a database on a backup client you would like to bring down, perform a database dump, bring the database back up after the dump, and then back up the dump file on the backup client. Another test may be to verify that a file exists before performing a backup on a client. In any case, you should be able to do something on the backup client before the back up, perform the backup of the client, and then do something after the backup of the client occurs.

Security Features

Permissions granted for restores

Back up something that belongs to one user, then log in as a different user and try to perform a restore. Try backing up something as one user from a folder that belongs to another user. If this succeeds, then try to restore it to your home directory. This restore should fail. These are minimum tests, and there are lots of other variations of permissions you can test.

Security for backups

Try to perform a backup from a client that has not been configured to perform a backup on the backup server. This should fail.

Authorization for administration and configuration functions

Logon to the backup server as a user with no administration rights for the backup software. Try to make a configuration change. This procedure should fail. Verify that your user ID has to be in the administration and configuration list to perform such tasks.

Encryption support

The best way to test this feature is by using a network sniffer. With the sniffer or other network monitoring tool, you should watch the network traffic to verify the data sent across the network for a backup and a restore is indeed encrypted.

Tape Features

Tape format

If the tape format is a standard format, then you should test this by taking the tape written to by the backup software to another system and read it with the standard utility.

Tape library features

The tape library features are discussed in the section "Tape Library Testing" later in this chapter.

Tape library media grouping support

The tape library media grouping feature is discussed in the section "Tape Library Testing" later in this chapter.

Tape drive or tape slot locking support

The tape drive or tape slot locking features are discussed in the section "Tape Library Testing" later in this chapter.

Tape library replenish support

The tape library replenish feature is discussed in the section "Tape Library Testing" later in this chapter.

Maximum tape drives supported

If it is possible that you may be using the maximum number of tapes drives supported by the backup software you are evaluating, then make sure that you test that configuration during your functionality testing. The maximum number may be very large. In this case, test the maximum number of drives you are likely to use.

Tape RAID support

If you plan on using the RAID feature, then you should perform multiple backups and restores to verify that the restored data matches the data that was backed up.

Tape verification support

The tape verification feature does affect performance and is therefore covered in the section "Performance Testing" later in this chapter.

Backup client multiplexing onto tape

Tape multiplexing is a performance issue and is covered in the section "Performance Testing" later in this chapter. This feature can enhance performance.

Tape duplicating support

The tape duplicating or cloning feature is discussed in the section "Tape Library Testing" later in this chapter.

Documentation Features

Online help

Use the online help as much as possible during your testing. If you use it whenever you have a question, you will quickly realize whether it is helpful.

Online tutorials

If a tutorial exists, it should be used at the very beginning. By using it first, before you really understand the backup software product, you will quickly learn if it was helpful in installation or configuration of the product.

Hard copy documentation set

It is sometimes hard to find quality time to read the documentation set, but try and take the time now to at least browse through these manuals.

Disaster recovery documentation

The process of restoring after a catastrophic data loss is handled as a separate step in this section. It is important enough for it to be explicitly listed as a test step. Use any documentation that the vendor provides in the steps listed to recover from a catastrophic loss of data.

Customer Support Features

Patches available via the Web or FTP sites

If the patches are available online, then access the Web or FTP site. Make sure that you don't need any special logins or passwords to get into the site and access the information required. Actually download a patch, just to verify that you can do it. If the patches are not available online, then test any patches you may receive from the vendor for ease of instructions and installation.

Problem identification / resolution facility via the Web

If you run across any problems during your testing and if there is a problem identification/resolution facility available online, test out their web site. Nothing like a real problem to test this facility out. Otherwise, at a minimum, visit the web site and step through it to see if there are any obvious problems with the site.

User groups

If there are any local user groups, contact them. Go to one of their meetings. Get a feel for what useful information you can get from the group. See if you can get names and numbers of individuals from the user groups who would be willing to help you, in a pinch, with the backup software installation, configuration, or questions.

Mailing lists available

If there is a mailing list available for the product you are using, subscribe to it while you are performing your testing. If you have any problems or questions during the evaluation, use the mailing list to see if your questions or issues can be addressed.

General customer support

> During your testing, call customer support at various times. Sometimes at night or during the weekend, vendors have answering machines or services taking support calls and no direct support individuals. You should be aware of how support works during these times.

Additional Features

Archiving support

> If there is a possibility that you will require the archiving feature in the future, then you should test this feature.

HSM support

> If there is a possibility that you will require the HSM feature in the future, then you should test this feature.

Customer references

> Call at least three references. You should prepare a list of questions to ask all the references and then keep notes on additional comments they provide. At a minimum, find out the number of backup servers they have, how many backup clients each backup server has, what operating systems they are backing up, what operating system is on their backup server, and any of their experiences in dealing with the vendor's help line. Ask them if they had to do it over whether they would choose the product again.

System Configuration

The following system configuration items should be taken into consideration as you prepare for the functionality testing:

- You may have the luxury of having multiple backup systems or servers to use for your testing. If so, start from scratch, installing the operating system, service packs, and each product to be tested on the separate backup systems. Multiple backup test systems give you the option of going back and forth between the different products to compare features. If you are testing with multiple backup systems, these backup systems should have identical hardware, operating systems, service packs, and tape devices.

- If you do not have multiple backup systems to test with, then chances are that the tests will be performed sequentially: first one backup software package, then another one, and so on. If this is the case, it is highly recommended that you reload the operating system and service packs after completing the evaluation of each backup software package. This guarantees that the environment begins in the same state for each set of tests.

You may just want to install a software package, evaluate it, remove it, and then install the next software package, thinking that you are saving time. However, there is no guarantee that the software removal process truly deleted all system references to the first software package. If the removal process was not entirely successful and entries were left on the system, these entries could affect the operation of the new software you load. You could potentially waste lots of time troubleshooting problems with the second software package because the removal of the first package was not clean. You may think the reinstallation of the system takes time, but troubleshooting can take much more time and effort. It is unlikely that you have the extra time to troubleshoot this kind of problem. You probably need all the time you can get just to perform the evaluation. If you format the hard drive and reinstall the system from scratch, you are eliminating this potential problem and saving time in the long run.

- On all test systems, install any other software you generally install on your systems in addition to the operating system and backup software. This provides a realistic system on which to perform the functionality testing. If there will be any compatibility problems between two products you intend to use in production, it is better to uncover these issues during the testing phase.

- If you intend to have a heterogeneous backup environment, you should perform the functionality testing on each of those backup client types. For example, if you intend to back up NT and Novell systems with the same backup product, perform the functionality testing on both.

If you are performing testing for networked backups, you should take the following notes into consideration for the backup clients:

- Feature testing commonly requires only one backup client. However, there are exceptions, like testing the remote restore feature. This is in contrast to performance testing, where you will need many backup clients.

- The hardware configuration of backup clients should be as close as possible to the configuration you will be using in production.

- The software configuration of the backup clients should match your production environment. If your backup clients have different operating system versions with different patch levels, they should all be represented for this testing. Also, if you intend on having a heterogeneous backup client environment, you should perform the feature tests on each of those backup client types. For example, if you intend to back up NT and Novell systems with the same backup server and product, make sure you perform the functionality testing on both.

- Make sure the backup clients also have any other application software loaded that will be used in production, in addition to the operating system and backup software.

Feature Evaluation

Using the systems you configured as described in the previous section, evaluate each feature you identified earlier. Keep thorough notes on what you experience with each product. Make sure you note positive as well as negative experiences. Go through your feature list first and try not to get too side-tracked with other features in the products. You can explore the additional features and variations of the different products after you have exhausted the initial feature list. You should be scientific in your approach and compare the products based on the same feature list you generated. This feature comparison can be supplemented with the other features you find, but always remember that it is important to have the initial baseline feature comparison.

Review Results

After you have tested or evaluated your initial feature list, review your results. At this point you should have a good idea of whether the backup software product(s) you are evaluating can meet the basic feature requirements. Don't be surprised if you decide that you need to eliminate a product or two and go back through the feature functionality testing with a different vendor's product. You want to continue with the rest of the steps in this section only with products that meet your feature requirements.

Catastrophic Data Loss Testing

In the area of backup and recovery, the worst possible situation is when you have a major failure and have to completely restore a system from scratch. During your test process, you should see how difficult or easy it is to perform a recovery from catastrophic loss of data. This is something you should experience before it is required for production. In addition, you need to see how the products you are considering behave under these conditions. Some products may be more difficult to use in a disaster than others, possibly because of poor documentation or excessive steps involved with the recovery.

The results of this testing should help you narrow down the product(s) best suited for your environment. This type of testing should be performed at sites of all sizes—small, medium, or large. The following sections list the steps you should take to perform this testing.

Backup Client, Catastrophic Data Loss

First, simulate catastrophic data loss on a backup client. There are two different parts to this step:

1. Perform a full backup of the system or backup client and then simulate a catastrophe on the backup client system by formatting the hard drive(s). This is the worst-case scenario and should be experienced firsthand during your testing process. You should fully document the steps you have to take to get the client system fully restored again. At this point, the speed of the restore isn't the most important thing to note. The important things are the steps involved and noting the level of difficulty you experience during this disaster scenario. There should be documentation available from the vendor for this type of restore. Use their documentation to evaluate how well it explains what needs to be done. If you use a combination of the vendor's documentation as well as other steps you discover need to be taken, make sure that you write all of this down.

2. Redo the disaster and then the recover, using the exact steps you documented. This second test is for timing purposes and also to verify that your notes from the first part are well done (you may want to have another individual perform this part). You should note the amount of time it takes from the very beginning to the very end of the restore, using your defined steps. Also, if needed, you should refine the steps you documented in the first part.

Backup Client, Partial Data Loss

Next, simulate a partial but large data loss. In this situation the entire disk is not lost, just a large amount of data (for example 30 GB). If possible, use a different client than the one used in the previous simulation. This will provide more real-world experience. For this test, use the same steps as listed previously, but remove a large amount of data, not an entire hard drive.

Backup Server, Catastrophic Data Loss

Simulate catastrophic data loss on the backup server. This step should only be performed for sites that are implementing networked backups with a backup server. This step has two different parts:

1. Perform a full backup of the backup client, and, as with the backup client, simulate a hard disk failure and then restore the original setup from a newly formatted disk. The backup server could lose a hard drive as easily as one of the client systems. The process of restoring the backup server will be different than restoring the backup client, so separately document the steps you have to take to get the server system fully functional. There should be vendor docu-

mentation on how to perform this type of restore, specifically for the backup server. You should use this documentation to make sure it is thorough and does not miss any important steps. If you use a combination of the vendor's documentation as well as other steps you discover need to be taken, make sure you write all of this down. Perform this part of this step without being concerned with the amount of time it takes to accomplish the full restore.

2. Redo the server disaster and then the recover, using the exact steps you documented. This second test is for timing purposes and also to verify if your notes from the first part are well done. You should note the amount of time it takes from the very beginning to the very end of the restore, using your defined steps. Also, you should refine the steps you documented in the first part, if needed.

Special Partition, Catastrophic Data Loss

Next, simulate catastrophic data loss on special partitions. Your site may have special formatted disks (not NTFS or FAT) that you would use for products such as SQL Server, Microsoft Exchange, or Lotus Notes. If so, you should test the process of backing up and recovering these types of partitions after a major loss of data. This is an important step to perform no matter what size backup site you are implementing. These special partitions are treated differently by the backup software package. Commonly, the software needed to perform this type of backup is a separate package. It is generally something you purchase in addition to the base product. There are two parts to this step:

1. Back up the special partition, then simulate a catastrophic failure. Without being concerned about how long it takes, document the steps to perform this restore. The vendor should provide documentation on how to restore the special partitions after a major data loss occurs. You should use the vendor's documentation to evaluate how useful it is for your situation. Also, document your steps or at least document any differences from the vendor documentation.

2. Redo the failure and restore, documenting how long this procedure takes. Use the notes you took in the first part. Make changes in your restore steps from the first part and note the exact amount of time it takes you to perform the restore from the very beginning to the very end.

Review Results

Finally, review all of your results. After you have gone through the catastrophic data loss scenarios, look at your results. At this point, you may have a definite preference for one product over the others. If this is the case, proceed into the library and performance testing with only the product(s) you prefer.

Tape Library Testing

Generally, only medium and large sites will use tape library technology. However, some small sites may have a limited number of huge systems that have lots of disk capacity. An extremely large system may require that a small tape library be used for backups. So this testing can apply to any size site.

Some of the tape libraries on the market have some sophisticated features that should be tested. Also, you should be comfortable with proper procedures for the tape library before you put the unit into production. The testing process should help you become more familiar with the tape library and how to use it properly.

During this testing, you should also take good notes. As has been stated before, backups run at night and on the weekend. It may be necessary for you to provide directions about the tape library to a night or weekend operator over the telephone. You may be at home, realize the library is having problems and need to use the operator as your hands and eyes. Having detailed notes and real experience on the behavior of your tape library will assist you in guiding this person through some basic troubleshooting. Some of the tape library problems may be able to be resolved without you visiting the tape library.

The features of a tape library that should be tested—at a minimum—are listed here. There may be other features of libraries that you think are necessary to evaluate. Don't hesitate, because the following list is just to get you started down the tape library testing path. The list contains tape library features and their suggested testing specifications:

Tape media grouping

    Some backup software packages allow you to group tapes within the tape library for backups. Configure the library to have multiple media groups, then perform backups using only one group at a time. Verify that the tapes in the specified groups were used for those backups. Then perform backups that use different groups at the same time. After the backups, confirm again that the appropriate tapes were used for those backups.

Tape drive or tape slot locking

    If your backup software has the ability to lock a tape drive so that it will not be used, test this feature. Lock a drive, then try and use that drive for a backup or a restore. Another test is to lock all drives and try backups. You should receive an error message that states there are no tape drive devices available for backups or something to that effect. Try the same testing with locking a tape slot.

Tape library replenish

If this feature is available, try to replenish the tape library with X number of tapes. This feature should also be tested between the different tape media groups. You may require X tapes from one media group and Y tapes from another media group within the tape library.

Hot-swappable drives

If the unit you have chosen has drives that can be changed while the rest of the unit is still running, this should definitely be tested. Start a backup session running, lock a tape drive so that it cannot be used by the backup software, and then remove it from the tape library. The backups should continue without any problems.

Entry/exit door

During your testing, move tapes into and out of the library using the entry/exit door. It may be easier just to open the library during the testing, but use the entry/exit door as often as possible to test this feature.

Cleaning tapes

Within the tape library, you should be able to configure certain slots (or use predefined slots) for cleaning tapes. Make sure you understand the tape technology well enough to understand when you should and should not clean tape heads. Some of the tape drive technology is conducive to having the tape drives cleaned as often as you like; other tape drive technology is not. Read the tape drive manuals or ask the hardware vendor what is best for the hardware you have purchased.

Bar code

Support for bar code labels may be tested naturally as you prepare the tape library and perform backups. The bar code labels are usually placed on the tapes before they are inserted into the tape library. Then the robotic arm reads and registers these bar code labels. You will probably have to configure the software to be aware of the bar code labels. This may be done though a process called tape labeling. After the software recognizes the tapes, the available tapes are noted in the backup software's database based on their bar code label. As the tapes are used, the use of the tape is tracked by updates to the backup software database.

Tape library inventory

When a tape library is shut down or rebooted or the access door is opened, the library must inventory the tapes in the tape library again. The time it takes to perform this task should be noted. You should perform this test when the tape library is empty or almost empty. It should also be tested when the library is full or almost full of tapes. Depending on the implementation of the robotic arm, these two times could be quite different, and the larger the tape library the larger the disparity in times. Basically, it is a matter of whether the robotic arm can automatically sense if a tape slot is empty. If the arm can automatically sense an empty slot, then there is no real inventory delay due to empty slots. If the robotic arm cannot automatically sense an empty slot, the arm has to physically probe to learn that the slot is empty. This physical verification is time-consuming with an empty library.

If you run into any problems with tape library testing, you may have difficulty determining whether the problem is with the tape library itself or the backup software you are using. Unfortunately, it may be a case where the hardware vendor says it is the fault of the software vendor and vice versa. This does happen, and it can be difficult to handle.

If the different vendors start pointing fingers at one another, you should contact someone using the same hardware and software configuration as you are to see if they've ever had the same problem. You may find someone through the software or hardware vendor's recommendation, through a user's group, or through a mailing list for the software or hardware vendor. Technical people are generally very open to discussing both positive and negative experiences they have personally had with a specific project. Talk to multiple people, so that you don't get one biased opinion. You should try to acquire many different opinions if you are experiencing problems. Having to describe your problem to someone by talking out loud or writing down email to others also sometimes helps you see the answer.

Performance Testing

Now that the functionality testing and library testing are completed, it is time to find out whether the backup server hardware and software will fit the size requirements you calculated in Chapter 4, *Requirements Definition*. At this point, you have to test in an environment that is the same as you will use in production. The closer you can get your performance testing backup server and client configurations the same as your production environment, the more realistic results you will be able to obtain.

As with the tape library testing, the medium and large backup implementations should undergo performance testing. However, some small sites may have a limited number of huge systems that have lots of disk capacity. The throughput and performance on these systems may be of concern and require testing. So this testing definitely needs to be done at any sites that perform backups across the network and may apply to small sites that have huge servers to back up.

The whole goal of performance testing is to determine the GB/h of your backup server or system. This is for the entire backup server, in the case of network backups. With backups that are not across the network, this applies to the backup system with large disk capacity. When testing, don't just test in brief intervals; make sure you test for sustained periods of time. If you can run tests and allow them to run for hours at a time, that will best represent what will actually occur when you put this system into production. By testing the environment for many hours, you will also be able to acquire your GB/h metric. It is important to take the actual GB/h you obtain and compare it to the value you calculated in Chapter 4.

If you can obtain the throughput required to meet your size requirements, then you will be able to back up all of the vital data you identified in your required time frame. If you cannot obtain the throughput required, you need to determine where your performance bottleneck is occurring. This bottleneck may be able to be eliminated, thus obtaining more throughput. Otherwise, you will need to install and configure multiple backup servers. Keep in mind that it may be less expensive to upgrade the backup server than it is to purchase another complete backup server with all the tape drives required.

General Considerations

When it comes to backing up medium and large environments, there are many different components of the systems and networks that can affect the backup test results. You may find someone who says: "The only difference the test lab has is a different manufacturer of the routers and that won't affect the performance." There is no way that you can guarantee that a particular router will or will not make a difference, and you need to be cautious. I have done testing and evaluation of different hardware and software on and off for over 12 years. Believe me, for your own good, be a bit skeptical during your testing and evaluation. This may seem like a negative attitude, but healthy skepticism will pay off in the long run.

When performing backups in a medium or large environment, there are many variables with roles in the performance testing results. A few of these variables are as follows:

Backup server hardware platforms

Make sure that your test backup server has the same type of CPUs, same number of CPUs, same network card, same amount of memory, same type of tape drives, and the same number of tape drives as your production backup server will have.

Backup server operating system and service packs

Whatever operating system version and service pack level you choose, use the same for your testing. If you intend to use NT 4.0 with service pack level 3 for your backup server, make sure that your test system has the same.

Backup client hardware platforms

The different hardware platforms you have in your production environment should also be in your test environment. You may choose to use the same systems for testing as you have in production, just using them during off hours. If you have Intel and Alpha hardware platforms, make sure you have some of each for testing.

Backup client operating system and service packs

Whatever the mix in your production environment, try to match that in your test environment. If you have a backup client environment with some NT 3.5x and NT 4.0 machines with varying service pack levels, make sure you have the same type of mix for your test backup clients. For larger sites, try to back up as many backup clients as possible, to be as realistic as possible.

Backup client network connections

If your backup clients are all on 10 MB/s Ethernet networks, make sure your test backup clients are as well. If your backup server is on a 100 MB/s network and your backup clients on 10 MB/s networks, make sure that your test environment reflects this type of configuration. If some of your backup clients are on the 100 MB/s network with your backup server, the test should reflect this too. Remember to take the same care if you intend to implement a heterogeneous environment.

Network backbone components

I suggest that during your testing you use the same network you will use for the production environment. Backups run constantly for hours at a time, and if there is a misconfigured router or some other piece of network equipment is misconfigured or not running correctly, the backups will stress the network enough to uncover these types of problems. At a minimum, connect your test backup server on the same network that your production system will be located on. If you are going to have your backup server on a 100 MB/s network, place your test server on that same network.

Systems Monitoring

System monitoring tools are the only way to gauge your backup environment's performance. How the backup server's system resources are being used is product-specific and is influenced by your site's hardware and software configuration. In medium and large sites, where the amount of time to perform the backups is rather precious, you should use the system's monitoring tools to determine where the backup environment's bottlenecks occur. You should not speculate about where the bottleneck is, but instead get tools to help you determine the bottleneck before implementing a solution. Throwing money and hardware at the problem without knowing the real bottlenecks is not smart.

Some of the important items to monitor on the backup server are the following:*

CPU utilization

> The load on your backup server CPU(s) is important. The CPU utilization should be substantial, but you also don't want it to be operating too high. If the CPU(s) are loaded too heavily, you won't be able to log into the backup server to make configuration changes or perform other tasks while the backups are running. About 80% utilization is recommended for CPU utilization while the backups are running.

Memory utilization

> You do not want memory utilization to be at its maximum. Basically, if memory utilization is too high, the system will begin swapping, and you definitely do not want it to become swap-bound. This is what happens when the system spends so much time swapping memory that the system's performance begins to degrade.

Network utilization

> With the faster tape drive technology, it is becoming easier to use all of the network bandwidth for backups. Watch your network to ensure that this is not occurring.

Tape drive utilization

> There are two schools of thought on tape drive utilization. The first says that you should use the tape drives to their fully rated speeds because you want to get the most throughput for your investment. The second says that you may have more tape drives, but should not use all of them at their fully rated speeds. This opinion may be appropriate if your site wants to have more tape drives available for restores while backups are being performed. With either approach, you should watch your tape drive throughput.

Once you know the bottlenecks, you may be able to configure the backup software to overcome or ease the bottlenecks. If that is not possible, you can then spend money on additional hardware for the backup server to overcome the bottleneck. The key is to have the monitoring software available so that you can first justify the hardware purchase, and second, see how the new hardware installation changes the equation. Once the appropriate hardware is installed, it is entirely possible that a different bottleneck will result. For example, removing a tape bottleneck may result in a network bottleneck.

---

* You can use the Windows NT Task Manager, CTRL-ALT-DEL →Task Manager... →Performance Tab, to monitor the CPU and memory utilization.

The whole idea is to understand what your bottleneck is and make a conscious decision to accept that particular bottleneck. The decision to accept a particular bottleneck may be a financial or technical decision

Poor Assumptions

When doing performance testing there are some assumptions that you should *not* make. It is important to be aware of the following scenarios so you don't make mistakes:

Multiple tape drives

You should not extrapolate the performance results of a backup server using one tape drive to determine the performance for multiple tape drives. If you are going to use multiple tape drives on a backup server, you should test multiple tape drives.

When backing up to a single tape drive, a certain amount of overhead is associated with using that tape drive. This overhead is associated with data that is taken off the network, information that is written to the backup database(s), and data that is written to tape. Using more than one tape drive results in more data to take off the network, more information to write to the backup database(s), and more tape drives. The overhead with the second tape drive will probably affect the original performance measured with the first tape drive and so on with more drives. There are limited system resources, and as you add tape devices, these resources have to be spread thinner.

Multiple backup servers

Do not assume that once one server works, the others will work just fine. Each server has its own personality. The personality of a backup server is derived from all different pieces, but most important are the backup clients. The backup servers back up a different set of backup clients; therefore, the personality of each backup server varies. This personality includes performance. The performance among different backup servers will be different, and each backup server should be tested independently to determine its GB/h.

Network backups

Do not perform local backups of a system and assume that you will obtain the same performance across the network. Backups across the network cause a lot more system overhead because of the processing of the network data. This overhead does affect the overall performance of the backups.

Full backups versus differential backups versus incremental backups

Do not assume that the speed of the differential or incremental backups is proportional to the speed of the full backups. The difference is that for differential and incremental backups, the software on the backup client has to take the time to determine what files and folders have changed before performing the backups. That takes some time, and it does not have to be made with full backups. When performing full backups, everything is backed up and there is no checking of when the folders or files were last modified.

Performance Testing Steps

The suggested steps associated with performance testing are broken into setup and actual testing and are provided in the following lists.

Setting up the tests

1. *Backup server hardware.* Install and configure the backup server hardware. This includes the network connection and the tape device(s) you intend to use in production.

2. *Backup client list.* Generate the list of backup clients you will be using for the performance testing. If you cannot get the exact ratio of backup clients you intend on backing up with the backup server, try to get as close as possible. For example, if you have 20 backup clients at your site, try and test with all 20 of those exact systems. If not, then get as close to 20 of them as possible.

3. *Backup time.* Determine when you can perform backup testing on your network. For best results, you should try to find a time frame in which the network is quiescent as possible. Many times this is either late at night or early in the morning.

4. *Backup server software.* Install and configure the backup software. It is recommended that you actually reinstall the complete operating system and service pack in addition to the backup software on the server system. Also, if there are other applications loaded on your servers, make sure that those applications are also loaded. This gives you a clean slate to begin your performance testing. It also gives you a realistic server configuration to test with. Once all the software is loaded, you should configure the backup software to include the backup clients you listed in step 2.

5. *Backup client software.* The software for the backup clients should be installed on each backup client in step 2. If possible, reinstall these clients from scratch, like you did with the backup server. If it is not possible, just make sure any versions of backup software you will not do performance testing with is removed from the backup clients.

Performing the tests

1. *Full backup testing.* You should perform a full backup to begin with. While backups are running, note the speeds you are obtaining on the tape drive(s).

You should be able to accomplish this through the backup software monitoring tool. If you observe the tape speed for a while, you will see a tendency for it to run at a particular speed. Then, after the backups complete, you should be able to use the total amount of data backed up divided by how long it took to perform the backup to calculate GB/h achieved on the backup server. The total amount of data that was backed up should be part of the software reporting mechanism. You may want to repeat this step many times to find an average GB/h over multiple runs.

2. *Differential backup testing.*[*] Using the same backup clients as you did in step 1, perform a differential backup. Once again, while the backups are running, note the throughput you are obtaining on the tape drive(s) on your backup server. After the backup completes, calculate the GB/h achieved during this test step. Again, you may want to run a differential multiple times to find an average GB/h.

3. *Restore testing.* Choose one of your backup clients and perform a restore from the full backup. Note the total amount of data to restore and the amount of time it takes to perform this restore. Calculate the MB/s to perform the restore. Use the metric MB/s for restores, because generally they include smaller amounts of data than the backups, and therefore the MB/s is a better measurement.

4. *Compare results.* You should compare the GB/h achieved with full and differential backups. You should also compare these values to the numbers calculated in Chapter 4.

   If you can achieve the GB/h required to meet your backup window, then you should not introduce multiplexing and should skip ahead to step 6. Remember that multiplexing does affect the speed of the restores. So if your backup performance is adequate without multiplexing, don't use it.

   If you cannot achieve the GB/h required to meet your backup window, then go to step 5. Multiplexing may be able to help you achieve your required GB/h.

5. *Multiplexing testing.* If the chosen backup product supports multiplexing, you should test it further, based on two other conditions:

   • The first condition is whether you think that the results you compared in step 4 will meet your backup window. For example, you may have determined in Chapter 4 that you need to obtain an aggregate of 4.71 GB/h to be able to meet your backup window. Say your results from the previous

---

[*] The differential backups will back up what changed since the last full backup. You could also repeat this test for the incremental backup but there is a pretty good chance that the GB/s obtained by the differential backup should be the same as the incremental backups.

tests were only 2.5 to 3.0 GB/h. This indicates that tape multiplexing may be able to increase your overall throughput to meet your requirements.

- The second condition is whether the tape throughput values you saw during the testing in steps 1 and 2 are not as high as the rated performance for those drives. For example, say you are using DLT 4000 class drive(s) that has a rated speed of 1.5 MB/s. You may have noted during your full and differential backup tests that the tape drives were running between 500 KB/s and 1 MB/s. That means the tape device is not achieving the rated speeds, and therefore tape multiplexing may be able to increase your overall performance.

If you meet both of these conditions, then you should test the multiplexing feature. When performing this testing, you should increment the level of multiplexing slowly. You want the lowest multiplexing that allows you to achieve your requirements. The testing you performed in steps 1 and 2 is considered a multiplexing level of 1. Recognizing that, take the following steps to determine what level of multiplexing is best for your environment (note that if you used multiple tape drives in the tests in the previous steps, use the same number of drives for this testing):

a. Increment the multiplexing by 1 for all the drives you are using.

b. Rerun the test in step 1. Remember to note the drive speed and overall GB/s achieved.

   Rerun the test in step 2. Remember to note the drive speed and overall GB/s achieved.

   Rerun the test in step 3. Remember to note the restore MB/s speed. Compare the MB/s restore speed you achieved without the multiplexing compared to the MB/s restore speed with the multiplexing. If the restore speed becomes unacceptable (a site-dependent question), then note the last multiplexing value you had with an acceptable restore speed and proceed to step 6. Don't forget that you also have to consider the GB/h backup speeds with the last multiplexing value. If you can meet your backup window with that throughput, then nothing more needs to be done. If you cannot meet the backup window, then you may want to use monitoring tools to potentially find a bottleneck on your system (see the later section on monitoring) or you may decide to use an additional backup server to meet your required backup window.

c. Make the comparison noted in step 4. If you can meet your backup window with the GB/h you noted, then the level of multiplexing you have achieved at this point is right for your site. Note the level of multiplexing you have achieved and go on to step 6.

If you cannot meet your backup window and the drive speed you noted is not the rated speed for the tape drive you are using, then repeat this process by going back to step a.

If you have repeated step a multiple times and the tape drive speed is not increasing, then the backup software may not be driving the tape drive as fast as it can, or you may have a bottleneck on you backup server or network. If this happens, go back to the last multiplexing value you had where you noted a change in the tape drive throughput. The GB/h you achieved with that multiplexing value is the overall throughput you will achieve with the backup server you are currently testing. You may realize that the GB/h achieved with that multiplexing value may not be enough to meet your backup window requirements. If so, then you need to monitor your system to see whether you can determine where the bottleneck exists. If you find a bottleneck that you can remove, you may be able to drive the tape drives faster and gain more performance. Another option is to decide to use another backup server to meet your backup window requirements. Now record this multiplexed value and go to step 6.

6. *Tape verification testing.* If the backup product has tape verification or validation and you need this feature at your site, you should test the impact of this feature on performance. Note the multiplexing value and GB/h throughput (for both full and differential backups) you acquired from step 5. Now, turn the tape verification feature on, using the multiplexed value you determined to be best for your site, and rerun steps 1 and 2.

Compare the GB/h results for both the full and differential backups with the tape verification feature turned off and with the tape verification feature turned on. This comparison will indicate the performance hit you will take by using the tape verification feature. If this feature is on and you can still obtain the throughput required to meet your backup window, then you are good to go.

If you cannot meet your backup window, then you may want to increase the multiplexing value to see if you can get a faster throughput on the backup server. You may also decide that the throughput achieved is adequate for the full backup window, but not for the differential backup window. If this is the case, you may choose to turn tape verification on during the full backups but turn it off during the differential backups. Another option is to have tape verification turned on for only the most important backup clients.

You may wish to perform other performance tests at your site. If so, you should perform them with the multiplexing you determined best for your site, and with tape verification turned on if that is what was determined best for your site. Also remember to use the same backup client hosts for that testing.

Performance Testing Matrix

You must have a notebook or some other way to keep notes with the performance testing. It is extremely iterative and you need to do a lot of comparing and contrasting of values among the different tests. Table 10-2 provides you with a sample matrix to log your performance results, so you can later make a comparison.

Table 10-2. Performance Testing Matrix

Performance Test Step	Test 1 Results	Test 2 Results	Test 3 Results	Test 4 Results	Test 5 Results	Test 6 Results
Step 1: Full Backups						
Total GB Backed up						
Total Hours						
Calculated GB/h						
Tape Speed						
Step 2: Differential Backups						
Total GB Backed up						
Total Hours						
Calculated GB/h						
Tape Speed						
Step 3: Restore from Full Backup						
Total MB Restored						
Total Seconds						
Calculated MB/s						
Step 6: Tape Verification ON with Full Backups						
Total GB Backed up						
Total Hours						
Calculated GB/h						
Step 6: Tape Verification ON with Differential Backups						
Total GB Backed up						
Total Hours						
Calculated GB/h						

11

Integration Hints

Once you reach this phase, you have completed testing and should know what backup software and hardware is best for your site. It is time to integrate the vendor's products chosen into your production environment. With some projects, testing and integration are run together into one phase. Don't let this happen. Testing and integration are distinctly different phases and should be treated as such:

Testing

Chapter 10, *Testing*, is focused on evaluating product features, library features, and product performance and comparing different products. It also allows you to become familiar with the installation, configuration, and operation of the software and hardware. The goal of testing is to choose the hardware and software best suited for your environment.

Integration

Integration is focused on getting the backups operational in your production environment. You want the backup software and hardware integrated into production and then migrated to an administrative maintenance mode. The goal of integration is to perform the installation and configuration of the backup environment with production in mind at all times.

Integration hints can help you initially bring up the backup server(s). The details of the integration are very dependent on the hardware and software you have chosen. Therefore, no explicit instructions are provided in this chapter, but general directions are given here that can be applied to any product you are installing and configuring.

Documentation

The initial integration of the backup hardware and software is a big task. Once all of the nuances associated with your site are ironed out, however, adding new backup servers or systems becomes more routine. You should document the steps you take to accomplish the integration at your site. Additionally, you should document the rationale for the installation and configuration choices you make. It may seem time-consuming and sometimes obvious to you, but these types of notes are very useful down the road:

- When you add systems or backup servers to your backup environment at a later time, you can use these notes so that you don't have to figure everything out a second time.

- The documentation can be used for training. It may be that one group within your firm actually performs the integration, but another supports the backup implementation once it is operational. The documentation can be used to share the responsibility between these two groups.

- These notes can be used by others if you move to a different position in your company or leave your company. The individual that follows in your footsteps will be grateful to have this type of documentation.

Fresh Installation

The type of backup implementation (local or network) will dictate what is done at this point.

Local Backups*I*

If at all possible, you should do a fresh install of the backup software, and possibly the operating system you used for the testing, in preparation for production.

If you used a system in a lab for your testing that will not be used in production, you have not installed the backup software or hardware on any production system. The integration phase will be the first time the backup software and hardware are used on the production systems. Therefore, the fresh install is handled naturally.

If you used a production system for your testing, you should consider reinstalling the backup software and operating system. You may be thinking, "Reinstall my production system—you have got to be kidding!" You may be right, because the system used for testing may be a widely utilized system and has been highly customized. However, your basic rule should be this: if at all possible, you should reinstall the system during your integration phase. This includes the operating system, service packs, backup software, and any other applications from scratch. During the testing phase, you may have made changes that were never undone. To avoid problems that may surround these ad hoc changes made during testing, the reinstallation is important.

For the local backup configurations, you should take notes on how the installation is done. You should try to create a cookbook that can be followed on all the other systems to be installed. If there are variations on the installation between systems, these should be well documented, perhaps with general notes and a supplement for each system that has any differences.

Network Backups

For the sites implementing backups over the network, I do not recommend that you go directly from the testing into integration without cleaning up your backup server. Generally, the backup server is a system exclusively used for backups, so this should not affect other applications at your site. If the backup server is multipurpose, then you should also consider the reinstallation, but not until you take into consideration what impact you will have on the other applications or services.

You should reload the operating system, system packs, backup software, and any other server-based applications from scratch on the backup server. Sometimes, during the testing phase, you make system or application changes on the fly. Generally, these changes are not backed out, but are left on the system. These changes can cause problems at a later time. To make sure that you don't have any of these ad hoc changes on your backup server system, format all drives and reload everything. The reload process may seem time-consuming now, but troubleshooting problems later can take much more time.

If your backup server is Windows NT–based, you should load software on that server to check for viruses.* In medium and large backup implementations, the backup server will be handling lots of vital data. Your company is depending on this server in the event of catastrophic data loss. You do not want a virus to cause failure or damage on such an important system.

If it is possible, reload the backup clients that you used for testing. This would include a reinstall of the operating systems, patches, backup software, and any other application software used by the backup clients. This may not be possible in environments where clients that are used on a daily basis by real users were used for the testing. If the system cannot be reloaded from scratch, make sure that all backup software that is no longer required has been removed from those clients.

---

* Antivirus software should really be loaded on all of your systems.

Relabel Tapes

You should relabel and reuse all tapes that were used during the testing phases. This labeling is the magnetic label actually on the tape itself, not the label on the outside of the tape cartridge. Depending on the backup software product, tape labeling may be a manual process initiated by an administrator or an automatic process performed by the software itself.

If the labeling is a manual process, it should be done before backups begin in production. You don't want to confuse any of the tapes that were used during the testing with the tapes that will be used in production. By relabeling the tapes, you are starting fresh. When relabeling, you may be prompted with a message telling you that the tape was previously used. The use may have been during your testing phase. Don't be confused by this; overwrite and relabel any tapes used during testing. When labeling new tapes that have never been used, you will not receive this type of message from the software.

If the tape labeling process is done automatically through the backup software, you may just need to specify which tapes can be used or reused. In this situation, the tapes are automatically labeled as they are used.

Configuration

The configuration of the backup server software should be done very carefully. You are starting fresh and want to configure it as cleanly as possible. For any size site, configuring the backup software should be based on the information you obtained from your site survey and what you put into your backup policy. This information includes—but is certainly not limited to—the following items:

- The hosts that have to be backed up
- What priorities the backups have compared to other batch jobs running at your site
- Where the vital data is located on each host
- What data not to back up
- Possible regulatory requirements for tape-retention periods

During your configuration, you should make choices that allow you the most flexibility in the future. Your environment will grow and change and you need to try to anticipate this. It can be difficult, but do the best you can.

Unfortunately, this book cannot cover all of the issues surrounding configuration. This is another area that is extremely product-specific. However, this is an excellent time to ask for assistance from the backup software vendor, user groups, or email lists to make the best configuration decisions. These contacts were identi-fied during your vendor survey. Try to find assistance from sources in the same industry that have the same type of systems, have the same size site, and have implemented the same type of backup model as you.

It is very beneficial to learn from others' experiences. A good question to ask oth-ers is if they had to do it over, what they would do differently to configure their systems to better suit their environment. Learning from their mistakes and their experiences can save you lots of time. Don't hesitate to ask people you talk to if they know of any other references. By talking to many contacts, you can learn even more.

Scheduling

There are two meanings to scheduling as it relates to backups. There is schedul-ing within the backup software. This specifies what will be backed up and how often. This can also include when the backups are performed. In the larger con-text of your entire site, there is scheduling of the backups and other batch jobs that run during the same hours. For example, it may be important to have a batch job complete before beginning the backup of data related to the batch job.

Backup Schedules

Backup schedules are a common point of confusion, no matter which backup model you are implementing. There are lots of different schedule combinations that you can configure with the different backup software packages. It is a trade-off to determine what schedule best suits your environment. The trade-off has to do with the amount of time and number of tapes it takes to perform the restore versus the time and number of tapes you are willing to use to get the backups completed.

When deciding what schedule is best for your site, remember that the more tapes involved for a restore, the more difficult and time-consuming the restore can become. When performing the restore, you are dependent on being able to find all tapes required, on having are no physical problems with reading all the tapes, and on the actual time required for the tape drive to go through each of the tapes. As you can see, it is a matter of balancing the time to perform the restore versus the cost of using extra tape to make the restore easier.

The following is a list of four possible backup options with the advantages and disadvantages of each.

Option 1

If you have a site with a relatively small amount of data, you may choose to perform full backups every night and on weekends. This means that no matter what data changed during the day, all data is backed up.

Example

Each night, every piece of data on every backup client is put to tape, whether or not the data has changed.

Advantage

This option makes restores very easy. All data is generally on one tape or set of tapes. If you need a restore today, you get the backups that were performed last night.

Disadvantages

One disadvantage is the extra cost of tapes for backing up data every night that does not change on a daily basis. This type of schedule requires the greatest amount of tape. A second disadvantage is that you may not have enough time each night (a large enough backup window) to perform full backups. The larger your site, the more these two disadvantages are an issue.

Option 2

The other extreme to performing full backups every day is to perform a full backup once a month and then incremental backups every day.

Example

The full backup was performed on the first of the month. Then on the fifteenth of the month a full restore of a backup client is required. This means that the full backup tape is required and every single incremental from the second of the month through the fourteenth of the month is required.

Advantages

One advantage is that this option only backs up what was changed on a day-to-day basis. Another advantage is that you will most likely be able to fit this schedule into the weekday backup window requirements.

Disadvantage

The disadvantage with this option is that a recover can be very cumbersome. You have to get the tape involved with the full backup and every incremental backup tape since the full backup. This can be tedious and lead to restore failures due to one bad tape or human error.

Option 3

Another, less extreme, schedule is to perform a full backup once a month, differential backups during the weekends, and then incremental backups the weeknights.

Example

The full backup was performed on the first weekend of the month. Then on the third Thursday of the month a full restore of a backup client is required. This means that the full backup tape, the most recent weekend differential backup tape, and then the Monday, Tuesday, and Wednesday incremental backup tapes are required.

Advantages

One advantage to this option is that it requires fewer tapes than the backup schedule described in Option 1. Another advantage is that you probably will be able to meet your backup window requirements, especially during the weekdays.

Disadvantages

One disadvantage is this option does require more tapes than in Option 2. A second disadvantage is that the recovers can still be a little bit cumbersome. As with Option 2, there are many tapes involved and therefore greater potential for restore failures.

Option 4

Another schedule is to perform a full backup every weekend and differential backups on the weeknights. This is a popular option because it represents a compromise between the amount of tape used, the time it takes to perform backups, and the number of tapes required for a restore.

Example

On the last Wednesday in a month, a full restore of a backup client is required. This means that the full backup tape from the most recent weekend and the differential tape from the night before, Tuesday night, are required. It requires more tape to be used than some of the other schedules, but by no means as much tape as required for a full backup every night. The major advantage of this schedule is that it requires relatively few tapes to perform the full restore.

Advantages

One advantage is that it requires fewer tapes than the backup schedule described in Option 1. Another advantage is that you probably will be able to meet your backup window requirements, especially during the weekdays. Yet another advantage is that recovers are not as cumbersome as in Option 2 or 3. A recover requires one full backup and one differential backup.

Disadvantage

This option uses more tape than Options 2 and 3.

Scheduling Backups and Other Jobs

Generally, scheduling within the backup software allows backups to begin only at a particular time. There are times when it would be better to have backups actually start after another event has finished. For example, say your site has a calculation engine that uses information from a database, calculates certain values based on that information, and then places the results back into the database. It may be important to back up the database after the calculation ends. This is actually a very simplistic example, because it shows only the backups dependent on one other job. There may be a series of batch jobs that have to be done one after another, possibly on completely different systems. This type of dependencies can become complex quickly.

There are third-party products for centrally controlling automated jobs. Products such as AutoSys from Platinum Technologies can perform this type of tightly coupled batch jobs. What would be ideal is if the backups could be integrated into the centrally managed job scheduling, so that administrators wouldn't have to manage the scheduling using the backup software and the central batch job scheduler.

If this type of scheduling is important to your site, take some time to investigate what the backup software can do and how it may integrate with schedulers outside of the backup software itself.

Overlap, New with Old

For sites where it is appropriate, overlap your old backups with the new backups for a minimum of one month. For example, your site may have a backup procedure in place and may be planning on replacing it with a more central backup implementation. If possible, keep the original backups in place for a month until you are confident that the new, more centralized backups are up and running properly.

During this overlap period, get all of your administrative tasks and procedures in place. Watch the new backups for errors and perform frequent restores. You may start slowly performing all of your production restores from the new backup environment, weaning yourself from the old environment.

Also during this overlap period, in addition to getting the administrative tasks in place, there are some other things that must be accomplished. These must be done to prepare for the day on which you completely switch over to the new backup environment:

- The change-over process must be well defined and laid out. This process should include which systems will be switched over and when. You should ensure that the process is not going to interfere with other projects. Sometimes systems involved with a major project deadline require that their backups not change until the deadline is met. This can be quite a coordination effort, but for a smooth transition, it is worth taking the extra time for planning.

- It is a given that you must be able to restore the data from the old backup environment. Therefore, you must outline procedures that explain how to perform restores for data from the old backup environment. Don't forget to thoroughly test these procedures, too. How to restore data from the old backup tapes should be part of your backup policy.

Migration, Old to New

Once the overlap period is over, you can start the migration process to the new backup environment. This may take a month or two or longer; it depends on how large your site is.

When the old backup environment is not performing backups, you should schedule a full backup the first time the new environment is completely responsible for the backups. This allows for a clean starting point for the new backup environment. Once the new backup system is in place, you have two options with the old backup data. You can either maintain both environments for restores or you can migrate the data from the old backup environment to the new backup environment.

Maintaining Two Restore Environments

Once the migration is completed, you should define the length of time the old backup tapes will be kept or whether you will actually migrate the old backup data into the new backup system. You will have a period of time where the new backup environment is in place and completely operational. However, you must retain the capability of restoring data from the old backup tapes. Eventually, after a certain number of months or years pass, the restore capability for the old backup tapes can be completely retired and is no longer needed. This period of time may be dictated by your legal or compliance departments.

You should clearly document the process of performing the restores from your old backup environment. It may involve installation of software or special configuration details. The operations staff responsible for the restores should be able to use this documentation without much assistance.

Additionally, your backup policy should clearly state for how long users can restore data from the old backup tapes. This may be more easily defined by giving a specific date after which the data from the old tapes will no longer be accessible.

Migrating Data

Migrating the backup data from the old backup environment to the new backup environment is a very difficult and time-consuming task. This should be considered only if you have no other option for your site. If maintaining multiple restore environments is a satisfactory answer to this problem, you should do so. Migrating the data is not recommended because of the time involved in doing so.

Monitoring

Traditionally, log parsing and error message monitoring has been the preferred method for watching systems. This type of monitoring is effective to a point. Beyond log parsing and error message monitoring, other system and infrastructure monitoring is becoming increasingly important. Corporations are investing lots of money in this area to more closely track the performance of their expenditures. This level of monitoring assists with future system purchases and adds confidence that money is being spent in the right area, not on just any area of the infrastructure.

Unfortunately, this type of monitoring "framework" is not widely installed and utilized. Only in the past few years has commercial off-the-shelf software been readily available, such as from Computer Associates or Tivoli. There are some sites with home-grown monitoring frameworks that were built before any commercial products were available. In any case, you should plan on integrating your backup implementation into this existing framework if it exists or is being planned at your site.

If the backup software or hardware you chose supports it, you can integrate SNMP or a MIB into your existing or planned monitoring framework. The SNMP and MIB concepts are described in Chapter 6, *Software Features*. However, to briefly recap, the SNMP manager/agent implementation can be in one of two forms. The first is in the form of traps. The SNMP agent can be implemented to trap events and send notifications to the manager. The second is in the form of polls. The SNMP agent can be implemented using a MIB that allows the manager to poll the agent as the manager sees fit. Basically, with traps, the agent provides information to the manager when the agent determines that it is necessary based on high- and low-water marks. With polling, the manager requests information from the agent when the manager wants to know what's happening. The traps push data to the manager and the polls pull information from the agent.

For example, it is technically possible for the backup software or a tape library to have a MIB for polling or traps for notification that watch tape drive performance or errors, backup or restore successes or failures, or tape utilization or capacity. It is possible to have a MIB that is polled at regular intervals with an SNMP manager that has the capability to perform a correlation of the information to determine whether there are potential problems. For instance, an important backup client has not been backed up for two days; therefore, the manager knows it should page someone immediately. As another example, the manager could note that a particular tape drive has had an excessive number of errors and thus send email, page, or call for hardware service the next business day.

While the technology is in place to perform this type of monitoring, it is not widely used. It is important for customers to ask about this type of monitoring. The software and hardware vendors will implement technology based on popular demand (the squeaky wheel gets the grease).

Notification

In addition to using SNMP for notification, many companies have implemented their own notification system. If your site is one of these, integrate the backup systems into this notification infrastructure. This is commonly a paging notification system for situations that warrant immediate attention. It could also be email, for non-emergency situations.

Trending

One thing that backup software packages are notoriously bad at is tracking information and performing trend analysis on that data. For example, you should know if a particular client increases or decreases the amount of data backed up if it is outside a particular window, such as a 20% increase or decrease. A drastic increase or decrease of data might indicate a problem with a backup client or the backup server. Another example is if a particular backup client has not been able to be backed up for x days. That client should be investigated, because it could have network problems or no longer be in service.

To watch for trends, you must determine what trends may be important. Then you must determine how to obtain that information from the backup software.

The information may be in the vendor's backup database. The problem is that it is sometimes difficult to get the response time needed using the vendor's database queries or the exact data needed from the vendor's own databases.

The information may be produced only in reports and never stored in a database. In this case, some sites write scripts to parse the reports generated when the backups finish. It may be possible to run these scripts at different times (once again, depending on the data needed). Some backup packages allow for postprocessing to be accomplished when the backup of a client is finished, and some backup packages allow for processing to be accomplished when particular groups of clients are completed or when all backups are completed.

With the data acquired from the parsing scripts, either on-the-fly analysis of the data can be done or the data can be stored in yet another database. You'll probably put the parsed data into your special site backup database that can be queried as needed at a later time. There are a couple of advantages to this approach. First, this may be the only way to store permanently certain data produced by the backup software. Second, the database you use for your information may be substantially faster to query than the vendor's database. This approach is very involved, but is sometimes the only way to manage trends at large sites.

Trending is another area, like the systems monitoring area, where customer demand will drive the backup software vendors to make changes. Trend analysis and tracking is possible. Most of the information is stored in the databases associated with the backup products. It is a matter of the backup vendors extending their databases and then writing their own software to perform the trend analysis. So ask for this feature; as more customers do, the vendors will be forced to add the functionality by popular demand.

Outside Integrator

You may choose to have an outside integrator help you with this phase of your backup project. The software vendor may have this service available, or you may find a third party to assist. If you use an integrator, work with them to define exactly what information you need for your site. Also, whatever they do needs to be fully documented. Finally, have the integrator train your staff members. Do not let the integrator come in and perform the work without including all three of these items in addition to the work itself.

12

Administration Hints

After you complete the integration, you should then change your focus to the administrative tasks involved with maintaining the backup environment. The administration is ongoing, and must be done no matter what size your site is or which backup model you are implementing. There are differences in the approach you should take, depending on the size of your site, and these will be noted throughout the chapter.

Administrative maintenance of the backup environment can be substantial work, depending on the size of your site; the larger the site, the larger the job. The administrative tasks can be broken into two categories: daily tasks and occasional tasks. This chapter highlights some of the tasks in these two groups, but by no means covers them all. You have to fine-tune the tasks and add others to best fit your site.

The specifics of how each of the tasks described in this chapter is performed are *very* software-specific. Therefore, this chapter can give you only general guidance to make sure that you don't overlook anything.

Daily Tasks

The daily tasks consist of a group of ongoing administrative chores that must be done to ensure the health and welfare of the backup system(s). These tasks help ensure backups are completed, so that you are able to perform the required restores. There are three very broad categories to describe the daily tasks:

Maintenance
> The maintenance tasks are those duties needed to keep the backup servers and associated tape libraries in proper working order.

Monitoring

> Monitoring of the backup system(s) is required to predict trends and growth. Every new system added to your site and every disk upgrade made to already existing systems at your site can potentially affect backups. Not only that, but disks are also continually getting larger. Users and applications are not using less disk space; they are using more. All of these items can affect backup and must be watched.

Troubleshooting

> Troubleshooting consists of dealing with any problems as they crop up. This is a very broad category and can consist of almost anything that affects backups in an unpredictable way.

The following sections examine some of the daily tasks that need to be performed. These by no means include all of the tasks. Once your backup server is in place and operational, you will develop a comprehensive list of tasks that are very specific to your site.

Check Backup Server Database

Every backup software package has some sort of database or group of databases in which all information about what was backed up, when it was backed up, and where it was backed up to is stored. Obviously, this information is vital to enable proper restores. Therefore, special attention should be given to the backup software database or group of databases.

Daily, or at least a few times a week, the database should be checked in the following manner:

- If the backup software has a consistency check utility for its database and if the backup software vendor agrees, run the consistency check on the database on a daily basis. The backup software vendor should provide specific instructions on what to do if this check fails.

- Confirm that the database was backed up properly to tape each day.

- From the backup server itself, query the database for random but predictable information to verify its contents.

- Choose a random but different backup client on a daily basis and query the backup server's database from that client. Choose a query that will provide predictable results and verify those results.

These tasks may seem excessive. However, the corporation's vital data is dependent on the backup system's reliability. You cannot be too careful with that level of responsibility.

These tasks are very package-dependent. Depending on the backup server software, these tasks may be automated. If not, it is important to perform them manually. This will help maintain confidence that the backup database is sound and capable of restores when necessary.

Log Management

Log files can cause some real problems. You don't want log files to get too large and cause full disk problems on your backup server, thus causing production failures, the worst of which is that your backups do not complete.

Most software packages (backup or other) do not manage their own logs. They may or may not have utilities in place that run regularly to truncate or rotate log files. This task is generally left up to the administrator. You may have to perform this task or write utilities to perform this task yourself.

For example, a common practice is to have a weekly utility run that rolls the log file(s) into another name and deletes the oldest log file after five weeks. Say the log file produced by your backup software is called *LOGS*:

- At the end of the first week:
  - the file *LOGS* is renamed *LOGS.1*
- At the end of the second week:
  - *LOGS.1* is renamed *LOGS.2*
  - *LOGS* is renamed *LOGS.1*
- At the end of the third week:
  - *LOGS.2* is renamed *LOGS.3*
  - *LOGS.1* is renamed *LOGS.2*
  - *LOGS* is renamed *LOGS.1*
- At the end of the fourth week:
  - *LOGS.3* is renamed *LOGS.4*
  - *LOGS.2* is renamed *LOGS.3*
  - *LOGS.1* is renamed *LOGS.2*
  - *LOGS* is renamed *LOGS.1*
- At the end of the fifth week and at the end of every week from that point on:
  - *LOGS.4* is removed
  - *LOGS.3* is renamed *LOGS.4*
  - *LOGS.2* is renamed *LOGS.3*
  - *LOGS.1* is renamed *LOGS.2*
  - *LOGS* is renamed *LOGS.1*

With this implementation, you always have four weeks of logs on hand to review in case of problems. Generally, that is enough for troubleshooting, and you can restore any logs necessary beyond that.

You should also browse the list of error messages that the software package may put into logs and watch for any particularly important ones. You may want to write scripts that will check the logs daily for specific messages and email the administrators with the results. This could be an early warning sign of a problem that is occurring or about to cause a worse problem.

Tape Management

For sites that do not have tape libraries, tape management is definitely a daily routine task. Each tape drive must be visited and the tapes changed, new tapes labeled and placed into the drive, and the old tape stored. Full procedures on how this is done should be written down and carefully followed. Multiple people at your site should be trained to perform these procedures. You do not want only one person aware of how this is accomplished.

For sites with tape libraries, the task is generally not performed daily. Of course, the smaller the library, the more often it must be visited. The management of the library is strongly tied to your backup policy for your site. The length of time the tapes stay online inside the library determines when they are rotated out of the tape library. Then they are rotated to a specified near-term storage for a defined length of time. Finally they are moved offsite. If any aspect of the tape management changes, remember to reflect the changes in your backup policy.

Review Backup Reports

Carefully go through all reports generated by the backup software. Remember that a successful restore cannot be done without a successful backup. Someone needs to be appointed as the individual who looks through the reports for successful backups as well as the backups that failed. You don't want someone to think someone else is reading the reports and vice versa.

As the reports are reviewed, it should be done with the backup policy in hand. This policy states what should be backed up and what will not be backed up. The reports generated by the backup software should reflect what is in the policy. If they do not, then the backups should be reconfigured or the backup policy changed.

Over time, you may find that this process is very tedious. It may be possible to automate a portion or all of this process with a program or script, depending on your site and the reports generated by the backup software. It is best to perform the process manually for a while and refine the steps before automating the procedures.

Successful backups

For successful backups within the report, make sure that you are backing up what you expected to. There is nothing worse than finding out you should have backed up something during the restore process. At that point, it is too late for that particular restore. It is easier to read the reports carefully, determine that data is missing from the backup, and then fix the backup configuration before the restore is required.

Failed backups

Check into every backup failure. This section cannot cover every possible combination and permutation of what can cause a backup to fail, but it does provide some small pointers on troubleshooting the problem. Usually there are error messages associated with the failure. These messages should be well documented in the vendor's manuals or through the online help. Reading the documentation associated with the error messages may help guide you to the problem and ultimately the solution. If the failure is persistent, contact the vendor's support to get help. Also, post the problem on the mailing lists related to the product. There is a good chance someone else on the mailing list will have had the same problem and can help you.

For all sites, the backup failure could be that the backup software was not properly installed or configured. It could also be possible that there is a hardware problem that needs to be addressed. Try performing an ad hoc backup. If the ad hoc backup is successful, then it is most likely a scheduling issue. If this is not successful, then it is probably not a scheduling issue, but some other configuration issue.

For medium or large sites, it could be any number of problems. The troubleshooting process is not straightforward, but there are some basic steps you can take to get going:

1. For all backup failures, first try to ping the backup client from the backup server and vice versa:

   — If the two computers cannot reach each other (going both ways), you have network connectivity or system configuration problems.

   — If the two computers can reach one another, then chances are that the network is not a concern.

2. If the pings are successful, try to perform an ad hoc backup from the backup client:

   — If this ad hoc backup fails, then examine the backup software configuration on the backup client itself.

   — If the ad hoc backup from the client works properly, the backup client software is probably all right.

3. Now try initiating an ad hoc backup of the backup client from the backup server:

— If that does not work properly, then it could be a configuration problem on the backup server.

— If this backup from the backup server works properly, there may be something wrong with the automated backup schedule or some other configuration detail on the backup server. It may also be possible that whatever was wrong is fixed and you are not aware of the fix.

Of course, not all cases are covered here, but this should help you narrow down the causes.

Watch for Anomalies and Trends

There are a number of items that should be watched and tracked on an ongoing basis to be able to see any anomalies or predict any trends. You may want to store this information in a database so that you can plot the data and perform queries against the data as necessary.

Most of the following tracking items can be automated. However, it is best to perform the process manually for a while and refine the steps before automating the procedures. Items to track initially include the following:

The total amount of data that is being backed up per backed-up system
This is especially important when you perform full backups. Generally, small sites do not have tape libraries. Therefore, if the amount of data backed up is larger than one tape, you must span tapes. Without tape libraries, spanning tapes requires human intervention to change tapes physically. As you see the total amount of data backed up approaching the total size of the tape, you can implement procedures to include the tape changes or remove data from the system that is no longer needed.

The license count at your site
The software vendors will generally provide *x* licences for backup software for your site. Once you exceed that number, you must buy more licenses to run backups legally. If you are watching the license count, you can better predict when the number of systems being backed up approaches the number of licenses your company owns. This then allows you to get more licenses on site, before you run into an emergency situation.

The total number of restore requests
As mentioned before, small sites generally do not have tape libraries. Without tape libraries, every time a restore request is issued, the tape(s) for that restore must be found and placed into the appropriate tape library. The more

restores, the more human intervention that is required. If you are tracking restores and the number drastically increases, this will help you justify more support individuals or a tape library, if necessary.

The total number of tapes used on a per-week or per-month basis

This tracking makes reordering tapes easier. Without this information, you may have to just guess when ordering the tapes and your guess could be wrong.

The time it takes to perform the backups

Generally, this is not part of the backup software product's features. This may be something that you need to plot out. You may find it desirable to write a script that extracts the start and stop time of the backups, the total amount of data backed up, and the total number of clients backed up, and that stores these values. Then another script or program could be written or a spreadsheet program could be used to provide plots of those values. You may also be able to configure the backup software to notify you or write a program that notifies you if the backup window, amount of data backed up, or the total number of backup clients jumps more than say a certain percentage of the last similar backup.

By tracking these items, you will be instantly aware of any anomalies and able to plot growth. Steady growth over time, plotted against the number of backup clients, will account for natural growth in the backup client count. However, overnight large jumps could account for a poor configuration decision on the backup server or a large number of backup clients added.

This information is also what you need to plan for and justify the next backup server. If you can present management with concrete growth paths and projections, they either need to tell their employees to use less disk space or plan on buying more backup servers, or you'll at least be able to cover yourself when things start failing. It is hard to dispute concrete growth figures.

Occasional Tasks

Occasional tasks are those that are performed on an as-needed basis, which may be weekly, monthly, quarterly, or annually. The frequency of these tasks depends on the task itself and how large or how dynamic your site is.

The tasks in this section are often overlooked or pushed aside. The daily tasks are so ingrained in the administrative staff that the tasks that need to be done only once in a while are commonly forgotten and sometimes not done. These tasks are just as important as the daily tasks and should not be left undone.

Operational Manual

By this point, you are probably thinking that all of the writing and documenting that is referred to in this book is getting a bit ridiculous. That is not true. Documentation can make your job easier and is helpful for your management. Since backups themselves are difficult to see or put your hand on, the operations manual helps people see what is in place, what is protecting the data at their site, and what procedures are required to maintain the backups. This type of manual can be useful for management to be able to justify your duties and your compensation as well as a larger head count as the backup environment grows.

This manual may duplicate information with the backup policy. That is acceptable because the audience for both documents will be very different. The operations manual should be done for any size site and, at a minimum, should have these major sections:

Current backup configuration
Exactly what is in place for the backups. This should include all of the hardware components and software components that make up the environment.

Daily tasks
Everything required to maintain the health and welfare of your backup environment on a daily basis. At a minimum, you should have all of the daily tasks mentioned in this chapter as sections in your manual (where appropriate). As you fine-tune and add administrative tasks that are site-specific, you should also add those procedures to the manual.

Occasional tasks
Tasks to be done on an occasional basis. As a matter of fact, a review of this operational manual should be listed as one of these tasks. This should list dates when the tasks should be accomplished. You may want to specify that something should be done twice a year, but with this approach, you will probably forget to do it or put it off. If you state that something must be reviewed or done by March 15th and September 15th, there is a much better chance it will get accomplished.

Future work
Any future work that is required to keep the backup environment moving forward. This could include, but is not limited to, a list of predicted upgrades to hardware or software.

The first draft of the operations manual will be a big job. Then, as procedures and the backup environment change, the operations manual must be updated. This manual will be a living document (like the backup policy document discussed in Chapter 5, *Policy and Politics*) and revised on a regular basis. It is recommended that the operations manual be reviewed a minimum of twice a year. If changes are required, they should be made at that time. You may want to keep a copy of the operations manual on your internal web site so that after the review cycle and after changes are made to the document, everyone can see the changes immediately.

Review the Backup Policy

Like the operational manual, the backup policy should be reviewed twice a year. You should make all required changes to the policy at this time. However, don't restrict policy changes to these times. Other events may occur and require changes to the policy. The scheduled review is commonly overlooked and not done regularly. You should try hard not to fall into that habit. With the rate of change in companies and in the technical industry, the backup policy review should not be put off.

The review process should include all individuals or job categories who participated in composing the original policy. Don't forget to include individuals from the legal and compliance departments. Also, don't limit your review group to management. The group should include some of the administrative staff members that take care of the backup environment on a daily basis. Commonly, these individuals best know the current state of the backup environment. Additionally, they are the ones who have to enforce the policy or operate within the constraints policy, so they should be able to provide input.

Once the initial group has reviewed and updated the backup policy, don't forget to distribute the new policy. The new policy should have a summary of the changes at the beginning of the document. Also, as mentioned in Chapter 5, you may want to put the policy on your internal web site for all employees to read. It is an effective way to distribute documents that change often.

Fire Drills

A fire drill is a test in which a particular restore request is made and the process surrounding the restore is graded on how long the restore takes, whether the restored data is valid, and what level of service is received. (Depending on your site, the fire drills may be referred to as audits.) The fire drills should be done for all sizes of sites.

At some sites, fire drills may be done by the compliance department. Whether or not the compliance department dictates when the fire drills are done, the administrative group managing the backup environment should perform their own fire drills as well. The level of the restore should vary from something very simple, such as a single file, to something very difficult, such as a complete system recovery. Each fire drill should be slightly different, so that the administrative staff does not become complacent.

You should have both scheduled and unscheduled fire drills of your backup system. You may also want unannounced fire drills. Basically, this is a restore request that is being graded, but the administrative group is not told that it is a drill. The frequency of the fire drills is completely up to individual preference. However, you should probably have them quarterly, at a minimum.

Downtime

The backup environment will need software and hardware upgrades as well as maintenance. Upgrades and maintenance to the backup systems should be planned for and anticipated. The upgrade downtime may be used to install a new version of backup software, a new version of the operating system, a new disk drive, or a new tape device. The maintenance downtime may be used to fix a tape drive. The upgrades and maintenance may or may not require the system to go down, but it is better to plan for the outage and not use it than not plan for it and need it. Of course, emergencies will crop up and force your backup systems to be down, but you should also schedule downtime.

For small sites with individual tape drives on systems, the downtime is relatively easy to schedule. When you bring a system down to perform an upgrade of some sort, you are affecting only that one system. Yes, the one system may be providing services to many users, but it is generally a well defined set of users. The downtime can be scheduled around that group's particular schedule and needs.

For sites implementing network backups, the scheduled downtime for backup servers is crucial. This downtime must be coordinated with either a single department, multiple departments, or the entire company, and must be announced far in advance. The downtime must be tightly managed, with very specific tasks that must be performed during the outage. When you schedule the time, don't hesitate to add a couple of hours to the anticipated outage time to hedge your bets in the event of problems. It is definitely better to get the backup systems up sooner than scheduled than to have to explain why the downtime was longer than scheduled.

You should schedule downtime quarterly, at a minimum. Having it regularly scheduled gets everyone into a routine, and they will eventually accept that the backup system is not available at these well-defined times. In the event that you don't need to use the scheduled downtime, consider it a bonus.

Sample Backup Policy

This appendix provides a sample backup policy. You can use this policy as a starting point for your policy and add to it or remove from it as you desire. The policy is for the company I have used for other examples, Genorff Engineering Inc. (GEI). GEI is implementing network backups. Their site consists of 200 user desktop workstations, each with 100 MB of vital data to be backed up, and 10 servers, each with 6 GB of vital data to be backed up.

GEI Information Technology Backup Policy

Document Comments and Questions

The document was written by and is maintained by the Information Technology group at Genorff Engineering Inc. (GEI). Please forward any questions or comments about this document to: Luke McCulloch, extension: 518, email: *lukem*.

Introduction

This backup policy outlines what data is backed up, how often it is backed up, what data is not backed up, why it is omitted from backups, data restore estimates, where data tapes are stored long-term, and who to contact if you have any questions with regards to backups or restores.

This document and the policy outlined within this document were produced in coordination with GEI's compliance department, legal department, and IT staff:

Compliance department

> In addition to participating in the backup policy, the compliance department has the authority to mandate periodic "fire drills." At unscheduled intervals, compliance will be able to request a random restore and verification. This is to verify and validate the data backed up as well as the restore procedures.

Legal department

> The legal department also participated in the creation of the backup policy. They are provided with weekly backup reports, which they scan to verify what data is backed up or not backed up. In addition to the reports, GEI's legal department has the capability to perform ad hoc queries of the data backed up to obtain more detailed backup information if they have the need to do so.

IT Staff

> This backup policy has been fully reviewed by all of GEI's IT staff. This includes the senior staff members and the Chief Information Officer (CIO).

Overview

The systems backed up at GEI are spread across two locations. The first location is in the downtown area of Wheaton. This location supports the sales and marketing departments, their administrative support, as well as a skeleton group of other support staff members. The second location, in the suburb of Daleville, is where the data center and additional support personnel are located. The computer systems backed up are almost evenly located at both sites (see Figure A-1).

GEI has implemented network backups with two central backup servers that each have a tape library. These severs are used exclusively for backups and restores. To maintain immediate offsite backups, the computers at the Wheaton location are backed up to the Daleville location and the systems in the Daleville office are backed up to the Wheaton office.

The backup servers are located in a secure and limited access room. This is to reduce accessibility, tampering, or theft. The physical location of the servers is as follows:

- The backup server, *bu11*, in Wheaton, is located in the 30th floor data center, rack A19.

- The backup server, *bu21*, in Daleville, is located in the 5th floor data center, rack B02.

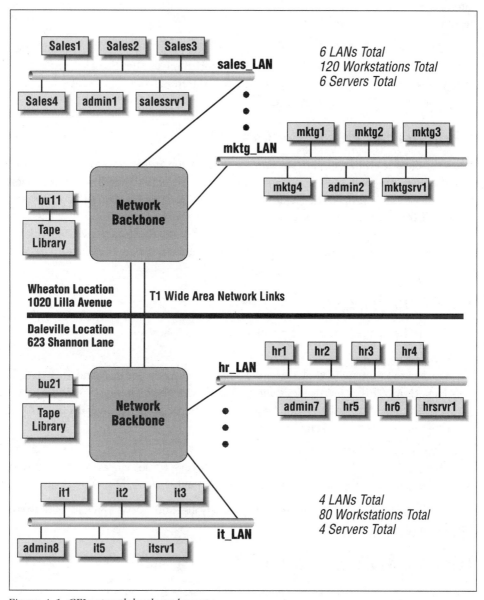

Figure A-1. GEI network backups layout

Document Life Cycle and Location

This document is a living document and will be updated quarterly. It will reflect any policy changes that have occurred in the past three months. When changes are made, an email notification will be sent to all individuals at GEI highlighting the backup policy changes and providing the location of the document on the internal web site. The document will be available for general review and comment.[*]

This document and its quarterly updates can be found on the GEI internal web site. Go to the *Information Technology* link and then to the *Backup and Restore Policy* link. From this link, you will find the different backup policies listed by month and year. The most current policy will be at the top of the list.

Computer Systems to Be Backed Up

The vital data at GEI is spread out and located on the user's desktop workstations and the departmental file, print, and application servers. Therefore, every computer will be backed up to one extent or another. There are a total of 120 workstations and 6 servers across 6 subnets in the Wheaton location that are backed up to the backup server, *bu11*. In the Daleville location, the totals are 80 workstations and 4 servers across 4 subnets that are backed up to the backup server, *bu21*.

Data to Be Backed Up

The data to be backed on each type of system is as follows:

Desktop workstations
> All desktops are where the user's home directory is located and this data is backed up. This is any folder called *C:\homedir* or *D:\homedir*. Anything outside of these locations is not backed up. There is an average of 100 MB of vital data on each workstation.

Print, file, and application servers
> All servers will be completely backed up (every folder on every hard drive). There is an average of 6 GB of vital data on each server.

There is approximately 80 GB total (workstations and servers) vital data to be backed up at GEI.

Data Not to Be Backed Up

The data not to be backed up on each type of system is as follows:

Desktop workstations
> On the workstations, the data that will not be backed up is any data that is not in the folders called *C:\homedir* or *D:\homedir*; that is, any data not

---

[*] Technology changes at a very rapid rate and making changes to the document quarterly should allow us to keep up with these changes.

stored in the user's home directory. It is the user's responsibility to make sure they store vital data in one of these two locations. The IT department is not responsible for backing up vital data left outside of the home directories.

Print, file, and application servers

There is no data on the servers that is not backed up. All servers will be completely backed up, except for core files and object files (every folder on every hard drive).

Backup Schedule Implemented

The backup window and backup schedule defined by the IT department is the following:

- Weekdays, 5 hours, 11:00 P.M. to 4:00 A.M, Differential Backup
- Weekends, 17 hours, Saturday 8:00 P.M. to Sunday 1:00 P.M., Full Backup

The backup schedule implemented at GEI consists of full backups performed on the weekends and differential backups performed each weekday. A differential backup is one in which the data changed since the last full backup is placed onto tape. Therefore, at GEI, on Monday all data changed that day is backed up. Then, on Tuesday, all data changed that day or Monday is backed up. The backup schedule continues like this until Friday when all data that was changed during the week, Monday through Friday, is backed up. Then, over the weekend, the full backup is performed and the differential backups start from that point on.

With this type of backup schedule, if a catastrophic disk failure occurs on Thursday then the full backup from the previous weekend and the differential backup from Wednesday night are required. A minimal number of tapes are required to perform the restore request.

Policy for Building/Updating Emergency Repair Disks

The Windows NT emergency repair disks will not be created or maintained by GEI's IT department. The IT department will rebuild any systems that have a failure and cannot recover from that failure. They use a custom-built application that makes rebuilding systems easier, faster, and more predictable than troubleshooting a corrupted system. After the initial rebuild of the failed system, a restore will be performed.

Tape Rotation Policy

Tapes will be kept in the tape libraries for a minimum of five weeks. This means restores from data up to five weeks old does not require human intervention for tape loads. After five weeks, the tapes will be rotated out of the library into on-site storage.

Full backup tapes are kept for a total of seven years. After seven years, the tapes are not reutilized; they are destroyed in accordance with GEI's compliance department. The differential backup tapes are reused after all of the data on the tape is over six months old. The tapes are reused once and then destroyed. Data older than six months will be able to be restored only from a full backup tape.

Onsite Backup Tapes

Once the tapes are rotated out of the tape library, they will be stored onsite. These tapes will be co-located with the tape library in racks in the corresponding data center. Since the backups are performed between sites and the backup data is immediately offsite, there is no threat of losing both the computer systems and the backup tapes in the event of a catastrophic site loss (for example, a building fire).

The tape racks in the data centers allow for two months of storage; this is in addition to the five weeks of storage in the tape libraries themselves, for a total of a little more than three months of onsite backup tapes. After this three-month window, the tapes will be moved offsite to a warehouse for long-term storage.

Anticipated Restore Response for Onsite Backup Tapes

Any restores of data that is less than five weeks old will be immediately responded to by the backup server and tape library. The average tape load time for the library is less than one minute. Therefore, the response to the restore will be very quick. The length of time it takes to perform the restore, once the tape or tapes are loaded into the tape drives, is a factor of the amount of data to be restored and the backup client requesting the restore.

Any restores that are older than five weeks but less than three months old will be responded to by a GEI staff member. The backup software will automatically notify the staff members that a tape is required that is not in the tape library. The tape or tapes required for the restore will be loaded into the tape library by hand.

If the restore request is between 8:00 A.M. and 6:00 P.M. during the weekdays, Monday through Friday, the tape load response time will be 30 minutes or less to load the tape in the library. The restore time itself is a factor of how much data is restored and the type of backup client requesting the restore.

If the restore request is between 6:00 P.M. and 8:00 A.M. during the weekdays, Monday through Thursday, or Friday from 6:00 P.M. through Monday 8:00 A.M. (over the weekend) the tape load response time will be 90 minutes or less. This is due to the reduced IT staff members available during non-business hours. The restore time itself is a factor of how much data is restored, the type of backup client requesting the restore, and if the restore itself has to compete with backups being performed. In the case when a restore is competing with backups, the restore speed will be negatively affected.

Offsite Location of Backup Tapes, Long-Term Storage

The backup tapes are stored in the tape library for five weeks, then placed in racks in the data centers for two additional months, and finally moved to a long-term facility. This facility is managed by Jed Davis Storage Specialists and is located at 9 Wyatt Way in Chatham.

Jed Davis Storage Specialists is a private company that has been in business for 18 years. It is owned by Eric Daniels and Wynn Smiley. They currently have 40 employees and handle long-term storage of tape media as well as paper documents. They support over 250 businesses in the downtown area and suburbs of Wheaton.

Anticipated Restore Response for Offsite Backup Tapes

When a restore request that requires tapes that were used for backups more than three months ago is issued, the tape or tapes required for the restore must be obtained from Jed Davis Storage Specialists. The IT staff is automatically notified that the tape is required and then a formal request is made to the storage facility. The storage facility must locate the tape and then send it to one of the two GEI facilities.

If the restore is requested from Monday through Friday, the tape load response time will be 12 hours or less to load the tape in the library. The restore time itself is a factor of how much data is restored, the type of backup client requesting the restore, and if the restore itself has to compete with backups being performed.

If the restore is requested on Saturday or Sunday, the tape load response time will be 24 hours or less to load the tape in the library. The restore time itself is a factor of how much data is restored, the type of backup client requesting the restore, and if the restore itself has to compete with backups being performed. GEI is charged $50 for each tape retrieved.

Offsite Tape Expiration

Before the tapes are shipped to the storage facility, they are separated into full backup tapes and differential backup tapes.

Full backup tapes are kept for a total of seven years at Jed Davis Storage Specialists. After seven years, the tapes are not reutilized; they are destroyed by the storage facility in accordance with GEI's compliance department's regulatory requirements at the time of destruction.

The differential tapes are stored for three months at Jed Davis Storage Specialists. After three months, the data is destroyed by the storage facility, the tape cartridge is marked, and they are shipped back to the GEI location to be reused once more (for differential backups).

Responsible Individuals for Backups and Restores

Responsibility for backups and restores at GEI lies with the IT operations department. The following information provides contact names and numbers in the event that an individual needs to be reached:

- Operations Department Manager, Alyssa James, extension: 620, email: *ajames*
- Weekday Shift Manager, Jan Swanson, extension: 604, email: *jswanson*
- Weeknight Shift Manager, Vivian Buxton, extension: 103, email: *vbuxton*
- Weekend Shift Manager, Jenny Adams, extension: 104, email: *jadams*

There is also a group email alias (*bures*) that can be used for any questions or comments relating tobackups or restores.

B

SCSI Fundamentals

The most popular type of interface and protocol used by tape drives is the Small Computer System Interface (SCSI). The SCSI protocol is a well-defined and popular ANSI industry standard. The SCSI bus is not part of the motherboard and is therefore not manufacturer-dependent, thereby providing standardization. SCSI is a cost-efficient, flexible protocol that provides good performance.

To help you weed through the tape hardware on the market today, a little introduction to SCSI is in order. For network backups, and probably for local backups, you will use SCSI tape devices. There are many variations of SCSI and different SCSI terminology used in the industry, so this appendix provides the basics to get you started.

Standards

The SCSI hardware and software standards emerged out of the need for universal interface standards. Before SCSI standards existed, devices such as hard disks had dedicated interfaces that were proprietary to the vendor who manufactured the device. This was expensive and difficult for the vendors to maintain, as well as expensive for the users who had to buy a different interface board with each device they purchased. As with any standard, the SCSI standards have evolved to what they are today:

SCSI-1

> SCSI-1 started in 1980 and was formalized in 1986. The major problem with the SCSI-1 standard was that it had too many vendor options, which resulted in incompatibilities among SCSI-1 vendors and the devices they designed and developed.

SCSI-2

SCSI-2 is the current standard, which started in 1986 and was formalized in 1994. SCSI-2 is an enhanced version of SCSI-1 and not an entirely new standard. SCSI-2 maintained backward compatibility with SCSI-1 devices and the transition between the two standards has been moving slowly and easily.

SCSI-3

SCSI-3 had not yet been approved at the time this book went to press. It is actually not a standard itself; rather, it is a collection of independent smaller standards. It is not anticipated that the SCSI-3 standards will replace the SCSI-2 standard; they will most likely coexist.

Compatibility among the standards is maintained because all devices, whether they are SCSI-1, SCSI-2, or SCSI-3, start up in the same mode. Before they can switch modes, the devices must negotiate how they will transfer data. The devices then switch to whatever mode is agreed upon.

Terminology

Before going any further into the SCSI discussion, a quick set of definitions is required. The terms listed here are commonly used when referring to parallel SCSI. They are in alphabetical order:

Fast or Fast Narrow SCSI

Both of these terms refer to the use of the synchronous transfer rates. This transfer rate is optional and is used only in the Data-In/Out Phase. See the later section "Protocol" for details on the synchronous transfer and the Data-In/Out Phase.

Fast Wide SCSI

This term refers to the combination of the two byte wide, plus parity, data width and the FAST transfer rate (synchronous transfer rate).

FAST-20

The FAST-20 standard doubles the throughput and the number of supported devices, compared to Fast Wide SCSI, with the use of the SCSI-3 protocol. This term replaced the older term Ultra SCSI. This change was due to trademark infringements with the company UltraStore, which owns the trademark for the term Ultra SCSI.

FAST-40

The FAST-40 standard also uses the SCSI-3 protocol, but doubles the throughput, compared to FAST-20, by using a wide data path. This term replaced the older term Wide Ultra SCSI. This change was due to trademark infringements with the company UltraStore, which owns the trademark for the term Ultra SCSI.

Logical Unit Number (LUN)

The LUN is the unique address assigned to the SCSI target. For regular SCSI, LUNs range from 0 to 7. For wide SCSI, LUNs range from 0 to 15.

Narrow or Regular or Slow SCSI

All three terms are used interchangeably with the term SCSI to refer to the width of data on the SCSI cable as one byte wide, plus parity.

SCSI initiator and SCSI target

The SCSI devices on the bus can be either initiators, targets, or both. The communications are started by the SCSI initiators, which request that a command be executed. The SCSI targets respond to the initiators and carry out the requested command. SCSI devices can act as either initiators or targets (but not both at the same time). The SCSI initiator is usually (not always) the host computer and the SCSI target is usually the peripheral attached to the host computer.

Wide SCSI

This term refers to the width of the data on the SCSI cable as two bytes wide, plus parity.

Table B-1 provides a quick reference to the different variations of parallel SCSI and includes the maximum bus throughput that can be achieved, the maximum data bits that can be used, and the maximum number of devices supported simultaneously.

Table B-1. SCSI Terminology Matrix

SCSI Term	SCSI Type	Maximum Throughput	Maximum Data Bus Width	Maximum Number of Devices
SCSI	SCSI-1	3 MB/s	8 bit	8
Slow SCSI	SCSI-2	5 MB/s	8 bit	8
Fast SCSI (a.k.a. Fast Narrow SCSI)	SCSI-2	10 MB/s	8 bit	8
Wide SCSI	SCSI-2	10 MB/s	16 bit	8
Fast Wide SCSI	SCSI-2	20 MB/s	16 bit	8
FAST-20	SCSI-3	20 MB/s	8 bit	16
FAST-40	SCSI-3	40 MB/s	16 bit	16

Protocol

The SCSI standard has two distinct sets of protocols: a top portion and a bottom portion. The top protocol defines the set of SCSI software commands; the bottom protocol defines the SCSI hardware specifications. As with any protocol stack, separating the two parts allows for the flexibility of changing one without affecting the other. An overview of the SCSI standard is provided in the following section.

SCSI Software Protocol

The top portion of the SCSI software protocol is well defined with a series in phases; the SCSI bus can be in only one phase at any time. These phases are divided into two basic groups.

The three following phases are grouped together because they are all required to initialize a connection. The phases below must happen in the order listed:

Bus Free Phase

> This phase is an indication that the SCSI bus is idle.

Arbitration Phase

> This phase is entered when the SCSI devices detect a Bus Free Phase. The devices attempt to gain control of the SCSI bus. Only one device can communicate with one other device on the bus at one time. If multiple devices try to gain control of the SCSI bus, the priority of the devices is based on the device's LUN. For regular SCSI, the highest priority is LUN-7 and the lowest priority is LUN-0 (7 to 0). For wide SCSI, the highest priority is LUN-7 down to LUN-0 and then LUN-15 down to LUN-8 (7 to 0, 15 to 8).

Selection/Reselection Phase

> The device that wins the Arbitration Phase enters into this phase. The Reselection Phase is entered if the target was previously connected, issued a command, disconnected to perform the slow task, completes the task, and is re-establishing the connection. Otherwise, the target is entering the Selection Phase. In either case, during this phase the initiator tries to contact the target. If the target cannot be reached, the initiator times out and enters the Bus Free Phase again.

Once the three previous phases are completed and the connection is established, the Information Transfer Phase starts. This phase is actually a group of multiple phases that are used to move the data on the SCSI bus. The phases may occur in any order and multiple times in one session:

Command Phase

This phase allows the SCSI initiator to transmit commands to the SCSI target to tell the target what needs to be done.

Data-In/Out Phase

This phase is actually two distinct phases and is used to transfer data between the initiator and target. The Data-In Phase is used to transfer data to the SCSI initiator and the Data-Out Phase is used to transfer data from the SCSI initiator.

Status Phase

This phase is entered when the data transfer is completed. The SCSI target tells the initiator whether the transfer was successful.

Message-In/Out Phase

This phase is two distinct phases and is used to provide a progress report. The Message-In Phase allows the initiator to receive a message and the Message-Out Phases allow the initiator to transmit a message.

The Information Transfer Phase, Command Phase, Message-In/Out Phase, and Status Phase all use asynchronous data transfer to accomplish their tasks. This is how the newer SCSI protocols remain backward-compatible. Once the Data-In/Out Phase begins, the initiator and target negotiate to determine whether they will use the default asynchronous data transfer or use the optional, higher-performance, synchronous data transfer. The two can be described as follows:

Synchronous data transfer

This type of transfer can typically provide a maximum of 3 to 4 MB/s throughput to the tape device. With synchronous data transfer, every block of data sent to tape must be acknowledged. Once the acknowledgment is received, the backup server goes to the next block of data. With high volumes of data, waiting for an acknowledgment for each block of data can result in a high overhead.

Asynchronous data transfer

This type of transfer can typically support a maximum throughput of 5 MB/s with narrow SCSI and 10 to 20 MB/s with wide SCSI. With asynchronous data transfer, after the initial handshake, the initiator and target agree upon a rate and maximum time delay. Then blocks of data are sent to tape and the backup software does not wait for individual acknowledgments. The longer the SCSI cable, the more noticeable the increased throughput gained.

The Information Transfer Phase lasts until the SCSI target releases. When the target releases, the SCSI bus is placed into the Bus Free Phase (back to the top again).

SCSI Hardware Protocol

The bottom portion of the SCSI protocol provides the standard for the transmission of commands and handshaking over the electrical wire itself. The transmission protocol widely used today is the parallel SCSI protocol; the emerging transmission protocol is serial SCSI:

Parallel SCSI

The industry is predominately using parallel transmission protocol for tape drive technology. As the name implies, data is transmitted over multiple wires at one time. This protocol is very fast, but is practical only for short distances. The hardware and device drivers required for implementation are available and well-known.

The terms single-ended and differential are used when referring to different types of parallel SCSI buses. The distinction between the two terms is the length of the bus itself. A single-ended bus can be a maximum of 3 meters (about 9 feet) long. A differential bus can be a maximum of 25 meters (over 80 feet). The differential bus uses a wider cable and more wires to compensate for any signal degradation due to distance. Therefore, the differential SCSI implementations are more expensive than the single-ended ones.

Serial SCSI

There are new requirements that cannot be accomplished with parallel SCSI, which include Plug and Play, increased throughput rates, guaranteed data delivery, and smaller cables and connectors. To meet these demands, SCSI-3 is introducing the serial SCSI transmission protocol. In contrast to the parallel SCSI implementation, data is sent in a sequential fashion. Even though the new protocol is not completely formalized, vendors are starting to implement what they believe the standard will become to get ahead of the market.

One serial protocol, Fiber Channel SCSI, is being used with external high-speed disk drive implementations. Another serial protocol, Serial Storage Architecture (SSA), is appearing in tape library implementations. Since SCSI-3 is not formalized, the SSA tape libraries are not very popular, so they are not discussed here. Once the SCSI-3 standard is formalized, serial SCSI will be more widely used because of the advantages mentioned earlier.

Advantages

SCSI is very popular and widely used. You could use SCSI based on just those two facts, but it is also nice to know about the following additional advantages:

Performance

The SCSI protocol utilizes a small amount of CPU to process its protocol. This is because the SCSI intelligence is located on the device (on the tape drive, for example) instead of primarily in the device driver on the computer. This makes the SCSI protocol very efficient. SCSI can also simultaneously process many requests, not just one request at a time. The SCSI commands can be interleaved (to different devices), and SCSI devices can disconnect and reconnect to allow slow operations to execute offline.

Extended device support

SCSI can support up to 8 (regular or narrow SCSI) or 15 (wide SCSI) devices on a single bus. These devices can be external or internal to the computer. Also, the same SCSI bus can be used by different types of devices. For example tape drives, hard disks, CD-ROM drives, scanners, and modems can all utilize a single SCSI bus.[*] The ability to use different devices is due in part to the fact that the SCSI bus has no clock signals. This means that the slower devices do not affect the faster devices.[†]

---

[*] One exception may be with the read/write CD-ROM drives. I have experienced a situation where that type of device had to be on its own SCSI bus, otherwise the writes were unexpectedly interrupted and not completed. This may change as the read/write CD-ROM drives become more popular and more heavily used. Of course, this is not relevant to tape backups, but is worth noting.

[†] For optimal performance, the SCSI devices on the same bus should be about the same speed (this is not required, though).

C

Hardware Vendors

To assist with finding hardware for your backup and restore implementation, this appendix provides a list of the backup tape drive hardware vendors and a list of the backup tape library hardware vendors.

Remember that the backup software must support your hardware. The hardware support lists are available at the software vendor's web sites.

Another point to remember is that many vendors repackage what they receive from the original equipment manufacturer and label the product as their own. So, don't be surprised over who you see listed. Also, there may be other vendors that you don't find in these tables. There may be local vendors in your area that are not commonly or widely known that sell tape drive and tape library equipment.

The tables are a starting point for you. You will note that some of the web site entries are empty. They were not forgotten; they are blank because I could not find the web site through my research. This could be because the company listed actually makes the drive, but does not package the drive for sale.

Tape Drive Table

Table C-1 contains a list of vendors that sell standalone tape drives.

Table C-1. Tape Drive Availability

Tape Drive Company	Web Site	QIC	4mm	8mm	DLT	AIT
ADIC	*www.adic.com*		yes	no	yes	yes
Aiwa	*www.aiwa.com/csd*		yes			
Andataco	*www.andataco.com*		yes	yes	yes	

Table C-1. Tape Drive Availability (continued)

Tape Drive Company	Web Site	QIC	4mm	8mm	DLT	AIT
Archive		yes	yes			
Boxhill	www.boxhill.com		yes	yes	yes	
Cipher	www.4cipher.com				yes	
Compaq	www.compaq.com	yes	yes		yes	
Conner	www.conner.com	yes	yes	yes	yes	
DEC	www.dec.com	yes	yes	yes	yes	
Dynatek		yes	yes	yes		
EMASS	www.emass.com				yes	yes
Emerald / NCE	www.ncegroup.com		yes	yes	yes	yes
Exabyte	www.exabyte.com	yes	yes	yes	yes	
Hitachi	www.hitachi.com			yes		
Hewlett-Packard	www.hp.com	yes	yes	yes	yes	
IBM	www.ibm.com	yes	yes	yes	yes	
Imation	www.imation.com	yes				
Iomega	www.iomega.com		yes			
Maynard		yes				
MDI	www.mdi.com		yes			
Overland Data	www.overlanddata.com				yes	
Quantum	www.quantum.com				yes	
Rexon		yes				
Seagate	www.seagate.com	yes	yes	yes		yes
Sony	www.sony.com		yes	yes		yes
Spectra Logic	www.spectralogic.com		yes	yes		yes
Storage Dimensions	www.storagedimensions.com		yes	yes	yes	
StorageTek	www.storagetek.com		yes	yes	yes	
Sun	www.sun.com	yes	yes	yes	yes	
Tandberg	www.tandberg.com	yes				
Tecmar	www.tecmar.com	yes	yes			
TTI	www.ttech.com		yes	yes	yes	yes
WangDAT			yes			
Wanttek		yes	yes			

Tape Library Table

The vendors included here sell tape libraries. Not all of the companies in Table C-1 are also in Table C-2. Some vendors specialize in tape libraries only and do not sell individual tape drives. The reverse is also true; some tape drive vendors do not sell tape libraries.

Table C-2. Tape Library Availability

Tape Library Company	Web Site	QIC	4mm	8mm	DLT	AIT
ADIC	*www.adic.com*		yes	yes	yes	yes
Aiwa	*www.aiwa.com/csd*		yes			
Andataco	*www.andataco.com*			yes	yes	
ATL (Odetics)	*www.atlp.com*				yes	
Boxhill	*www.boxhill.com*			yes	yes	
Breece Hill	*www.breecehill.com*				yes	
Compaq	*www.compaq.com*		yes		yes	
Conner	*www.conner.com*		yes	yes	yes	
DEC	*www.dec.com*		yes		yes	
EMASS	*www.emass.com*				yes	yes
Emerald / NCE	*www.ncegroup.com*		yes	yes	yes	
Exabyte	*www.exabyte.com*		yes	yes	yes	
Hewlett-Packard	*www.hp.com*		yes		yes	
IBM	*www.ibm.com*		yes	yes	yes	
Imation	*www.imation.com*	yes	yes		yes	
MediaLogic ADL	*www.adlinc.com*		yes	yes	yes	yes
Mountain Gate	*www.mountaingate.com*				yes	
Overland Data	*www.overlanddata.com*				yes	
QualStar	*www.qualstar.com*		yes	yes	yes	yes
Quantum	*www.quantum.com*				yes	
Seagate	*www.seagate.com*		yes			
Sony	*www.sony.com*		yes	yes		yes
Spectra Logic	*www.spectralogic.com*		yes	yes		yes
Storage Dimensions	*www.storagedimensions.com*		yes	yes	yes	
StorageTek	*www.storagetek.com*				yes	
Sun	*www.sun.com*		yes	yes	yes	
Tandberg	*www.tandberg.com*	yes				
TTI	*www.ttech.com*		yes	yes	yes	

Index

Numbers

4mm tape technology, 6, 194
8mm tape technology, 6, 195

A

administrative hints
  checking backup server database, 269
  daily tasks, 268
  downtime, 277
  fire drills, 276
  log management, 270
  occasional tasks, 274, 276
  operational manuals, 275
  review of backup reports, 271–273
  reviewing the backup policy, 276
  tape management, 271
  watching anomalies and trends, 273
administrative, configuration
        considerations, 18, 79–86
  backup exceptions and, 86
  backup restarts and, 80
  bulk information entry and, 85
  calendar-based scheduling and, 85
  client-based backup exceptions and, 86
  for commercial software (matrix), 181
  disk space and, 80
  GUI, command-line access and, 82
  host grouping and, 83
  information to be stored and, 79
  multilevel backups and, 85
  printable information and, 83

priority specification and, 84
restores and, 81
wildcards, regular expressions and, 82
ADSM (Version 3), 137–142
  backup server component, 138, 139
  configuration and backup
        information, 139–141
  log files, 141
Advanced Metal Evaporated (AME)
        media, 6, 8, 195
AIT (Advanced Intelligent Tape), 6, 196
alternative hardware, 20
AME media, 6, 8, 195
archiving, 3
ARCserve (Version 6.5), 142–147
  backup client feature, 144
  backup server feature, 143
  configuration and backup
        information, 144
  editions, 142
  log files for, 145
  special options, 145, 147
automatic software distribution
        mechanisms, 78

B

backup clients, 5, 77
  hardware platforms, 188
backup exceptions, 86
Backup Exec (Version 7.0), 147–152
  backup client feature, 149
  backup server feature, 148

About the Author

Jody Leber is the Chief Technical Officer for Genorff Engineering Inc., where she specializes in mass storage systems, performance tuning, and scalable system administration issues. Jody earned a B.S. in Computer Science from Northern Arizona University in 1984, an M.S. in Business Administration from East Texas State University in 1987, and a M.S. in Computer Science from the Naval Post Graduate School in 1994.

Before becoming a founding member of Genorff Engineering, Jody was Vice President, Unix Systems Developer at a major Wall Street financial firm. Jody's career spans a wide cross section of the computer industry, and she has held numerous engineering positions with both the government and private sectors.

Jody lives with her faithful dog Freda and cat Murphy in Summit, New Jersey, and struggles with learning the soprano sax.

Colophon

Our look is the result of reader comments, our own experimentation, and feedback from distribution channels. Distinctive covers complement our distinctive approach to technical topics, breathing personality and life into potentially dry subjects.

The animal appearing on the cover of *Windows NT Backup & Restore* is a spotted hyena (*Crocuta crocuta*). Hyenas live in flat, grassy plains of sub-Saharan Africa. An average adult female hyena weighs about 140 pounds and stands several feet high; the male is smaller and shorter. Females are also more aggressive than males. In other respects, it is not easy to distinguish between the sexes. This difficulty, along with the hyena's status as indiscriminate scavenger, has inspired much folklore about hyenas, frequently associating them with witches.

Though they have a dog-like appearance, hyenas are more closely related to cats than dogs, and their nearest relations are the mongoose and meerkat. Spotted hyenas are carnivorous, acting as predator or scavenger, eating every bone and shred of remains with their remarkably strong jaws. Hyena cubs fight viciously among themselves, significantly reducing the eventual adult population.

Hyenas live in loosely grouped matriarchal clans of up to 100 members. Most hunting is solitary, though groups do occasionally hunt together, relying on numbers and stamina. Spotted hyenas are social and vociferous animals with several distinct means of communication, including the notorious giggling laugh, which indicates not humor but fear or excitement when under attack.

Edie Freedman designed the cover of this book, using a 19th-century engraving from the Dover Pictorial Archive. The cover layout was produced with Quark XPress 3.32 using the ITC Garamond font. Whenever possible, our books use Rep Kover™, a durable and flexible lay-flat binding. If the page count exceeds Rep Kover's limit, perfect binding is used.

The inside layout was designed by Nancy Priest and implemented in FrameMaker 5.0 by Mike Sierra. The text and heading fonts are ITC Garamond Light and Garamond Book. The illustrations that appear in the book were created in Macromedia Freehand 4.0 by Robert Romano. This colophon was written by Nancy Kotary.

More Titles from O'Reilly

Windows NT System Administration

Windows NT in a Nutshell

By Eric Pearce
1st Edition June 1997
364 pages, ISBN 1-56592-251-4

Anyone who installs Windows NT, creates a user, or adds a printer is an NT system administrator (whether they realize it or not). This book features a new tagged callout approach to documenting the 4.0 GUI as well as real-life examples of command usage and strategies for problem solving, with an emphasis on networking. Windows NT in a Nutshell will be as useful to the single-system home user as it will be to the administrator of a 1,000-node corporate network.

Windows NT User Administration

By Ashley J. Meggitt & Timothy D. Ritchey
1st Edition November 1997
218 pages, ISBN 1-56592-301-4

Many Windows NT books introduce you to a range of topics, but seldom do they give you enough information to master any one thing. This book (like other O'Reilly animal books) is different. Windows NT User Administration makes you an expert at creating users efficiently, controlling what they can do, limiting the damage they can cause, and monitoring their activities on your system. Don't simply react to problems; use the techniques in this book to anticipate and prevent them.

Windows NT SNMP

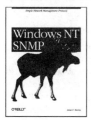

By James D. Murray
1st Edition February 1998
464 pages, Includes CD-ROM
ISBN 1-56592-338-3

This book describes the implementation of SNMP (the Simple Network Management Protocol) on Windows NT 3.51 and 4.0 (with a look ahead to NT 5.0) and Windows 95 systems. It covers SNMP and network basics and detailed information on developing SNMP management applications and extension agents. The book comes with a CD-ROM containing a wealth of additional information: standards documents, sample code from the book, and many third-party, SNMP-related software tools, libraries, and demos.

Essential Windows NT System Administration

By Æleen Frisch
1st Edition February 1998
486 pages, ISBN 1-56592-274-3

This book combines practical experience with technical expertise to help you manage Windows NT systems as productively as possible. It covers the standard utilities offered with the Windows NT operating system and from the Resource Kit, as well as important commercial and free third-party tools. By the author of O'Reilly's bestselling book, Essential System Administration.

Windows NT Backup & Restore

By Jody Leber
1st Edition May 1998
320 pages, ISBN 1-56592-272-7

Beginning with the need for a workable recovery policy and ways to translate that policy into requirements, Windows NT Backup & Restore presents the reader with practical guidelines for setting up an effective backup system in both small and large environments. It covers the native NT utilities as well as major third-party hardware and software.

Windows NT Server 4.0 for NetWare Administrators

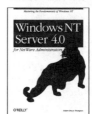

By Robert Bruce Thompson
1st Edition November 1997
756 pages, ISBN 1-56592-280-8

This book provides a fast-track means for experienced NetWare administrators to build on their knowledge and master the fundamentals of using the Microsoft Windows NT Server. The broad coverage of many aspects of Windows NT Server is balanced by a tightly focused approach of comparison, contrast, and differentiation between NetWare and NT features and methodologies.

O'REILLY™

TO ORDER: **800-998-9938** • **order@oreilly.com** • **http://www.oreilly.com/**

OUR PRODUCTS ARE AVAILABLE AT A BOOKSTORE OR SOFTWARE STORE NEAR YOU.

FOR INFORMATION: **800-998-9938** • **707-829-0515** • **info@oreilly.com**

Windows NT System Administration

Windows NT Desktop Reference

By Æleen Frisch
1st Edition January 1998
64 pages, ISBN 1-56592-437-1

A hip-pocket quick reference to Windows NT commands, as well as the most useful commands from the Resource Kits. Commands are arranged in groups related to their purpose and function. Covers Windows NT 4.0.

MCSE: The Core Exams in a Nutshell

By Michael Moncur
1st Edition May 1998 (est.)
300 pages (est.), ISBN 1-56592-376-6

MCSE: The Core Exams in a Nutshell is a detailed quick reference for administrators with Windows NT experience or experience administering a different platform, such as UNIX, who want to learn what is necessary to pass the MCSE required exam portion of the MCSE certification. While no book is a substitute for real-world experience, this book will help you codify your knowledge and prepare for the exams.

MCSE: The Electives in a Nutshell

By Michael Moncur
1st Edition June 1998 (est.)
550 pages (est.), ISBN: 1-56592-482-7

A companion volume to *MCSE: The Core Exams in a Nutshell*, *MCSE: The Electives in a Nutshell* is a comprehensive study guide that covers the elective exams for the MCSE as well as the Internet requirements and electives for the MCSE+Internet. This detailed reference is aimed at sophisticated users who need a bridge between real-world experience and the MCSE exam requirements.

Learning Perl on Win32 Systems

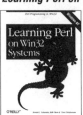

By Randal L. Schwartz, Erik Olson & Tom Christiansen
1st Edition August 1997
306 pages, ISBN 1-56592-324-3

In this carefully paced course, leading Perl trainers and a Windows NT practitioner teach you to program in the language that promises to emerge as the scripting language of choice on NT. Based on the "llama" book, this book features tips for PC users and new, NT-specific examples, along with a foreword by Larry Wall, the creator of Perl, and Dick Hardt, the creator of Perl for Win32.

Managing the Windows NT Registry

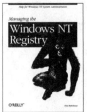

By Paul Robichaux
1st Edition April 1998
470 pages, ISBN 1-56592-378-2

The Windows NT Registry is the repository for all hardware, software, and application configuration settings. This is the system administrator's guide to maintaining, monitoring, and updating the Registry database. A "must-have" for every NT system manager or administrator, it covers what the Registry is and where it lives on disk, available tools, Registry access from programs, and Registry content.

Perl

Mastering Regular Expressions

By Jeffrey E. F. Friedl
1st Edition January 1997
368 pages, ISBN 1-56592-257-3

Regular expressions, a powerful tool for manipulating text and data, are found in scripting languages, editors, programming environments, and specialized tools. In this book, author Jeffrey Friedl leads you through the steps of crafting a regular expression that gets the job done. He examines a variety of tools and uses them in an extensive array of examples, with a major focus on Perl.

The Perl Cookbook

By Tom Christiansen & Nathan Torkington
1st Edition June 1998 (est.)
600 pages (est.), ISBN 1-56592-243-3

This collection of problems, solutions, and examples for anyone programming in Perl covers everything from beginner questions to techniques that even the most experienced Perl programmers might learn from. It contains hundreds of Perl "recipes," including recipes for parsing strings, doing matrix multiplication, working with arrays and hashes, and performing complex regular expressions.

Perl

Perl Resource Kit—UNIX Edition

By Larry Wall, Nate Patwardhan, Ellen Siever,
David Futato & Brian Jepson
1st Edition November 1997
1812 pages, ISBN 1-56592-370-7

The *Perl Resource Kit—UNIX Edition* gives
you the most comprehensive collection of
Perl documentation and commercially
enhanced software tools available today.
Developed in association with Larry Wall,
the creator of Perl, it's the definitive Perl distribution for webmasters, programmers, and system administrators.

The *Perl Resource Kit* provides:

- Over 1800 pages of tutorial and in-depth reference documentation for Perl utilities and extensions, in 4 volumes.
- A CD-ROM containing the complete Perl distribution, plus hundreds of freeware Perl extensions and utilities—a complete
snapshot of the Comprehensive Perl Archive Network (CPAN)—
as well as new software written by Larry Wall just for the Kit.

Perl Software Tools All on One Convenient CD-ROM
Experienced Perl hackers know when to create their own, and
when they can find what they need on CPAN. Now all the power of
CPAN—and more—is at your fingertips. *The Perl Resource Kit*
includes:

- A complete snapshot of CPAN, with an install program for
Solaris and Linux that ensures that all necessary modules are
installed together. Also includes an easy-to-use search tool
and a web-aware interface that allows you to get the latest
version of each module.
- A new Java/Perl interface that allows programmers to write
Java classes with Perl implementations. This new tool was
written specially for the Kit by Larry Wall.

Experience the power of Perl modules in areas such as CGI, web spi-
dering, database interfaces, managing mail and USENET news, user
interfaces, security, graphics, math and statistics, and much more.

Perl in a Nutshell

By Stephen Spainhour, Ellen Siever &
Nathan Patwardhan
1st Edition July 1998 (est.)
600 pages (est.), ISBN 1-56592-286-7

The perfect companion for working programmers, *Perl in a Nutshell* is a comprehensive reference guide to the world of Perl. It contains
everything you need to know for all but the most
obscure Perl questions. This wealth of informa-
tion is packed into an efficient, extraordinarily usable format.

Programming Perl, 2nd Edition

By Larry Wall, Tom Christiansen &
Randal L. Schwartz
2nd Edition September 1996
670 pages, ISBN 1-56592-149-6

Coauthored by Larry Wall, the creator of
Perl, the second edition of this authorita-
tive guide contains a full explanation of
Perl version 5.003 features. It covers Perl
language and syntax, functions, library
modules, references, and object-oriented features, and also
explores invocation options, debugging, common mistakes, and
much more.

Perl 5 Desktop Reference

By Johan Vromans
1st Edition February 1996
46 pages, ISBN 1-56592-187-9

This is the standard quick-reference guide for
the Perl programming language. It provides a
complete overview of the language, from variables to input and output, from flow control to
regular expressions, from functions to document formats—all packed into a convenient,
carry-around booklet. Updated to cover Perl version 5.003.

Learning Perl, 2nd Edition

By Randal L. Schwartz & Tom Christiansen
Foreword by Larry Wall
2nd Edition July 1997
302 pages, ISBN 1-56592-284-0

In this update of a bestseller, two leading
Perl trainers teach you to use the most
universal scripting language in the age of
the World Wide Web. Now current for Perl
version 5.004, this hands-on tutorial
includes a lengthy new chapter on CGI programming, while
touching also on the use of library modules, references, and
Perl's object-oriented constructs.

Perl

Advanced Perl Programming

By Sriram Srinivasan
1st Edition August 1997
434 pages, ISBN 1-56592-220-4

This book covers complex techniques for managing production-ready Perl programs and explains methods for manipulating data and objects that may have looked like magic before. It gives you necessary background for dealing with networks, databases, and GUIs, and includes a discussion of internals to help you program more efficiently and embed Perl within C or C within Perl.

Developing Web Content

Web Client Programming with Perl

By Clinton Wong
1st Edition March 1997
228 pages, ISBN 1-56592-214-X

Web Client Programming with Perl shows you how to extend scripting skills to the Web. This book teaches you the basics of how browsers communicate with servers and how to write your own customized web clients to automate common tasks. It is intended for those who are motivated to develop software that offers a more flexible and dynamic response than a standard web browser.

JavaScript: The Definitive Guide, 3rd Edition

By David Flanagan & Dan Shafer
3rd Edition June 1998 (est.)
800 pages (est.), ISBN 1-56592-392-8

This third edition of the definitive reference to JavaScript covers the latest version of the language, JavaScript 1.2, as supported by Netscape Navigator 4.0. JavaScript, which is being standardized under the name ECMAScript, is a scripting language that can be embedded directly in HTML to give web pages programming-language capabilities.

Developing Web Content

CGI Programming on the World Wide Web

By Shishir Gundavaram
1st Edition March 1996
450 pages, ISBN 1-56592-168-2

This book offers a comprehensive explanation of CGI and related techniques for people who hold on to the dream of providing their own information servers on the Web. It starts at the beginning, explaining the value of CGI and how it works, then moves swiftly into the subtle details of programming.

Information Architecture for the World Wide Web

By Louis Rosenfeld & Peter Morville
1st Edition January 1998
226 pages, ISBN 1-56592-282-4

Learn how to merge aesthetics and mechanics to design web sites that "work." This book shows how to apply principles of architecture and library science to design cohesive web sites and intranets that are easy to use, manage, and expand. Covers building complex sites, hierarchy design and organization, and techniques to make your site easier to search. For webmasters, designers, and administrators.

Dynamic HTML: The Complete Reference

By Danny Goodman
1st Edition June 1998 (est.)
1000 pages (est.), ISBN 1-56592-494-0

Dynamic HTML: The Complete Reference is an indispensable compendium for Web content developers. It contains complete reference material for all of the HTML tags, CSS style attributes, browser document objects, and JavaScript objects supported by the various standards and the latest versions of Netscape Navigator and Microsoft Internet Explorer.

O'REILLY™

TO ORDER: **800-998-9938** • **order@oreilly.com** • **http://www.oreilly.com/**
OUR PRODUCTS ARE AVAILABLE AT A BOOKSTORE OR SOFTWARE STORE NEAR YOU.
FOR INFORMATION: **800-998-9938** • **707-829-0515** • **info@oreilly.com**

Developing Web Content

WebMaster in a Nutshell, Deluxe Edition

By O'Reilly & Associates, Inc.
1st Edition September 1997
374 pages, includes CD-ROM & book
ISBN 1-56592-305-7

The Deluxe Edition of *WebMaster in a Nutshell* is a complete library for web programmers. It features the Web Developer's Library, a CD-ROM containing the electronic text of five popular O'Reilly titles: *HTML: The Definitive Guide*, 2nd Edition; *JavaScript: The Definitive Guide*, 2nd Edition; *CGI Programming on the World Wide Web*; *Programming Perl*, 2nd Edition—the classic "camel book"; and *WebMaster in a Nutshell*, which is also included in a companion desktop edition.

HTML: The Definitive Guide, 2nd Edition

By Chuck Musciano & Bill Kennedy
2nd Edition May 1997
552 pages, ISBN 1-56592-235-2

This complete guide is chock full of examples, sample code, and practical, hands-on advice to help you create truly effective web pages and master advanced features. Learn how to insert images and other multimedia elements, create useful links and searchable documents, use Netscape extensions, design great forms, and lots more. The second edition covers the most up-to-date version of the HTML standard (HTML version 3.2), Netscape 4.0 and Internet Explorer 3.0, plus all the common extensions.

Learning VBScript

By Paul Lomax
1st Edition July 1997
616 pages, includes CD-ROM
ISBN 1-56592-247-6

This definitive guide shows web developers how to take full advantage of client-side scripting with the VBScript language. In addition to basic language features, it covers the Internet Explorer object model and discusses techniques for client-side scripting, like adding ActiveX controls to a web page or validating data before sending it to the server. Includes CD-ROM with over 170 code samples.

Frontier: The Definitive Guide

By Matt Neuburg
1st Edition February 1998
618 pages, 1-56592-383-9

This definitive guide is the first book devoted exclusively to teaching and documenting Userland Frontier, a powerful scripting environment for web site management and system level scripting. Packed with examples, advice, tricks, and tips, Frontier: The Definitive Guide teaches you Frontier from the ground up. Learn how to automate repetitive processes, control remote computers across a network, beef up your web site by generating hundreds of related web pages automatically, and more. Covers Frontier 4.2.3 for the Macintosh.

WebMaster in a Nutshell

By Stephen Spainhour & Valerie Quercia
1st Edition October 1996
374 pages, ISBN 1-56592-229-8

Web content providers and administrators have many sources for information, both in print and online. WebMaster in a Nutshell puts it all together in one slim volume for easy desktop access. This quick reference covers HTML, CGI, JavaScript, Perl, HTTP, and server configuration.

Designing for the Web: Getting Started in a New Medium

By Jennifer Niederst
with Edie Freedman
1st Edition April 1996
180 pages, ISBN 1-56592-165-8

Designing for the Web gives you the basics you need to hit the ground running. Although geared toward designers, it covers information and techniques useful to anyone who wants to put graphics online. It explains how to work with HTML documents from a designer's point of view, outlines special problems with presenting information online, and walks through incorporating images into web pages, with emphasis on resolution and improving efficiency.

How to stay in touch with O'Reilly

1. Visit Our Award-Winning Web Site

http://www.oreilly.com/

★ "Top 100 Sites on the Web" —*PC Magazine*
★ "Top 5% Web sites" —*Point Communications*
★ "3-Star site" —*The McKinley Group*

Our web site contains a library of comprehensiveproduct information (including book excerpts and tables of contents), downloadable software, background articles, interviews with technology leaders, links to relevant sites, book cover art, and more. File us in your Bookmarks or Hotlist!

2. Join Our Email Mailing Lists

New Product Releases

To receive automatic email with brief descriptions of all new O'Reilly products as they are released, send email to:
listproc@online.oreilly.com
Put the following information in the first line of your message (*not* in the Subject field):
subscribe oreilly-news

O'Reilly Events

If you'd also like us to send information about trade show events, special promotions, and other O'Reilly events, send email to:
listproc@online.oreilly.com
Put the following information in the first line of your message (*not* in the Subject field):
subscribe oreilly-events

3. Get Examples from Our Books via FTP

There are two ways to access an archive of example files from our books:

Regular FTP

- ftp to:
  ftp.oreilly.com
  (login: anonymous
  password: your email address)
- Point your web browser to:
  ftp://ftp.oreilly.com/

FTPMAIL

- Send an email message to:
  ftpmail@online.oreilly.com
  (Write "help" in the message body)

4. Contact Us via Email

order@oreilly.com
To place a book or software order online. Good for North American and international customers.

subscriptions@oreilly.com
To place an order for any of our newsletters or periodicals.

books@oreilly.com
General questions about any of our books.

software@oreilly.com
For general questions and product information about our software. Check out O'Reilly Software Online at **http://software.oreilly.com/** for software and technical support information. Registered O'Reilly software users send your questions to: **website-support@oreilly.com**

cs@oreilly.com
For answers to problems regarding your order or our products.

booktech@oreilly.com
For book content technical questions or corrections.

proposals@oreilly.com
To submit new book or software proposals to our editors and product managers.

international@oreilly.com
For information about our international distributors or translation queries. For a list of our distributors outside of North America check out:
http://www.oreilly.com/www/order/country.html

O'Reilly & Associates, Inc.
101 Morris Street, Sebastopol, CA 95472 USA
TEL   707-829-0515 or 800-998-9938
       (6am to 5pm PST)
FAX   707-829-0104

O'REILLY™

International Distributors

UK, EUROPE, MIDDLE EAST AND NORTHERN AFRICA (EXCEPT FRANCE, GERMANY, SWITZERLAND, & AUSTRIA)

INQUIRIES
International Thomson Publishing Europe
Berkshire House
168-173 High Holborn
London WC1V 7AA
United Kingdom
Telephone: 44-171-497-1422
Fax: 44-171-497-1426
Email: itpint@itps.co.uk

ORDERS
International Thomson Publishing Services, Ltd.
Cheriton House, North Way
Andover, Hampshire SP10 5BE
United Kingdom
Telephone: 44-264-342-832 (UK)
Telephone: 44-264-342-806 (outside UK)
Fax: 44-264-364418 (UK)
Fax: 44-264-342761 (outside UK)
UK & Eire orders: itpuk@itps.co.uk
International orders: itpint@itps.co.uk

FRANCE

Editions Eyrolles
61 bd Saint-Germain
75240 Paris Cedex 05
France
Fax: 33-01-44-41-11-44

FRENCH LANGUAGE BOOKS
All countries except Canada
Telephone: 33-01-44-41-46-16
Email: geodif@eyrolles.com
English language books
Telephone: 33-01-44-41-11-87
Email: distribution@eyrolles.com

GERMANY, SWITZERLAND, AND AUSTRIA

INQUIRIES
O'Reilly Verlag
Balthasarstr. 81
D-50670 Köln
Germany
Telephone: 49-221-97-31-60-0
Fax: 49-221-97-31-60-8
Email: anfragen@oreilly.de

ORDERS
International Thomson Publishing
Königswinterer Straße 418
53227 Bonn, Germany
Telephone: 49-228-97024 0
Fax: 49-228-441342
Email: order@oreilly.de

JAPAN

O'Reilly Japan, Inc.
Kiyoshige Building 2F
12-Banchi, Sanei-cho
Shinjuku-ku
Tokyo 160-0008 Japan
Telephone: 81-3-3356-5227
Fax: 81-3-3356-5261
Email: kenji@oreilly.com

INDIA

Computer Bookshop (India) PVT. Ltd.
190 Dr. D.N. Road, Fort
Bombay 400 001 India
Telephone: 91-22-207-0989
Fax: 91-22-262-3551
Email: cbsbom@giasbm01.vsnl.net.in

HONG KONG

City Discount Subscription Service Ltd.
Unit D, 3rd Floor, Yan's Tower
27 Wong Chuk Hang Road
Aberdeen, Hong Kong
Telephone: 852-2580-3539
Fax: 852-2580-6463
Email: citydis@ppn.com.hk

KOREA

Hanbit Media, Inc.
Sonyoung Bldg. 202
Yeksam-dong 736-36
Kangnam-ku
Seoul, Korea
Telephone: 822-554-9610
Fax: 822-556-0363
Email: hant93@chollian.dacom.co.kr

SINGAPORE, MALAYSIA, AND THAILAND

Addison Wesley Longman Singapore PTE Ltd.
25 First Lok Yang Road
Singapore 629734
Telephone: 65-268-2666
Fax: 65-268-7023
Email: daniel@longman.com.sg

PHILIPPINES

Mutual Books, Inc.
429-D Shaw Boulevard
Mandaluyong City, Metro
Manila, Philippines
Telephone: 632-725-7538
Fax: 632-721-3056
Email: mbikikog@mnl.sequel.net

CHINA

Ron's DataCom Co., Ltd.
79 Dongwu Avenue
Dongxihu District
Wuhan 430040
China
Telephone: 86-27-3892568
Fax: 86-27-3222108
Email: hongfeng@public.wh.hb.cn

ALL OTHER ASIAN COUNTRIES

O'Reilly & Associates, Inc.
101 Morris Street
Sebastopol, CA 95472 USA
Telephone: 707-829-0515
Fax: 707-829-0104
Email: order@oreilly.com

AUSTRALIA

WoodsLane Pty. Ltd.
7/5 Vuko Place, Warriewood NSW 2102
P.O. Box 935
Mona Vale NSW 2103
Australia
Telephone: 61-2-9970-5111
Fax: 61-2-9970-5002
Email: info@woodslane.com.au

NEW ZEALAND

Woodslane New Zealand Ltd.
21 Cooks Street (P.O. Box 575)
Waganui, New Zealand
Telephone: 64-6-347-6543
Fax: 64-6-345-4840
Email: info@woodslane.com.au

THE AMERICAS

McGraw-Hill Interamericana Editores, S.A. de C.V.
Cedro No. 512
Col. Atlampa 06450
Mexico, D.F.
Telephone: 52-5-541-3155
Fax: 52-5-541-4913
Email: mcgraw-hill@infosel.net.mx

SOUTH AFRICA

International Thomson Publishing
South Africa
Building 18, Constantia Park
138 Sixteenth Road
P.O. Box 2459
Halfway House, 1685 South Africa
Telephone: 27-11-805-4819
Fax: 27-11-805-3648